My Daily Devotion

My Daily Devotion

God's Promises for Joyful Living

Stephen J. Carter

Publishing House
St. Louis

Copyright © 1988 Concordia Publishing House
3558 S. Jefferson Avenue, St. Louis, MO 63118-3968
Manufactured in the United States of America

Library of Congress Cataloging-in-Publication Data

Carter, Stephen J., 1941-
    My Daily devotion: God's promises for joyful living/by Stephen
  J. Carter.
      p.   cm.
    ISBN 0-570-03077-3
    1. God—Promises—Mediations. 2. Devotional calendars—Lutheran Church. 3. Lutheran Church—Prayer-books and devotions—English.
  I. Title.
  BT180.P7C37 1988
  242' .2—dc19
                                          87-37386

2 3 4 5 6 7 8 9 10   97 96 95 94 93 92 91 90 89

Preface

In this devotional book I offer to you God's promises for joyful living. He has strengthened my faith through His Word. In Scripture verse after Scripture verse God has exposed my sin and pointed me to the cross of His son Jesus Christ for forgiveness. The writing has challenged me to open my heart and mind to His powerful, life-changing Gospel and to see His presence in the world of robins, mountains, family quarrels, church windows, baseball games, and prison cells.

As you read the devotions privately or in the family circle, read the Scripture sections suggested, because the devotional thoughts flow from the chosen verses. Before reading each devotion, take time to focus your thoughts and heart on the living God. Pray that He will use my words to point you to His Son and to illumine His Word. Pray that you will be receptive in your inner being to be shaped by His Word—convicted of sin, comforted with forgiveness, laid bare before Him, covered with the blood of Christ.

Hymn verses are used frequently as prayer thoughts. I rejoiced to discover how beautifully the hymns of God's people echo the words of Scripture and speak to the problems and joys of daily living. The hymns also remind us that personal and family devotions belong in the context of God's people gathering together around Word and Sacrament. In that spirit, the rhythm of the church year guides the devotional selections, although the church year can't be matched with the calendar year.

Modern life presents many difficulties, discouragements, and temptations. You and I struggle to live with faithfulness and compassion. I pray that these daily devotions will help to strengthen you in the Word as you receive God's promises for joyful living!

A Fearless New Year

Reading: Romans 8:28–39

Text: Deuteronomy 31:6—"Do not be afraid or terrified . . . for the Lord your God goes with you: he will never leave you nor forsake you."

Israel has reason to be afraid. They camp on the eastern banks of the Jordan River. Within eyesight, the Promised Land flowing with milk and honey. But strong, hostile tribes rule Canaan. Israel must defeat these alleged giants. Moses has just dropped the bombshell that he will not enter the new land with them. They feel desperate without his leadership. They fail to seek God for courage and strength.

On the threshold of a new year, with the parties over, the noisemakers silent, and the business of daily living ahead, we need the words of Moses as greatly as Israel did. The events of the new year lie hidden from our gaze. Perhaps the international situation will worsen or nature will unleash its fury to destroy buildings and people. Perhaps your family will experience major troubles. Like Israel we often face the future anxiously and fearfully. We too frequently fail to look to God for strength and courage.

But Moses reassures Israel. And we know that the God of Moses will likewise enter the new year with us. We have the even greater assurance that God's Son, born in Bethlehem's manger, permitted Himself to be forsaken by the Father so that we might never be forsaken by God. Jesus experienced the fear and despair of being alone as He shouldered our burdens on Calvary. We can say with the confidence of Moses: "The Lord our God will not fail us nor forsake us." So bring on the new year, unknown, fraught with trials, filled with challenges, but marked by God's presence and promise. A fearless new year to all of you!

Prayer

Dear Lord, help me to face the New Year trusting Your sure promises. Amen.

Trust the Lord for Help

Reading: Psalm 37:8–19

Text: Psalm 37:9—"Those who hope in the Lord will inherit the land."

What a struggle American farmers have endured in recent years, many losing their land or at least plagued by staggering debt and decreasing land values. Israel in David's day faced similar problems. Many righteous people saw the wicked prospering at their expense. They were filled with anger and worry. But the anger and worry only led them deeper into trouble.

We survey the past year and see many difficult and discouraging events. We cry out for help. All the while we notice that the wicked seem to be prospering. Anger fills our heart. "It's not fair. Why should they prosper while I struggle by trying to do what is right? Why, God, do You permit these things to happen?" Worry consumes us. "What will I do now? How can I make ends meet?" Anger and worry only lead us deeper into trouble. Self-pitying, we feel helpless.

But the psalmist suggests that we trust the Lord for help. He knows that God alone gives the victory. True happiness comes from the Lord and not the desires of our heart. Ultimately the wicked will destroy themselves, while the Lord upholds the righteous. We need to wait patiently for the Lord to act.

God, our Help in ages past and our Hope for years to come, sent His Son Jesus Christ to live on this earth and die for the world's sins. He gives us an inheritance which will not fade. He freely gives us trust in His promises. Anger and worry aside, we trust the Lord for help now and eternally.

Prayer

We gather up in this brief hour
The mem'ry of your mercies:
Your wondrous goodness, love, and pow'r
Our grateful song rehearses;
For you have been our strength and stay
In many a dark and dreary day
Of sorrow and reverses.

Trust the Lord for Guidance!

Reading: Psalm 37:23–31

Text: Psalm 37:23—"He makes his steps firm."

We look to the new year with all sorts of plans and intentions. Relying on God's help, the psalmist wants us to trust the Lord for guidance.

The wicked scheme, plot, and manipulate. They know how to steal from others, amass land, and accumulate wealth. They seek and gain power over others and laugh at the helpless. They go their own way.

We deplore such conduct on the part of others and agree with the psalmist that the wicked should be punished. But do we not often chart our own course and resort to scheming and manipulating in order to get our own way—all for a good cause, we think?

How beautiful the person who trusts the Lord for guidance. "Though he stumble, he will not fall, for the Lord upholds him with his hand." Admitting our waywardness, we place ourselves in the strong hands of the God who sent His only Son to go the way of the cross. Resting in Him, we seek God's guidance for the new year.

God supplies the direction in His Word. He leads us to glorify Him by serving others. We live the love of Jesus Christ on the job, in our homes and neighborhoods, in our community, and in our church. We will stumble because of our sin and weakness, but we will not fall, because the Lord upholds us with His hand.

Prayer

Then, gracious God, in years to come,
We pray your hand may guide us,
And, onward through our journey home,
Your mercy walk beside us
Until at last our ransomed life
Is safe from peril, toil, and strife
When heav'n itself shall hide us.

Sleepless Nights?

Reading: Psalm 131

Text: Psalm 4:8—"I will lie down and sleep in peace, for you alone, O Lord, make me dwell in safety."

Sleepless nights lately? Worried about job or school or family? Fretting about providing enough food for the table, meeting high mortgage payments, paying for those college educations, setting aside enough savings for retirement? Stewing about people who unfairly criticize you and seem to prosper despite their disregard of God's commands?

The psalmist suggests: "Lie down and sleep in peace," for God alone makes us "dwell in safety." Aware of unfair treatment by others, prone to anger and resentment, sometimes depressed by worry, the psalmist nevertheless discovers a peaceful rest in the sure protection and promises of God.

Sleepless nights may call for confession of sins—doubts, self-pity, resentments, bitterness, misguided reliance on self. Confession leads to God's peace and God's rest, for the Obedient One, who slept in a boat amidst a storm, also went to the sleep of death in order to win the victory and bring lasting peace.

As He woke from death, victorious over His enemies, so we wake, refreshed each day, from peaceful sleep in His protection, ready for a life of service until we awake in heaven to serve Him forevermore.

Problems remain. Worries abound. Evil appears to triumph. Long nights and tired eyes remain. Tranquilizers fall short. Counting sheep gets old. But sleep beckons for the child of God— safe, forgiven, sustained, refreshed, quiet and at rest, trusting in Christ Jesus.

Prayer

Oh, may my soul in thee repose,
And may sweet sleep mine eyelids close,
Sleep that shall me more vig'rous make
To serve my God when I awake!

Troubled or Joyful about His Birth?

Reading: Matthew 2:1–12

Text: Matthew 2:3, 10—"When King Herod heard this he was disturbed, and all Jerusalem with him . . . .When they saw the star, they were overjoyed."

Herod was troubled at the news of a king's birth. Known as the fox, he gained and kept power by clever politics and ruthless cruelty. He could not afford a pretender to his throne. So he sweet-talks the Wise Men about wanting to worship the newborn king and then prepares to slaughter the innocent children in Bethlehem.

Horrible, brutal—and yet, are we troubled at the Christ Child's birth? Since Eden and the raised fist of rebellion against God, we have an obsession for power and a desire to be king— king of the snow hill, king or queen of the family with New Year's Day television rights, top of the ladder at work. Sometimes we sweet-talk others to get our own way, and sometimes we resort to ruthless techniques with carefully chosen words and actions. So we may well be uncomfortable at the birth of a Child who is King of kings and Lord of lords.

Herod was troubled, but the Wise Men were overjoyed. They see the star at Bethlehem and rejoice "with exceeding great joy." Their joy at finding the Infant King leads them to kneel down in worship and to bring Him costly gifts. They claim no kingship but honor Christ as King of their lives. Their source of joy: God's revelation through His Word and the guiding of the star. God's good news fills them with joy.

How about you? Are you troubled like Herod or joyful like the Wise Men at His birth? Confessing our desire to be kings, we look to that same revelation of God. He speaks to us in the star, the Word, the water, the wafer and wine. He points us to a King who became a servant for us—born in a manger, nailed to a tree for our sins. God fills us with exceeding great joy. Our kingship discarded, we kneel to worship and bring the costly gifts of our very lives to Him.

Prayer

As with joyful steps they sped, Savior to thy lowly bed,
There to bend the knee before Thee, whom heav'n and
earth adore;
So may we with willing feet Ever seek thy mercy seat.

11

Arise, Shine!

Reading: Isaiah 60:1–12

Text: Isaiah 60:1—"Arise, shine, for your light has come, and the glory of the Lord rises upon you."

I'll never forget the closing candle ceremony in the Cotton Bowl during Explo '72 in Dallas. Following a stirring message to take the evangelism zeal back home, each of the 85,000 youth and adult counselors in the audience lit a candle. The flames grew until the Texas night was aglow with the light. It was certainly symbolic of the Epiphany message of God to Zion through the prophet Isaiah: What does God want us to do? "Arise, shine!" The words were spoken to Israel in exile, ready to return home.

In Matthew's gospel the Wise Men from the East saw the light of a special star and journeyed to Bethlehem to see the infant King. And the words speak to our hearts as well: "Arise, shine!" Hold up Jesus as the Light of the world, for everyone to see.

Why are we to arise and shine? The world lies in darkness. Isaiah goes on: "See, darkness covers the earth and thick darkness is over the peoples." Israel had lived in the darkness of rebellion and ended up in the darkness of heathen Babylon. Today our world suffers from an energy crisis called sin, which extinguishes all lights.

How can we arise and shine? God has shined in our dark world with the light of His Son Jesus Christ. He brought Israel home to Jerusalem and sent the Messiah in the fullness of time. In the darkness of Good Friday, Jesus, the Light of the world, could not be extinguished. Victorious and risen, He shines brightly as Savior and Lord. His Word illumines us. Drawing upon that unfailing light each day, we let God shine through us with the light of His Son.

Prayer

Arise and shine in splendor,
Let night to day surrender;
Your light is drawing near.
Above, the day is beaming,
In matchless beauty gleaming;
The glory of the Lord is here.

12

Jesus as the True Israel

Reading: Matthew 2:13–15, 19–23

Text: Matthew 2:15b—"And so was fulfilled what the Lord had said through the prophet: 'Out of Egypt I called my son.' "

The well-known story of the holy family's flight to Egypt tells us much more than God's protection of the Christ Child. Matthew clearly presents Jesus as the true Israel. The original Israel (Jacob, son of Isaac, grandson of Abraham) fathered a great nation intended to be a blessing. But Israel failed miserably in rebellion and sin. Now God sends us His own Son to be the true Israel and hope of the world.

Note the comparisons. Pharaoh ordered the slaughter of all Hebrew male children. King Herod orders the slaughter of male infants under two years old in Bethlehem. God preserved Moses and Jesus. Matthew quotes Hosea 11:1, "Out of Egypt I called my son." God led Israel out of Egypt through the mighty Exodus. He led Jesus out of Egypt and back to the Promised Land. Before Jesus began His public ministry, He was baptized in the Jordan and tempted in the wilderness. God provided manna and quail in the wilderness. Jesus fed 5,000 in the wilderness. God gave the Law on Mt. Sinai. Jesus preached a sermon on the mount. The parallels mount. Yes, Jesus is the true Israel.

And in spite of our frequent rebellion, He chooses us as His people. He frees us from our slavery in Egypt by the Exodus of His suffering, death, and resurrection. He leads us through the waters of Baptism into the wilderness of temptation and the Promised Land of eternal life. He helps us, called out of darkness into His marvelous light, shine for the world as part of the new Israel. In this Epiphany season we praise and proclaim Jesus, called out of Egypt into Galilee, as the true Israel!

Prayer

Dear Father, thank You for the fulfillment of the Old Testament prophecies in the life, death, and resurrection of Jesus Christ, the true Israel. Amen.

Misguided Trust?

Reading: Exodus 15:1–21

Text: Psalm 20:7—"Some trust in chariots and some in horses, but we trust in the name of the Lord our God."

We live in a day of powerful weapons—nuclear submarines, laser beams, sophisticated computer technology, and deadly missiles. Raw force is pitted against raw force with boasts of superiority. We struggle to understand the meaning of the arms race and pray that the world will not be reduced to ruins. We feel personally powerless in the face of such military might.

The psalmist recognizes the importance of chariots and horses, the dreaded war machines of that day. Both Israel and her enemies possess armies and weapons. However, he lauds Israel for trusting not in chariots and horses but "in the name of the Lord our God." Conscious of the great Red Sea victory of Yahweh over Pharaoh's chariots and horses, aware of the stunning victories of Joshua and Gideon over seemingly superior forces, thankful for God's grace in his own life as commander and king, David relies on the powerful name of God, who will bring ultimate victory through the death and resurrection of His Son Jesus Christ, the Suffering Servant. Nothing can stop the kingdom of God bringing grace and salvation to a world in desperate need.

Empowered by God's forgiving love in Jesus Christ, we dare to speak His name to others in a world of mighty superpowers, knowing the Gospel will penetrate hungering hearts and the kingdom of God will continue to come with salvation.

Prayer

With might of ours can naught be done,
Soon were our loss effected;
But for us fights the valiant One,
Whom God himself elected.
Ask ye, Who is this? Jesus Christ it is,
Of sabaoth Lord, And there's none other God;
He holds the field forever.

The Taste Test

Reading: Isaiah 55:1–13

Text: Psalm 34:8—"Taste and see that the Lord is good; blessed is the man who takes refuge in him."

Within the last few years a major soft drink company changed the formula of its most popular cola. Immediately, strong reaction was forthcoming from lovers of the old taste and from consumers of rival colas. The bottom line was not expensive advertising or colorful packaging but the taste test.

In our Scripture verse for today David suggests the taste test for experiencing the true God. He writes, "Taste and see that the Lord is good; blessed is the man who takes refuge in him." David has personally experienced the mercies of God in his life—protected as a shepherd boy from wild animals, able to slay mighty Goliath, preserved from the jealous wrath of Saul, now David looks for deliverance in the promised Messiah and asks others to taste the sure promises of the living God and find refuge in Him.

From the seed of David came the Messiah to experience life in our stead. He tasted rejection, ridicule, suffering, and death on a cross for the sins of a rebellious world. David's challenge rings out to us too. We admit that selfishness, materialism, and thrill-seeking leave a flat taste in our mouth. We turn quietly to the living Word of God, where we taste and see that the Lord is good.

We taste the body and blood of Jesus Christ in the bread and wine. And we know that for time and for eternity we have refuge in Him. The ultimate taste test never fails—for David or for us.

Prayer

I come, O Savior, to your table,
For weak and weary is my soul;
You, Bread of Life, alone are able
To satisfy and make me whole.
Lord, may your body and your blood
Be for my soul the highest good!

A Path to the Future

Reading: Psalm 119:97–104

Text: Psalm 25:4—"Show me your ways, O Lord, teach me your paths."

In our world of rapid change people spend great sums of money trying to discern the future. Futurism is a big business. Trends, forecasts, economic predictions abound. Fortunetellers, astrologers, palm readers market their shadowy views of the future. We feel we must find the right path for our lives. Who will guide us?

The psalmist knows where to turn. He recognizes that the Word of God is a lamp unto his feet and a light to his path. Obedience to the law of God marks the right path. But the psalmist also confesses the sins of his youth and his rebellious ways (v. 7). Going his own way leads only to confusion, fear, and uncertainty about the future.

God makes known His ways to us just as clearly today as He did to Israel of old. His Word reveals the Law, which is good and just and true. But the psalmist also remembers the Lord's great mercy, as in the next verse he writes, "For you are God my Savior, and my hope is in you all day long." He clings to the forgiveness of a Covenant God who not only shows the way but sends His Son to be "the way, the truth, and the life" (John 14:6). Jesus walked the path of the Father all the way to Calvary, where He fully paid for the sins of the world.

We turn to God's Word, where we are reminded of what Christ has done for us. Trusting Him for salvation, we daily seek His ways and His paths. The future holds no fear, for our journey will lead to the heavenly mansions.

Bring on rapid change. Bring on the future. Jesus Christ is our Way.

Prayer
You are the way; to you alone
From sin and death we flee;
And he who would the Father seek
Your follower must be.

A View from Alcatraz

Reading: Isaiah 60:1–3

Text: Psalm 27:1—"The Lord is my light and my salvation—whom shall I fear?"

I remember visiting Alcatraz, the former island prison in the San Francisco Bay area. As part of the prison tour, we were invited to step into the solitary confinement vault and have the door briefly closed. I experienced total darkness and isolation. What would it be like to spend days or weeks alone in that darkness?

The psalmist knows the darkness of sin and rebellion, and the darkness of hiding in a cave from dangerous pursuers. But rather than succumb to paralyzing fear, he boldly proclaims, "The Lord is my light and my salvation." He remembers the Creator God who spoke the word that first brought light. He believes that God will ultimately shine in the world's darkness with the light of the Messiah.

From a human standpoint we have much to fear—the darkness of terrorism, violent crime, nuclear war, and perplexing personal problems. At times the darkness closes in on us.

But then the reassuring words of the psalmist flood our consciousness. We remember that the God who caused the light to shine out of darkness has shined in our hearts with the light of His Son Jesus Christ. In the darkness of Good Friday, when it seemed that evil had triumphed, the Son of God died to pay for our sins so that the light of salvation would continue to shine in an Easter world. Jesus, our Light, can penetrate every corner of darkness in our life, exposing and forgiving our sin, restoring hope and joy. Rekindled by the light of God's Word, we go forth to shine as lights in a dark world.

After that brief stay in solitary darkness, the Alcatraz door swung open, and we walked out into the dingy prison light and then out into a sunswept view of the bay. Similarly, the Lord has not left us in darkness.

Prayer
Dear Lord, lead me to your eternal light! Amen.

Tunnel Vision Transformed

Reading: Isaiah 60:1–7

Text: Psalm 48:10—"Like your name, O God, your praise reaches to the ends of the earth."

Some people suffer from an eye problem called tunnel vision. The eyes can only see straight ahead with no peripheral vision at all. So much of God's creation goes unseen. One cannot drive a car safely or participate successfully in athletics. With a world to see, reality lies only straight ahead.

Unfortunately, Christians often view God's church and the Christian life through tunnel vision. Reality is limited to my home, my work, and my church. I see no one else. I fail to see other Christians, other countries, other peoples in need of the Gospel. I insist that God operate only within my field of vision.

The psalmist widens our vision tremendously by speaking of "the ends of the earth." Israel often suffered from tunnel vision. Jonah suffered God's wrath by refusing to preach to Nineveh and trying to run in the opposite direction. But God's name and His praise reach "to the ends of the earth." He made the world. He sent His Son to die for the world. And He spreads His Gospel Word over all nations.

My tunnel vision broadens considerably when I hear about a wonderful Savior from the Japanese Lutheran Hour speaker or work with fellow Lutherans from South Africa and Tanzania or talk to enthusiastic Haitian students or learn of exciting Christian fellowship groups in Communist China. Indeed, God has made me a world Christian and transformed my tunnel vision into eyes which see a universe alive with His name and His praise.

Prayer

Can we whose souls are lighted With wisdom from on high,
Can we to those benighted The lamp of life deny?
Salvation! Oh, salvation! The joyful sound proclaim
Till those of ev'ry nation, Have learned Messiah's name.

Ready to Explain the Hope Inside

Reading: 1 Peter 3:8–16

Text: 1 Peter 3:15b—"Always be prepared to give an answer to everyone who asks you to give the reason for the hope that you have."

Outside: hopelessness. Inside: hope. I sit in a warm, comfortable family room looking out at a snow-covered lawn with barren trees and a wind-chill factor below zero. I am aware that outside there are evils like homelessness (made all the worse by the cold), hunger, violence, abortion, homosexuality, immorality, opposition to Christianity, and a host of others. Outside: hopelessness.

But we also know God's hope. A fallen world redeemed by the blood of the Lamb without blemish, new birth into a living hope through the resurrection of Jesus Christ from the dead, an inheritance that can never perish, spoil, or fade, an incorruptible Word that stands forever, status as a chosen people. St. Peter's words meant for our heart. Inside: hope.

And so Peter writes to us the words of our text. We Christians live differently from the world. We too suffer, sometimes struggle, and live in the midst of hopelessness. But we have a living hope which generates a smile, a caring touch, a vitality and energy that shows. We know Christ as our Savior. We rejoice in Word and sacrament. We treasure the fellowship of God's people. And we eagerly anticipate eternal life in heaven.

All Peter asks—be ready to explain the hope inside. Know how to talk about your faith, your God, your hope. Tell the story of God's faithfulness in your life. No fancy words needed. No major education needed. Use the Apostles' Creed. Use John 3:16. Use your favorite hymn. Use your own words. Practice on your family and Christian friends at the supper table, in the coffee hour, at church. Outside: hopelessness. Inside: hope. Let God help you bring that hope from inside to outside.

Prayer

If you cannot speak like angels,
If you cannot preach like Paul,
You can tell the love of Jesus;
You can say he died for all.

Mr. Inside and Mr. Outside

Reading: Romans 1:8–17

Text: Romans 1:16—"I am not ashamed of the gospel, because it is the power of God for the salvation of everyone who believes: first for the Jew, then for the Gentile."

Back in the 1940s, Army had an outstanding football team under Coach Red Blaik. Anchoring their undefeated team in 1946 were the "touchdown twins," Doc Blanchard and Glen Davis. Known as Mr. Inside and Mr. Outside, they combined powerful inside running with fleet, shifty, outside running.

Evangelism points to the necessary combination of Mr. Inside and Mr. Outside. The target for evangelism is "first for the Jew" (Mr. Inside) and "then for the Gentile" (Mr. Outside). The powerful Gospel of salvation aimed first at the Jew, self-satisfied by birth into God's people, often self-righteous, sometimes entrenched in tradition. Church members today often fall into a similar category. The same Gospel aims secondly at the Gentile, often nonreligious or idolatrous and immoral. The unchurched person today often displays similar characteristics.

Evangelism provides impressive power. The Greek word for power is related to our word "dynamite." Dynamite for the Jew. Look how God transformed the apostles into dynamic witnesses. Look how Saul was dramatically changed to Paul, the great missionary. Church members today are likewise transformed as they live in their baptism and listen to God's Word.

Dynamite for the Gentile. The church grew by leaps and bounds as the Gospel changed people like the jailer at Philippi and his household. The same change occurs with the unchurched today as sin is exposed and needs are met in the death of Jesus Christ.

Whom does God tap as the messengers of evangelism? You and I minister to one another with the good news of Jesus Christ. You and I can be equipped by God to share the Gospel of Christ.

Prayer

Dear Lord, use me to reach those inside and outside the church with Your power unto salvation through Jesus Christ. Amen.

Encounters with Jesus: Andrew

Reading: John 1:35–42

Text: John 1:41—"The first thing Andrew did was to find his brother Simon and tell him, 'We have found the Messiah.' "

Andrew—the story of his encounter with Jesus is a simple, powerful one that can help us as we seek to share the faith.

Andrews are needed to hear about Jesus. A little-known disciple of John the Baptizer sees the man from Nazareth and hears Him identified as the Lamb of God. He believes and rejoices. Before going out to witness, we need to see Jesus as the Lamb of God. By His grace we believe and rejoice. Again and again we hear His Word.

Andrews are needed to follow Jesus. Andrew, having seen Jesus, asked where He was staying and followed Him to learn more. He obeyed and became one of Jesus' disciples. We also need to follow Jesus. Believing, we want to hear Him again and again. We hear and obey and hear and obey. He makes us His disciples. We regularly grow through Word and Sacrament. We study the Word personally and in groups. We serve as Jesus leads.

Andrews are needed to bring others to Jesus. The minute Andrew left Jesus, he hurried to tell his brother, "We have found the Messiah." Then he brought Simon to Jesus. And Simon Peter became a powerful spokesman for the early church. Andrew: a quiet witness, a relatively unknown follower of Jesus, an important instrument of God's love.

God needs us also to bring a brother or sister to Jesus. He brought us to faith in our baptism. We see Jesus, crucified and risen for us. We follow Him by hearing and obeying.

He provides us with power to witness. Very simply and quietly we go to the family member, the neighbor, the co-worker, the friend and say, "We have found the Messiah." And we bring that person to Jesus through His church. Yes, Andrews are needed today. That means you and me.

Prayer

Lord Jesus, use me like Andrew to bring someone to You. Amen.

Encounters with Jesus: Philip

Reading: John 1:43–51

Text: John 1:43—"Finding Philip, he said to him, 'Follow me.' "

During the Epiphany season our eyes focus on Jesus as the Light of the world, revealed in many miraculous ways. In John's gospel many people had encounters with Jesus. How did they respond?

Jesus finds Philip and simply says, "Follow me." No other introductions. So far only Peter and Andrew have been called as disciples. An absolute call. No strings attached. No explanations given. Simply "Follow me."

Philip obeyed. He accepted Jesus' call. Immediately he went to Nathanael and told him that they had found the Messiah. A response of faith in Jesus as Savior, and witness to a friend.

Jesus likewise finds us and simply says, "Follow me." He comes to us in our baptism, in His Word, and in Holy Communion. "Follow me." For life. Day-by-day. Without reservation.

How do we respond? We may insist on knowing more details, on qualifying our answer, but He continues calling, "Follow me."

The motion picture *The Hiding Place* recounts a real call to discipleship. During World War II the ten Boom family lives in the Nazi-occupied Netherlands, where Jews are being captured and exterminated. They are faced with the decision of whether to hide Jews in their home. They decide they must obey by hiding Jewish refugees in a secret room. Ultimately, when detected, they pay dearly.

God worked in Philip's heart to follow Jesus. He moved Corrie ten Boom and her family to do the same. And He sent His Son to pay for our sins by dying on the cross so that we might follow Him as well.

Prayer

Jesus, still lead on Till our rest be won;
And although the way be cheerless,
We will follow calm and fearless;
Guide us by your hand To our fatherland.

Encounters with Jesus: Nathanael

Reading: John 1:43–51

Text: John 1:46—" 'Nazareth! Can anything good come from there?' Nathanael asked."

Another encounter with Jesus. Philip follows by going to Nathanael and telling him about Jesus of Nazareth, the Messiah. Rather than following Jesus immediately, Nathanael questions, "Nazareth! Can anything good come from there?" Notice that Nathanael is not an atheist or agnostic, but a God-fearing man, "a true Israelite, in whom there is nothing false" (v. 47). Yet he questions Jesus and His credentials.

In the motion picture *The Hiding Place,* while the ten Boom family decides to follow Jesus at great risk by harboring Jewish refugees in their home, the local pastor visits them and wrestles with the moral choices involved. He questions. Finally, out of fear he decides not to get involved.

But Jesus reaches out to a questioning Nathanael. Philip answers Nathanael with the simple invitation, "Come and see." As Nathanael approaches, Jesus identifies him as a true Israelite. Still questioning, Nathanael asks, "How do you know me?" Jesus replies, "I saw you while you were still under the fig tree before Philip called you."

Now Nathanael responds in faith and is ready to follow, "Rabbi, you are the Son of God." Jesus leads him on to greater understanding and greater service.

In the same way Jesus answers our many questions, with the simple invitation, "Come and see." He then lets us know that He has called us by name. We belong to Him. He lived and died for us. He knows our potential for service. And He has a wonderful plan for our future as we follow Him. Our questioning is turned into a simple confession of faith, "Rabbi, you are the Son of God."

Prayer

Dear heavenly Father, forgive my endless questioning of Your love, Your Word, and Your plan for my life. Help me like Nathanael to confess Jesus as Lord and Savior. Amen.

Bearing Witness to the Lamb

Reading: John 1:29–34

Text: John 1:29b—"Look, the Lamb of God, who takes away the sin of the world!"

All of us treasure events we have personally witnessed—a presidential inauguration, a World Series, or a Superbowl game. We freely tell about our experience.

John's gospel records a dramatic moment in history. John the Baptist watches a man walk among the crowds of Israel. It is the long-awaited moment when the Messiah begins His public ministry. John, aware of this decisive moment, bears joyful witness: "Look, the Lamb of God, who takes away the sin of the world!" The phrase "Lamb of God" may have sprung from a recollection of Isaiah 53, where the Messiah is described as a lamb led to the slaughter. Clearly John labels Jesus as the Savior of the world.

We also need to bear witness. Each of us has seen the Lamb of God, crucified and risen, in the pages of Holy Scripture. By our lives of service and our words of witness we can say to others, "Look, the Lamb of God!" Yet we often fail. Our witness fades when the going gets rough. Sometimes it loses steam. Or we fall into the trap of witnessing to ourselves—our faithfulness, our commitment—instead of to the Lamb of God.

John could have experienced the same witness problems. But God chose John, empowered him through the Word, and disciplined his life so that his witness to the Lamb never faded. He would not bend, nor would he permit the crowds to give him the honor that was due Jesus. He focused steadfastly on the Lamb of God.

The same God who sent the Lamb to be sacrificed on our behalf also makes us His strong, unwavering disciples through a disciplined life of Word and prayer. Refusing honor for ourselves, we steadfastly bear witness to the Lamb of God who takes away the sin of the world!

Prayer
See, the Lamb, so long expected,
Comes with pardon down from heav'n.
Let us haste, with tears of sorrow,
One and all, to be forgiv'n.

24

Follow Me!

Reading: Mark 1:14–20

Text: Mark 1:17—" 'Come, follow me,' Jesus said, 'and I will make you fishers of men.' "

Out of nowhere comes a man, walking beside the Sea of Galilee. Born in obscure Nazareth, baptized 30 years later in the Jordan, just beginning to proclaim the kingdom of God, He approaches four fishermen, hard at work with their nets, and asks them to follow Him. Incredibly they follow, leaving their vocation behind. Who is this man? What authority elicits such a total response from these rugged fishermen?

We live in a skeptical age. Many voices call us to follow—endless sales people, TV evangelists, political leaders, etc. Generally we tune out the voices and follow the line of least resistance. Year after year we keep the same job, live in the same home, observe the same traditions.

When the Man from Galilee visits you and says, "Follow me," how do you respond? Turn His voice off as one more sales pitch? Listen halfheartedly and respond with a polite affirmative to get rid of Him? Agree to follow Him on some Sundays and when it seems convenient? Who is He? With what authority does He speak?

Admitting our lethargy and rebellion, we meet Him face to face, Jesus Christ, the Son of God and Savior of the world. We cannot follow on our own. But He has blazed the path of personal self-giving and death on a cross to pay for our sins. His call to follow carries with it the power for us to leave our nets and follow Him.

The adventure begins—loving Him, fishing for others to follow Him as well, finding new meaning and sparkle in our daily routines, living and loving with purpose and joy. Troubles and persecution may lie ahead. Temptations will abound. Other voices will try to lead us astray. But the forgiving, loving, empowering Man from Galilee continues to sound the gentle, life-changing call, FOLLOW ME!

Prayer
Lord, help us to follow You. Amen.

The Need for Refreshment

Reading: Mark 1:29–39

Text: Mark 1:35—"Very early in the morning, while it was still dark, Jesus got up, left the house and went off to a solitary place, where he prayed."

A typical day in the ministry of Jesus! He taught and expelled a demon in the synagogue. He spent the lunch hour healing Peter's mother-in-law of a fever. In the evening He was mobbed by townspeople who came to the door with the sick and demon-possessed.

Exhausted by the day's labors, does He sleep late the next day and eat a leisurely breakfast? On the contrary, Jesus gets up in the predawn darkness and goes to a solitary place for prayer. As true man He needs refreshment and finds it in a devotional communion with the heavenly Father. Immediately the demands of the next day's ministry crowd in on Him. Everyone is looking for Him. Refreshed, He continues His preaching throughout Galilee.

What kind of typical days do you have? Hectic demands from family and co-workers. Hurried banking and shopping for supper. Endless trips to piano lessons and dental appointments. The telephone ringing off the hook. Evening meetings. Another similar day to dread. Do you need refreshment?

Many say, "With my impossible schedule I don't have time for a daily devotional period with God. I know I need it, but I can't work it out." Jesus needed the refreshment of prayer precisely because the demands of His ministry were so great. In obedience He steadily moved to the cross, where He died for our sins, including our devotional failures. He makes available His Word and also other Christians to encourage us in our devotional life.

Picture that quiet time—early morning, midday, or late at night—a few moments alone in the presence of a loving, strengthening God, an oasis for refreshment, a new surge of energy and enthusiasm for the rest of the day, direction and guidance for loving ministry to others.

Prayer

Dear Lord, refresh me with Your Word and support me in my daily devotional time with You. Amen.

Need a Doctor?

Reading: Mark 2:13–17

Text: Mark 2:17—"It is not the healthy who need a doctor, but the sick. I have not come to call the righteous, but sinners."

How sad when a desperately sick person refuses to admit the need for help! A cancer may be growing inside, but everything seems normal on the outside. The increasingly sharp pains or a suspicious lump are ignored. Doctors stand ready to help, but the fatally diseased person continues pretending health.

Jesus serves as the Great Physician of physical and spiritual diseases. Approaching Levi at a tax collector's booth, He summons him to follow. Recognizing his spiritual alienation, Levi forsakes his questionable occupation and receives spiritual healing from the Savior. Jesus then eats with other tax collectors and notorious sinners to offer them similar healing.

Meanwhile the self-righteous Pharisees protest His associating with such people.

Where are you, my friend? Do you pretend health, though desperately sick with sin? Do you feel righteous because of a decent moral life, membership in a church, service to your community—while looking with disdain at alcoholics and drug addicts, divorced couples and unwed mothers, poverty-level families on welfare, and minority groups? Or do you let the Great Physician probe your innermost heart, diagnose a fatal disobedience and rebellion against God, and offer you Himself as the full payment for sin, the only treatment for your disease?

Jesus came for you. He loves you. He offers you life, now and for eternity. NEED A DOCTOR?

Prayer

We deserve but grief and shame,
Yet his words, rich grace revealing,
Pardon, peace, and life proclaim.
Here our ills have perfect healing;
We with humble hearts believe
Jesus sinners will receive.

Power Source Unlimited

Reading: Ephesians 1:18–23

Text: Ephesians 1:18b–19a—" . . . in order that you might know . . . his incomparably great power for us who believe."

Today our world knows limits. We need tremendous power every day to drive industrial machines, light cities and homes, fuel cars, and heat buildings. What power sources can we find? Power in great demand. Power sources limited.

How exciting are the words of Paul in the spiritual realm! We need tremendous spiritual power in our world to carry out God's saving plan for humanity. Writing to the Ephesians, Paul describes a power source unlimited, " . . . his incomparably great power for us who believe. That power is like the working of his mighty strength, which he exerted in Christ when he raised him from the dead and seated him at his right hand in the heavenly realms."

We have power for Christian living, God's power. He demonstrated that power by raising Christ from the dead. The resurrection powerfully announces God's acceptance of Christ's sacrifice for our sins. Weak and helpless on our own, inept to help others, we receive God's power when He works faith in our hearts at our baptism. In short, Christ's resurrection power becomes available "for us who believe." Christ continues to reign in power at the right hand of the Father. Therefore, plugged into Christ by faith, we possess a power source unlimited.

In the next three devotions we explore how that power of God can be unleashed in our lives for the blessing of many. But what a comfort to know that God's spiritual power source will never run low!

Prayer
All hail the pow'r of Jesus' name!
Let angels prostrate fall;
Bring forth the royal diadem
And crown him Lord of all.

Word Power

Reading: Romans 1:8–17

Text: Romans 1:16—"I am not ashamed of the gospel, because it is the power of God for the salvation of everyone who believes."

Dynamite packs terrific power. Atomic and hydrogen bombs contain terrifying power. Modern technology sports an impressive array of powerful machines. But words perhaps convey even greater power. A word triggers the dynamite in the bombs and instructs powerful machines to operate.

We looked yesterday at God's spiritual power source unlimited, focusing on the resurrection of Jesus Christ from the dead. Romans 1:16, our text, describes the Word that unlocks that power source.

Gospel—the Word. Good news. God's good news about a Savior who took upon Himself our unrighteousness. Righteous, He paid the price on the cross. God declares the world righteous for Christ's sake. That righteousness comes to us by faith in Christ.

And Paul calls that Gospel the power of God for salvation, "dynamite" according to the Greek word for power. Word power. Gospel power. What sheer joy as a believer to have in our possession such Word power. The church preaches that Word and administers the sacraments as visible words.

We hear the Gospel every day for our own assurance and power. We speak the Gospel every day for the salvation of others. We live the Gospel because we have been instructed to operate with power for others. Word power unlocks God's spiritual power source unlimited.

Prayer

The Gospel shows the Father's grace,
Who sent his Son to save our race,
Proclaims how Jesus lived and died
That man might thus be justified.
It is the pow'r of God to save
From sin and Satan and the grave;
It works the faith, which firmly clings
To all the treasures which it brings.

Go Power

Reading: Matthew 28:16–20

Text: Matthew 28:19–20a—"All authority in heaven and on earth has been given to me. Therefore go and make disciples of all nations."

America, a nation on the go. We work, travel, exercise, play, and celebrate. We get up early, work through lunch, and stay up late. We live by the clock and the digital watch and the odometer. And we need "go power" to keep moving—breakfast cereals, fruit juices, vitamins, candy bars, and pep pills. Nevertheless, we frequently run out of gas and lie exhausted in front of the television.

Most of us would agree that some of this "going" makes little sense. There is one going, however, that is of the utmost importance. Jesus speaks of it when He says, "Therefore go and make disciples of all nations, baptizing them in the name of the Father and of the Son and of the Holy Spirit, and teaching them to obey everything I have commanded you." Not a going to get rich or to find thrills, but a going to make disciples of all nations, to share that Gospel Word power with family members, neighbors, co-workers, golfing partners, church friends, and people in other lands. Good reason for going.

But where do we get the power for such going? Jesus answers that question on the Great Commission mountain. "All authority in heaven and on earth has been given to me," He says. He supplies the go power from His limitless supply. Crucified and risen from the dead, He offers forgiveness and endless refreshment. Through Word power—His Gospel—we receive all the go power we will ever need. He promises to be with us always, to the very end of the age. What comfort!

Prayer

Send now, O Lord, to ev'ry place
Swift messengers before your face,
The heralds of your wondrous grace,
Where you yourself will come.

Staying Power

Reading: 2 Corinthians 12:7–10

Text: 2 Corinthians 12:9—"But he said to me, 'My grace is sufficient for you, for my power is made perfect in weakness.' "

True power needs to last. Many distance runners start with a burst of energy but fade on the stretch. The best athletes sometimes lose to a steadier team which takes better conditioning into the final quarter or overtime period. We are describing staying power.

Yes, God provides a power source unlimited in the resurrection of His Son. He also supplies Word power, the Gospel, to unlock that power source. And He intends for us to use His resources to keep going over the long haul, to have staying power.

Paul, the great on-the-go missionary, learned the importance of staying power when God sent him a thorn in the flesh, some illness or physical handicap that simply wouldn't go away. Paul prayed and hoped, but the problem remained. Discouraged and frustrated, Paul finally got the message of our text. Paul was being conditioned for the long haul. He felt weak and unable to continue. At that point he learned to accept his weakness and rely totally on God's grace and power. Now he could face any troubles, because Christ was always there for him.

Similarly we will experience discouragement and frustration after our initial "going." We will experience God's testing in our personal lives as well as in our witnessing efforts. But God says also to us, "My grace is sufficient for you, for my power is made perfect in weakness." We look to the weak and helpless Son of God, nailed to a cross for us, and then experience His resurrection power flowing from the empty tomb to us in our weakness.

Prayer

Sing, pray, and keep his ways unswerving,
Offer your service faithfully,
And trust his word; though undeserving,
You'll find his promise true to be.
God never will forsake in need
The soul that trusts in him indeed.

Snow for Slowing Down

Reading: Psalm 131

Text: Psalm 46:10—"Be still, and know that I am God; I will be exalted among the nations, I will be exalted in the earth."

In many parts of America, now is the time for heavy snowstorms. Snow for building snow forts and snowmen—the delight of all red-blooded American children. Snow to be shoveled and reshoveled—the plague of all middle-aged men.

A little four-year-old boy named David recently asked his mother, "Why does God let it keep snowing so much?" The mother's answer is worth pondering. She told David, "God is making it snow because He thinks we've been going too fast and should slow down." It's true that snow slows us down. We complain because snow-covered streets prolong our drive to work. Some of our planned trips or evenings of entertainment need to be canceled.

Could such delays be good for us? Are you spending some time with your family? Have you taken the time to play with your children and really get to know them as human beings? The snow may be a blessing in disguise. Use the time to relax at home. Light up a fire and pop some popcorn. Have some real enjoyment with the family. Try relaxing and reflecting a little on your life.

Perhaps God is saying to us: Slow down and think. Through our text He reminds us how great He is and how much in control. When we slow down, God has a chance to enter our thoughts. He can point us to the passing of time and to our many shortcomings. He can remind us that His own Son Jesus Christ came into this world to bring us salvation. Jesus did not always hurry. He took time out to go on a mountain alone to pray. He relaxed at the home of His friends Mary, Martha, and Lazarus. Even His suffering and death were basically passive. He did not concoct some activist plot to conquer the world. Rather He remained silent while His captors put Him to death.

Perhaps we need more snow time to think about God and His Son Jesus Christ and to make Him a part of our family life.

Prayer Thoughts

Thank God for the snow and for the opportunity to slow down for time with Him and each other.

Snow for Serving Others

Reading: Philippians 2:5–8

Text: Galatians 5:13c—"Serve one another in love."

More thoughts on snow today. I notice that heavy snow seems to bind people together and moves them to help each other. Sunday morning two men shoveled out their entire court so that all of the apartment residents could get their cars out. When a car got stuck in the parking lot of our school, two adults plus several teenagers shoveled and pushed to get the car going.

Perhaps we have a second answer to the little boy's question: "Why does God let it keep snowing so much?" God is sending snow to encourage us to serve others in need. Or as Paul says in Galatians, "Serve one another in love." The two answers are complementary. We need to slow down and recognize our need for God. He alone can make us His own and forgive our sins through Jesus Christ. Then when we realize that He has done everything for us, we are moved in turn to start helping others.

So often we show indifference to others. Perhaps a snowstorm is needed to wake us up to people obviously in need of assistance. Even snowstorms provide no panacea. I suspect that if snow continues for an extended period, our initial enthusiasm for pushing stalled cars and shoveling whole parking lots might quickly fade.

Nevertheless, helping others can be a real joy. The comradeship and enjoyment you experienced from helping your neighbor in the snowstorm can become a permanent part of your life. Stop thinking only of your own problems. Get involved in the lives of others. That's the meaning of serving one another in love.

Remember why you serve and how you are able to serve—because God sent His Son Jesus to be a servant and to humble Himself and become obedient unto death, even death on a cross. He served you and frees you to serve others. Let it snow!

Prayer Thoughts

Consider ways to serve others in small practical ways.
Ask God's strength and guidance for Jesus' sake.

Needed—a Gospel Partnership

Reading: Philippians 4:14–16

Text: Philippians 1:4–5—"In all my prayers for all of you, I always pray with joy because of your partnership in the gospel from the first day until now."

Lonely, depressed Christians. Paul writes to the Philippian Christians from prison in Rome. A lonely Christian? Persecuted and suffering for his faith, Paul could be lonely and depressed. But he writes the joyful words of our text.

Paul knows he is not alone, for he has the Philippian Christians as partners in the Gospel. They heard and believed the message of Christ Crucified when he first visited Philippi. No wonder Paul rejoices and continues his own Gospel ministry with power.

Are you a lonely Christian, wallowing in self-pity and despair, afraid to stand up for the Gospel, helpless before the onslaught of a rebellious world? Or do you see the partnership in the Gospel from the first day until now—the Christian pastor faithfully proclaiming the Gospel and administering the sacraments, the retired factory worker with years of Gospel experience amidst the trials of life, the teenager excited about telling friends about Jesus? Sinful, struggling believers, to be sure, but Gospel partners, washed clean by the blood of the Lamb, sustained by God through suffering, and giving of themselves to others with a quiet joy, rooted in the Gospel promises.

Jesus Christ endured a lonely death on the cross so that you might be forgiven and drawn into the fellowship of the Gospel. And you, yes, you, can be a partner in the Gospel every day.

Prayer
Blest be the tie that binds
Our hearts in Christian love;
The unity of heart and mind
Is like to that above.

Promised—Continued Partnership Power

Reading: Philippians 1:6–11

Text: Philippians 1:6—". . . being confident of this, that he who began a good work in you will carry it on to completion until the day of Christ Jesus."

How many partnerships begin with great hopes and dreams only to end in failure and broken promises? A wagon train heads west with the common goal of finding a good location to settle, with green pastureland, fresh water, and perhaps gold. The train thins out as desert, Indian raiders, and illness take their toll. Finally, a crude settlement develops at journey's end, complete with general store, blacksmith shop, saloon, bank, school, and church. The future looks bright, but a few years later—bypassed by railroads, battered by severe winters, empty of gold—the original wagon train partnership ends in a ghost town, doors flapping in the wind, tumbleweeds blowing in the deserted street.

Paul knows the temptations threatening the Philippian Christians—persecution, strife and jealous bickering from within, discouragement over his absence and imprisonment. Therefore he adds the precious Gospel promise that God will bring His work in us to completion. By human efforts even the closest fellowship will eventually disintegrate. But the God who sent His Son to the cross will continue nurturing His church through the Gospel.

Your Gospel partnership will be threatened both from without and from within. People move out. Neighborhoods change. Pastors come and go. Buildings age. Sometimes Biblical mission is neglected. But Paul's confidence applies to you as well. Centered in the Word and sacraments, you see again that the same God who began the Gospel partnership around His crucified and risen Son will continue that good work until Jesus comes again.

Prayer

The Church's one foundation Is Jesus Christ, her Lord;
She is his new creation By water and the Word.
From heav'n he came and sought her To be his holy bride;
With his own blood he bought her, And for her life he died.

A Backwards Desire

Reading: Philippians 1:20–26

Text: Philippians 1:23—"I desire to depart and be with Christ, which is better by far."

We live backwards, trying to avoid death at any cost. Anxiously we review the holiday death tolls on the highway, shudder at tragic air crashes and tornado, earthquake, and flood disasters, and tremble at dreaded terminal diseases like cancer and leukemia. We try to hide death behind nice-sounding words and cosmetic surroundings.

Paul didn't view death or life that way. Imprisoned in Rome, uncertain as to whether he would be put to death by his captors, he welcomed the thought of death with these words, "I desire to depart and be with Christ, which is better by far." Earlier he wrote the Philippians, "To me . . . to die is gain." Paul knew that Jesus Christ endured death on a cross to pay for the sins of the world. Alive from the dead, Jesus was preparing a place for Paul in heaven, a glorious way to spend eternity. Believing in Christ, confident of a far better eternal life in heaven, Paul had a zest and a purpose for living.

Do you desire to "be with Christ, which is better by far"? Do you kneel penitently at His cross, recognizing the full forgiveness of your sins? Do you joyfully see the empty tomb and anticipate the heavenly celebration around the throne of the Lamb? God supplies a foretaste of the heavenly feast through His Holy Meal. As the desire grows to be with Christ forever, the zest returns for living joyfully today in humble service to others.

A backwards desire to the world, but a life-giving approach to life and death for the Christian. Death may be near, but with faith in Christ the future is secure. We are free to live for others backwards from death to life.

Prayer

If death my portion be, It brings great gain to me;
It speeds my life's endeavor To live with Christ forever.
He gives me joy in sorrow, Come death now or tomorrow.

Profit or Loss?

Reading: Philippians 3:1–10

Text: Philippians 3:7—"Whatever was to my profit I now consider loss for the sake of Christ."

How we guard and cultivate our assets in life—degrees, promotions earned, civic honors, financial balance sheet, club memberships! While wanting to appear humble, we secretly savor our accomplishments and expect to profit from our assets, perhaps even in God's heavenly ledger.

Paul understood our drive for profit. He was a Hebrew of Hebrews, a Pharisee, a persecutor of the church, and a faultless observer of legal principles. He honestly sought to please God by his actions—until he found himself in the dust of the Damascus road, at odds with Jesus Christ, whom he persecuted. Blinded, alone, convicted of his many sins before God and men, Saul of Tarsus is baptized and comes to know Jesus as the crucified and risen Savior.

Now Paul sees all his own righteousness, however humanly impressive, as mere rubbish. He gladly lays it aside for the priceless righteousness that comes from God and is by faith in Christ. He now lives with reckless abandon for Christ, his only profit.

A painful review of our assets is in order. Before God we are weighed in the balance and found wanting. Selfish, rebellious, manipulative, we find ourselves with mere rubbish before God and others. But Christ's righteousness, demonstrated by His sinless life and sacrificial death, stands for us as profit before the Father. Trusting in Christ alone for salvation, we live unburdened, using our assets by His grace to proclaim Jesus Christ and the power of His resurrection. What gain when we count our profit as loss and His sacrificial loss as our profit!

Prayer

Dear Lord, help me to count all as loss for Your sake. Amen.

Daily at the Door

Reading: Proverbs 8:1–36

Text: Proverbs 8:34—"Blessed is the man who listens to me, watching daily at my doors, waiting at my doorway."

Many successful people started out at the doorstep of those they admired. Many children in American history came to the doors of printers, blacksmiths, and bakers to apprentice themselves for a career. Young men followed Socrates and other philosophers to gain morsels of wisdom.

Proverbs 8 personifies wisdom and declares, "Whoever finds me finds life and receives favor from the Lord." Pride and arrogance stand condemned. Evil behavior and perverse speech are hated. But simple, humble willingness to come to God and let Him guide into all truth brings wisdom. Daily at the door of God's wisdom brings life.

Today's world provides many competing doorsteps—scientific knowledge, business acumen, psychological success strategies, secular philosophies. Each beckons for a daily visit at the door. Wisdom's door described by Proverbs may appear less appealing.

But that wisdom leads to Christ, the Power of God and the Wisdom of God. Try reading Proverbs 8, substituting Christ for wisdom and its pronouns. Wait at the door of Bethlehem, the temple, the Nazareth synagogue, the home of Mary and Martha, the upper room. Follow Him on the dusty roads, along the seashore, through the Jerusalem streets to Calvary, to the mountain in Galilee. Read the Word. Worship in His house with bread and wine. Daily at the door—His door—means life, eternal life, for you and those you bring to Him.

Prayer
Wisdom's highest, noblest treasure,
Jesus, is revealed in you.
Let me find in you my pleasure,
Make my will and actions true,
Humility there and simplicity reigning,
In paths of true wisdom my steps ever training.
If I learn from Jesus this knowledge divine,
The blessing of heavenly wisdom is mine.

The Saving Boast

Reading: Galatians 6:12–18

Text: Galatians 6:14a—"May I never boast except in the cross of our Lord Jesus Christ."

We boast. Family pictures quickly available in our wallet for everyone to see. Trophies in our family rooms of past athletic glory. Service awards proudly displayed on the wall behind our desk. Country club luncheons for clients where the head waiter knows us. Fashionable clothing with the right labels displayed. We boast. Sadly, we boast about externals which provide nothing permanent.

They boasted in Paul's day too. The Judaizers came with requirements for the new believers in Jesus Christ. A return to Jewish laws and customs for authentic faith. Circumcision most of all. The external mark which counts. Something to boast about. Sadly, they missed the mark because all the external customs in the world provide nothing permanent.

Paul, a Hebrew of the Hebrews, one of the circumcised, could have joined the external boasting. But instead, he writes powerfully, "May I never boast except in the cross of our Lord Jesus Christ, through which the world has been crucified to me, and I to the world. Neither circumcision nor uncircumcision means anything; what counts is a new creation." Paul describes the saving boast, the only legitimate boast—clinging to the cross of Jesus Christ for full and free salvation.

We boast. Not of ourselves nor of our accomplishments nor of our pedigree. We boast that Jesus Christ renounced all boasting and went to the shameful cross to pay for our sins. We belong to Him. We have been crucified with Christ. Therefore we live. No, Christ lives in us. We belong to His new creation. Thank God for the saving boast!

Prayer

Till then—nor is my boasting vain—
Till then I boast a Savior slain;
And oh, may this my glory be,
That Christ is not ashamed of me!

Skin-Deep Beauty

Reading: 1 Samuel 15:10–26

Text: 1 Samuel 9:2—"He had a son named Saul, an impressive young man without equal among the Israelites—a head taller than any of the others."

We place great value on outward beauty. Teenage magazines sponsor dream guy and beauty queen contests with emphasis on looks and personality. Men and women of all ages work, sweat, diet, and exercise to remain trim and avoid wrinkles. As for the inevitable aging process, cosmetic and fashion companies provide expensive ways to cover it up and make us appear more beautiful than we look in the morning mirror. In short, we emphasize skin-deep beauty.

Saul filled the bill as an attractive king for Israel. But Saul's beauty turned out to be only skin-deep. Shortly after becoming king, he revealed his inner character by disobeying God on two successive occasions. To make matters worse, he tried to cover up his sin by lying and blaming others. The Lord came to Samuel and said, "I am grieved that I have made Saul king, because he has turned away from me and has not carried out my instructions" (1 Sam. 15:10).

Saul's skin-deep beauty and inner ugliness make us look at our own lives. Are we guilty of devoting major attention to our outward appearance while neglecting our relationship to God? Do we cover up physical blemishes so artfully that we also cover up our sins against God and others? In honesty, we need to confess a beauty that is only skin-deep and sinful hearts, deserving the clear label of ugly.

God knows our hearts and sent His Son to die for our sins. He covers our sins with Christ's righteousness. No need for us to cover up. He makes us truly beautiful in Christ. As His children we have no need to concentrate on a beauty that is only skin-deep.

Prayer

Forgive us, dear Father, for pursuing skin-deep beauty. Point us to Your Son, who died on the cross to make us truly beautiful. Amen.

His Ugly Beauty

Reading: Isaiah 52:13–53:12

Text: Isaiah 52:14b—"His appearance was so disfigured beyond that of any man and his form marred beyond human likeness."

Yesterday we described the world's fascination with outward beauty. "Dress for success," we are told. A political candidate's television image rates as all-important for a winning campaign. By the same token, society shudders at ugliness. We try to hide the sick and handicapped behind the walls of institutions.

But God reverses the process. In Isaiah, God describes the Suffering Servant as physically ugly: "He had no beauty or majesty to attract us to him, nothing in his appearance that we should desire him" (Is. 53:2b). Jesus Christ, the beautiful and all-powerful Son of God from eternity, became a true human being at Bethlehem. Though a king, He chose to serve by suffering. "He was despised and rejected by men" (v. 3a). Arrested, tried, and convicted, he was nailed to a cross, the most despised death available. From a human standpoint His birth, life, suffering, and death were ugly.

Yet God saw beauty in His ugliness. He came for us, for a world trapped in the ugliness of sin. "He took up our infirmities and carried our sorrows . . . . But he was pierced for our transgressions, he was crushed for our iniquities; the punishment that brought us peace was upon him, and by his wounds we are healed" (vv. 4a, 5). God says, "I will give him a portion among the great . . . because he poured out his life unto death" (v. 12). God raised Jesus Christ from the grave to His right hand. Unsurpassed beauty.

We look at Him amazed. Ugly beauty. We bow in humble adoration before His nail-pierced hands and crown of thorns. We rejoice in His ugly beauty.

Prayer

Beautiful Savior, Lord of the nations,
Son of God and Son of Man!
Glory and honor, Praise, adoration,
Now and forevermore be thine!

Inner Beauty

Reading: 1 Peter 3:1–9

Text: 1 Peter 3:4b—". . . the unfading beauty of a gentle and quiet spirit, which is of great worth in God's sight."

Full circle. We looked at skin-deep beauty, so appealing to the world but masking the inner ugliness of sin. Then we focused on Jesus Christ, whose humble, suffering life and death appeared ugly to the world but provided a beautiful salvation for us. Today the apostle Peter describes inner beauty as he pens words to husbands and wives.

He writes to wives, "Your beauty should not come from outward adornment, such as braided hair and the wearing of gold jewelry and fine clothes. Instead, it should be that of your inner self, the unfading beauty of a gentle and quiet spirit, which is of great worth in God's sight" (vv. 3–4). He proceeds to describe beautiful inner qualities for husbands and all believers, including consideration, respect, sympathy, love, compassion, and humility. True beauty lies in the heart, not on the surface.

Do we display inner beauty to others in our daily lives? As husbands or wives, as parents or children, as employers or employees, as pastors or laity, do we radiate God's love? You see, inner beauty comes only from God. We do not manufacture or buy it. No catalog or cosmetics company can guarantee it to us. In fact, our nature will lead us to sin and ugliness.

But God sent His own dear Son to live and die for us. Jesus demonstrated humility, a quiet spirit, compassion, and love as He ministered to the multitudes and went obediently to the cross. He died for our inner ugliness.

Now Christ lives in us through our baptism. Clothed with Christ's righteousness, we also, by His grace, display the inner beauty which comes from Him. Through our daily example others see Christ, and His beauty becomes theirs as well. Inner beauty—His gift to us for others!

Prayer

Dear Father, give us the inner beauty of a life yielded to You. Amen.

A Mouthful

Reading: Psalm 71:14–18

Text: Psalm 71:8—"My mouth is filled with your praise, declaring your splendor all day long."

Picture a delightful, tasty morsel filling your mouth—a juicy filet mignon, a tangy lemon meringue pie with flaky crust, or a superb pasta with zesty meat sauce. What a mouthful to be savored and then swallowed with delight. But before long, the stomach grows full and the appetite wanes.

The psalmist describes a different kind of mouthful, no less delightful, "My mouth is filled with your praise, declaring your splendor all day long." Struggling with evil around him, needing deliverance from the grasp of wicked and cruel men, he nevertheless remembers the marvelous blessings of God from the moment of his birth. He sees God as his Hope, Refuge, and Rescue. Therefore his mouth is filled with God's praise, not just for a hungry moment, but all day long. The more he declares the splendor of God, the more he enjoys his mouthful of praise.

And what of us? Do we fill our mouth only with fattening foods? Do we fill our mouth with complaining, profaning, slandering words all day long? Or can we say with the psalmist, "My mouth is filled with your praise, declaring your splendor all day long"? How often our indulgent mouthfuls turn flat and indigestion follows. How often our negative words leave our mouth stale and empty, with an emotional hangover remaining.

But God spoke His joyful word at creation, at Bethlehem, at Jordan, and at the empty tomb. He still speaks at the baptismal font, the lectern, and the altar table that our sins are forgiven as we eat Christ's body and drink His blood. Indeed, by His grace—from birth to death and beyond—our mouth is filled with His praise all day long. What a mouthful!

Prayer

"O Lord, open my lips, and my mouth will declare your praise" (Ps. 51:15). Amen.

Who Do You Say I Am?

Reading: Mark 8:27–33

Text: Mark 8:29b—"Who do you say I am?" Peter answered, "You are the Christ."

A pivotal question in the Gospel of Mark: "Who do you say I am?" Jesus stands with His disciples at Caesarea Philippi and raises the question of His Messiahship. They have been listening to Him for some time now and observing his miracles. How will they answer?

Peter answers simply and clearly, "You are the Christ." A beautiful confession, right on target, a life-giving answer. Peter at least has listened, watched, and believed. But shortly thereafter, when Jesus describes what kind of Messiah He is, namely one who will suffer, die, and rise again, Peter rebukes Him for such foolish talk. Much to learn.

A pivotal question today. "Who do you say I am?" Jesus stands in our midst and raises the question about His Messiahship. We have learned about Him over a period of years. We belong to churches, listen to sermons, study the Bible, talk with one another about our faith, participate in Holy Communion. How will we answer? Some say Jesus was a great teacher, a brilliant philosopher, a bold prophet, a fiery revolutionary, a great martyr, and a wonderful, loving man to be emulated.

We answer simply, "You are the Christ." We know that He is the Son of God, the promised Messiah. But are we prepared for Jesus' description of the kind of Messiah He is—a rejected, suffering, dying Christ? Do we rebuke Him and choose a prosperous life also for ourselves? Much to learn.

Jesus has shown us who He is and why He came. He went to the cross for us to pay for our sins. He has given us new life in Baptism. He gives us a life to lose and a cross to bear for His sake. Peter later preached on Pentecost: "God has made this Jesus, whom you crucified, both Lord and Christ." He learned to answer the pivotal question, and so have we. Thank God!

Prayer

Lord Jesus, confirm in our hearts that You are the Christ, our crucified and risen Savior. Amen.

Mountaintop Experiences

Reading: Mark 9:2–9

Text: Mark 9:5—"Peter said to Jesus, 'Rabbi, it is good for us to be here.' "

Mountaintop experiences. Easter Sunday morning—Easter lilies, full choir, trumpets, a rousing message. Confirmation—questions and answers, white robes, special flowers, standing before the altar, public confession of faith, special Bible verse, the joy of Holy Communion. "It is good for us to be here."

Mountaintop experience. Near the end of His ministry Jesus takes three disciples with Him on a high mountain. Suddenly He is transfigured before them with clothes dazzling white. Moses and Elijah appear with Jesus, attesting that He is indeed the beloved Son of the Father, the promised Messiah. Frightened and overwhelmed, the disciples fumble for words. Peter says to Jesus, "It is good for us to be here." No doubts about Jesus as Messiah or His power to save. Far above the mundane daily problems, privileged to bask in the presence of God Himself—why not stay?

But they could not stay on the mountain. Soon they saw only Jesus in His normal state and returned down the mountain to problems with a demon-possessed boy. Soon would come the cross. Nevertheless, the three were strengthened for the coming events.

Rejoice in your mountaintop experiences with Jesus, where you see Him clearly as exalted Lord and Savior. Relish those moments. Say without reservation, "It is good for us to be here."

But recognize that the valley awaits, with routine drudgery and knotty problems. The cross looms ahead even as it provides for us the complete atonement for our sins. We take up our crosses and follow Him by faith, not by sight. But we are confirmed in our faith by the risen Lord Jesus, who promises a heavenly mountaintop experience that will never end.

Prayer
How good, Lord, to be here!
Yet we may not remain;
But since you bid us leave the mount,
Come with us to the plain.

The Reason We Misunderstand Jesus

Reading: Mark 9:30–37

Text: Mark 9:32—"But they did not understand what he meant and were afraid to ask him about it."

The saying goes: "To be great is to be misunderstood." Certainly these words would apply to Albert Einstein and Thomas Edison. The saying also describes Jesus of Nazareth, who confounded not only the crowds but also His disciples.

Shortly after His transfiguration Jesus spoke privately to His disciples, "The Son of Man is going to be betrayed into the hands of men. They will kill him, and after three days he will rise." Mark simply records that the disciples didn't understand.

What was the reason for their misunderstanding? Not because Jesus spoke unclearly. He spoke with simple words and repeated His message. Why then the misunderstanding?

When they reached Capernaum, Jesus asked what they had been arguing about on the road. They kept quiet because they had been arguing about who was the greatest. In short, the disciples misunderstood because they were selfish. They wanted success and fame. They couldn't understand Jesus' talk about suffering, service, and a cross.

Do we misunderstand Jesus? We have the benefit of the Holy Scriptures. We know much more about Jesus' life, death, and resurrection than did the disciples at the time of this text. Yet we misunderstand as badly as the disciples.

Why do we fail to understand Jesus? Because so often we are in effect arguing about who is the greatest. Forgetting about our suffering Savior, we tend to push for success and recognition. When Jesus talks about suffering, service, and a cross, we screen out His words with our selective filters.

What can we do to understand Jesus? In the text Jesus takes a little child in His arms and says that whoever welcomes one of these little, humble children welcomes Him. God will give us the humility of a child. Exposing our selfishness and stopped-up ears, He gives us His Son, who humbled Himself unto death, even death on a cross! By God's grace we understand Jesus.

Prayer
Lord, open my heart to understand Your Word. Amen.

Like a Child

Reading: Mark 10:13–16

Text: Mark 10:15—"Anyone who will not receive the kingdom of God like a little child will never enter it."

Children like to dress up like Mom and Dad, donning dresses and shoes several sizes too large and wearing jewelry. We think it's cute to see them playing adults. Jesus reverses the process, suggesting that adults should become like children.

Today we often have no time for children or for the child in each of us. We forget what we experienced as children. We bury feelings and spontaneous joys because we have learned not to show our feelings. We wear masks.

Jesus, on His final journey to Jerusalem, could have rejected the children brought to Him. But He says, "Let the little children come to me, and do not hinder them, for the kingdom of God belongs to such as these." He took the children in His arms and blessed them.

For the moment forget your busy schedule and your self-importance. Picture yourself as a child in your favorite room. As you sit there playing, Jesus enters the room and comes to you. You are excited to see Him. He looks at you with a kindly sparkle in His eyes, a smile on His face. He holds out His arms to you. You run to Him with a big hug and then sit in His lap, talking with Him and listening to Him telling you stories. You feel so happy, secure, and relaxed. You know He loves you.

God can make you like a child. He has sent His Son to take the burdens for you. He knows how you hurt inside. Humbly depending on Him like a child, you can face the world's problems with new strength and determination. Jesus, who had time for the children, taught us to call God our Father. Martin Luther commented on this as follows:

Prayer Thoughts

"God would by these words tenderly invite us to believe that He is our true Father and that we are His true children, so that we may with all boldness and confidence ask Him as dear children ask their dear father."

(Small Catechism, "Lord's Prayer," Introduction)

Surprising Greatness

Reading: Mark 10:35–45

Text: Mark 10:43—"Whoever wants to become great among you must be your servant."

Who is the greatest? How would you answer that question? Muhammed Ali repeatedly said, "I'm the greatest!" You could survey the public for their choices—politicians, journalists, religious or business leaders. You could turn to historians for their estimate based on the historical contributions of great individuals.

James and John were working for a prominent place in Jesus' kingdom, one on His right and the other on His left. They were measuring greatness by prestige or status. The other disciples were furious when they heard about that request, probably because they wanted the same greatness for themselves.

Are we any different? Do we not strive for greatness in our own way—formal college degrees, title or position on the job, net worth and material possessions, social standing, number of celebrities we know personally, community organizations we join, or even church positions we hold. We struggle, climb ladders, cultivate the right kind of friends, and hope to achieve greatness.

Jesus must have shocked the disciples when He spoke the words of our text. As the greatest man who ever lived, He described His mission in life: "For even the Son of Man did not come to be served, but to serve, and to give his life as a ransom for many" (v. 45). He washed the disciples' feet and "humbled himself . . . to death, even death on a cross!" (Phil. 2:8). Surprising greatness in humble service.

Jolted by Jesus' words, we confess our fond ambitions and manipulative struggles to achieve greatness and accept His service for us. Redeemed, restored, forgiven, we pick up the towel and ready the basin of water for a life of service. We reach out to others and help them. Surprising greatness!

Prayer

Lord, make me great in service, as You served on the cross for all. Amen.

To See Again

Reading: Mark 10:46–52

Text: Mark 10:51—"The blind man said, 'Rabbi, I want to see.' "

I'll never forget the first time I put on glasses to correct my near-sightedness. I walked out into the bright sunlight and saw the whole world clearly. Oh, how great to see again!

My experience pales in comparison with that of blind Bartimaeus sitting by the roadside outside the city of Jericho. Somehow he knew about Jesus and was willing to ask for help. Helplessly blind, he cried out, "Jesus, Son of David, have mercy on me!" Even when others rebuked him, Bartimaeus persevered and cried out all the louder. With Jesus near, the man threw his cloak aside, jumped to his feet, and came to Jesus, asking for help. Jesus immediately restored his sight, and Bartimaeus followed Jesus along the road.

What an example for us who are blind in sin. Are we willing to ask for help in our deepest need? Are we willing to persevere in asking Jesus? When He calls us, are we willing to go quickly and ask for specific help? And when Jesus supplies our need, do we willingly and immediately follow Him?

When Jesus, the Sight-Giver, was on His way to the cross, no mission or crowd was too important for Him to help an individual in need. When Bartimaeus came forth, Jesus asked a penetrating question, "What do you want me to do for you?" He let Bartimaeus admit his specific need and ask for help. Then, by His almighty power, Jesus restored the blind man's sight.

What an example for us. Jesus, having restored our spiritual eyesight, can use us to help others see again. He can help us to place individual needs first, ahead of crowds of people and goals we pursue. With His help we then use God's power through His Word and sacraments to restore people's spiritual sight.

Prayer

Amazing grace! How sweet the sound
That saved a wretch like me!
I once was lost but now am found,
Was blind but now I see!

Reach Out

Reading: Mark 6:7–13

Text: John 17:18—"As you sent me into the world, I have sent them into the world."

REACH OUT—and touch the stars in the dark winter sky.

REACH OUT—and feel a snowflake melt in your hand or on your eyelashes.

REACH OUT—and breathe in the cold heady air of February.

REACH OUT—and let Him touch you— gently, lovingly, firmly, permanently.

REACH OUT—and let the love of Jesus sink deep into your inner self.

REACH OUT—and let the fresh wind of the Spirit sweep the cobwebs from your mind, body, and spirit.

REACH OUT—and come alive in the newness of an exciting life and a brand-new day.

REACH OUT—and let the Word speak to you as it has never spoken before, with words of power, conviction, meaning, depth, truth, love, joy, and life.

REACH OUT—and breathe your new life—His life—into another.

REACH OUT—and place your arm around the one you love.

REACH OUT—and touch them all—the untouchable, the unlovable, the lost, the frightened, the weak, the overbearing, the cocky, the falling, the aging, the dying, the comic, the remote, the phony—with His love and your love and care.

REACH OUT—and sing a new song from the bottom of your soul and from the top of your soaring spirit.

REACH OUT—and march side by side with the searchers, the mourners, and the helpers.

REACH OUT—and tell the truth about yourself, your triumphs, your Leader, your Savior, your Power, and your Joy.

REACH OUT—and don't ever stop reaching out until you have embraced the whole world, until your arms have become His arms, your love His love, His death your death, His resurrection your resurrection, and until every man, woman, and child has come to know and believe that He is reaching out to them forever.

Prayer

Lord, help me to reach out! Amen.

Jesus' Exodus and Ours

Reading: Luke 9:28–36

Text: Luke 9:30–31—"Two men, Moses and Elijah . . . spoke about his departure, which he was about to bring to fulfillment at Jerusalem."

One Greek word in Luke's account of the Transfiguration stands out. The word for "departure" is "exodus." Moses, who led God's people out of slavery in Egypt, talks with Jesus "about his exodus. "

Jesus was called to a new exodus from slavery to freedom. Moses had been called to a heavy responsibility. He had to face mighty Pharaoh and ask him to let the people go. Jesus was called to deliver the world from slavery to sin, death, and the devil. He bore a far greater responsibility. Standing on the Mount of Transfiguration, Jesus faces the journey to Jerusalem, where He will suffer and die. With the call of the Father at His baptism fresh in mind, He willingly shoulders the world's sin and begins His exodus.

We also are called to a new exodus from slavery to freedom. Moses took Israel with him on the journey, grumbling and complaining though they were. Jesus took His disciples with Him on that final journey also, confused and resistant though they were. Called in our baptism as children of God, we stand free in Christ. We bear a heavy responsibility to bring Gospel freedom to the world. Like Moses and the disciples, we often make excuses, complain, and even long for our former slavery.

But God supplies strength and guidance for our new exodus. He strengthened Jesus on the mount, filled Him with glory, reassured Him through Moses and Elijah, the cloud and the voice. Jesus strengthened the disciples following His resurrection and poured out His Holy Spirit upon them. He strengthens us as we worship together, hear His Word, and receive His body and blood. What a joy to follow Jesus on the journey from slavery to freedom!

Prayer

Jesus, still lead on Till our rest be won;
Heav'nly leader, still direct us,
Still support, console, protect us,
Till we safely stand In our fatherland.

51

Compassion for the Lost

Reading: Mark 6:30–34

Text: Mark 6:34—"When Jesus landed and saw a large crowd, he had compassion on them, because they were like sheep without a shepherd."

In the abstract we can feel compassion for lost sinners the world over. In the concrete, however, compassion comes with much greater difficulty. We lead our daily lives to meet personal needs, earn a living, and keep family together. On occasion we may respond to a mission sermon and make calls for a new adult class. But normally we don't think much about the lost. If they intrude on our comfortable lives, we may even resent them.

How different the single-minded compassion of Jesus for the lost sheep. By example He also challenged His disciples to a similar compassion. They had just returned from a successful preaching mission in the villages of Galilee. As they are reporting to Jesus, so many people crowd around them that they don't even have a chance to eat. Jesus, recognizing the need for rest, suggests that they go by boat to a quiet place. However, when they arrive they discover that multitudes have gone around the lake on foot to meet them. Does Jesus send them away until a more convenient time? No, He teaches them and later feeds the 5,000.

Compassion for the lost. Only God can fill us with it. Jesus sought us out as sheep needing a shepherd. He gave His life for us on the cross. He personally binds up our wounds and forgives our lack of compassion. He knows our need for rest with Him. But He also places before us constantly, in the concrete, people who need His love and forgiveness, lost sheep. And He wants to use us to teach, feed, and heal them. How we need Jesus' compassion for the lost!

Prayer

Raise up, O Lord the Holy Ghost,
From this broad land a mighty host;
Their war cry, "We will seek the lost
Where you, O Christ, will come."

Preventive Prayer

Reading: Mark 14:32–42

Text: Mark 14:38a—"Watch and pray so that you will not fall into temptation."

"An ounce of prevention is worth a pound of cure." So goes the saying. Preventive measures are stressed in many areas today. Diet and physical fitness gurus promote aerobics, jogging, exercise machines, health foods, weight reduction programs, and special cookbooks. Anti-smoking campaigns target prevention of cancer and heart disease. Some people, however, ignore all preventive efforts.

Jesus sees danger ahead as He visits the Garden of Gethsemane with His disciples. He knows that suffering and death await Him. He realizes that the disciples will also be tested severely. He asks them to pray with Him. Preventive prayer works, not to remove problems and temptations but to tap God's powerful resources for handling them.

Note the outcome. The disciples fall asleep, despite Jesus' efforts to rouse them. They do not pray. Consequently, when the hostile crowd comes, they fall into temptation. They desert Jesus and flee. Peter denies his Lord three times.

Observe the contrast. Jesus practices preventive prayer. His soul overwhelmed with sorrow, He prays three times for the Father's will to be done in His life. The Father equips Him to bear the intense suffering. Instead of falling into temptation, Jesus steadfastly and silently goes to Annas, Caiaphas, Pilate, Herod, and Calvary. He fully and completely bears the sins of the world and wins the victory.

How many times we fail to pray! Without the regular habit of communing with God, we are in danger of falling into sin when the crisis comes to test our faith. Thank God that Jesus did not fail but won the victory for us. Through His Word and sacraments He strengthens also our prayer life.

Prayer

Go to dark Gethsemane, All who feel the tempter's pow'r;
Your Redeemer's conflict see. Watch with him one bitter hour;
Turn not from his griefs away; Learn from Jesus Christ to pray.

Small in Number—Large in His Love

Reading: Deuteronomy 7:1–9

Text: Deuteronomy 7:7a–8a—"The Lord did not . . . choose you because you were more numerous than other peoples . . . but it was because the Lord loved you . . . ."

The motion picture *Hoosiers* describes a small-town high school with only 64 students which fielded an amazing basketball team. The team managed to defeat school after school on its way to the state championship game in Indianapolis. Pitted against a large city school with players several inches taller, the embattled team worked together, came from behind, and at the buzzer scored an outside jump shot which gave them the coveted state championship. Small town, tiny high school, outsized team, but a large heart and a great victory.

Moses reminds Israel on the east bank of the Jordan waiting to enter the Promised Land that they face a major challenge— seven nations larger and stronger. He assures Israel that the Lord has chosen them as a special people, His treasured possession. Israel, small in number but large in God's covenant love, crossed the Jordan and by God's power won the victory.

Often today we feel outnumbered as Christians. We see evil gripping our society and our world. Sex outside of marriage. Abortion on demand. Broken homes and child abuse. Pornography. Crime. Unfettered use of drugs and alcohol. Many scoff at religion and especially Biblical Christianity.

God promises us victory. He sent His own Son into a sinful world. Originally popular, He gradually lost His following as opposition mounted, and He ended up alone on a cross, forsaken even by His friends. But against all odds He won the victory over sin, death, and Satan for us and our salvation. He chose us in Baptism to belong to His special people and sends us out to win the world with His love. Like that tiny Hoosier basketball team and Israel of old, we will win the victory.

Prayer

Lord, thank You for choosing us by Your loving grace. Help us, though small in numbers, to win the victory by sharing Your love with others. Amen.

Living Simply

Reading: Luke 18:18–30

Text: Luke 18:22—"Sell everything you have and give to the poor, and you will have treasure in heaven."

At the 1964 World's Fair, General Electric featured a Carousel of Progress, now on permanent display at Disney World. As the audience revolves on a carousel, four scenes are presented, each showing material progress in its own era—turn of the century, the 1920s, the 1940s, and the modern age. From a pump in the sink to a fan blowing over a block of ice in the bathtub, to refrigerators and color television sets, the carousel moves on. Yesterday's luxury becomes today's necessity. Jesus confronts the rich young ruler with the startling call for a simpler life. Faced with giving up his extensive wealth, the man goes away sorrowing.

We find purpose and security in money and possessions. We work hard to attain them and then often work harder to maintain and protect what we own. These possessions complicate our lives, often failing to make us happy. At the same time we rationalize about our need to provide for our family and our old age.

Look at Jesus' simple living. Though not wealthy, He enjoyed life with good friends, with sufficient food and clothing. He furnished the Passover meal for His disciples, visited with Mary and Martha, and fed 5,000 people. Yet He placed all material possessions in service to His father and other people. And Jesus willingly gave up all possessions in death. He went to the cross, where they divided His garments and gambled for His seamless robe. He died simply for the sins of the world, including greed and the selfish use of possessions.

Only Jesus Christ counts in life. Saved by His death, we receive full forgiveness and rejoice as His followers. Material possessions serve as gifts from Him to be enjoyed and used in His service. The struggle continues, but He makes it possible for us to live simply as we follow Him.

Prayer

Dear Father, reorient my complicated use of possessions into a simpler life of service based on the life, death, and resurrection of Your Son for me. Amen.

Love Your Enemies

Reading: Matthew 5:43–48

Text: Matthew 5:44a—"Love your enemies . . . ."

You may know the story of Dave Wilkerson, the country preacher from Pennsylvania who came to New York City to start a ministry among street gangs. In one dramatic episode he approached Nicky Cruz to show concern, and the hardened gang fighter drew a knife to attack him. Dave simply said, "I love you and Jesus loves you." Those words haunted Nicky Cruz and eventually led to his conversion. Dave Wilkerson loved his enemy.

Who is your enemy—fanatic leaders in faraway lands who threaten our security, local or national groups which oppose our interests, or the people we face day by day like the boss, a neighbor, a church member, or our own husband or wife? The closer the enemy, the more difficult the relationship. Love our enemy? Love with a self-giving, long-suffering love?

Our problem: We often live selfish, undisciplined lives, controlled by our feelings. When the other person treats us unfairly, we want to lash back with bitter, vindictive actions. We sin. Our veneer of decent living is stripped from us. We hate our enemies.

Enter Jesus Christ. Though He loved everyone, enemies abounded in His life—enemies out to trick Him, badger Him, damage His reputation, and ultimately destroy Him. Yet His words of love ring out from the cross, "Father, forgive them, for they do not know what they are doing." His death on the cross made all the difference. God changed us from His enemies into His friends through the sin-atoning sacrifice of Jesus.

Now the Spirit stands ready to help us. By Dave Wilkerson's words Nicky Cruz was changed from an enemy of God into His friend. Similarly transformed by God's "I love you," we can begin to love our enemies with God's own self-giving love. We can say to them with life-changing power: "I love you and Jesus loves you."

Prayer

Dear Father, as you have loved us "while we were still sinners," help us to love our enemies with the sacrificial love of Your Son Jesus Christ. Amen.

Fruit-Bearing Required

Reading: Luke 13:6–9

Text: Luke 13:9—"If it bears fruit next year, fine! If not, then cut it down."

Jesus tells a harsh parable about required fruit-bearing. He reminds the people of His time that they have a mission to bear fruit with their lives. This particular fig tree had failed to bear fruit for three years, so the owner ordered it cut down. Jesus warns the people that they have failed to live for God.

God has made us beautiful fig trees in our Baptism, nurturing us to a growing faith in Jesus Christ as our Savior. He intends us to bear the fruit of Christ in our lives by His grace. Yet often we, like Jesus' contemporaries, fail to produce fruit. We may have a poor credit rating, conduct ourselves poorly at sporting or social events, use foul language and unkind words, fail to care for others, to attend church regularly, and to share our faith in Christ. Like the people to whom Jesus spoke, we need to repent.

In the parable the owner gives the fig tree another chance, a year of grace to bear fruit. The gardener plans special nourishing care to give the tree every chance. God's grace and mercy pours forth to us as well. We have no need to despair. Because of Christ's death on the cross, God gives us another chance. He provides maximum nourishment. As we come humbly to Him, He forgives and restores us. His love alone can produce fruit in us. What the church needs most is fig trees receiving nourishment and by God's grace continuing to bear fruit in word and deed. Fruit-bearing is required and supplied through Jesus Christ!

Prayer
He like a tree shall thrive,
With waters near the root;
Fresh as the leaf his name shall live,
His works are heav'nly fruit.

Tested by Flood

Reading: Luke 6:46–49

Text: Luke 6:48b—"When a flood came, the torrent struck that house but could not shake it, because it was well built."

Normally Fort Wayne, Ind., provides peaceful living, with houses nestled among three rivers which converge in the downtown area. In March of 1982 the town was tested by flood. The spring thaw and steady rainfall brought rising rivers. Dikes started to give way. Water poured over the banks and submerged residential areas despite the efforts of sandbaggers. How solidly built were the homes and dikes? The flood of 1982 put them to the test.

Jesus describes the believer's life in terms of wise and foolish builders. The one digs deep and lays the foundation on rock. The other builds on the ground without a foundation. During normal times both homes appear safe and livable. But when the flood comes, the house built on rock endures the torrent, while the house built on the ground collapses.

How securely are you building your life? Have you concentrated on external features like wealth, popularity, success? Or have you been building on the bedrock of Jesus Christ? As Paul writes, "No one can lay any foundation other than the one already laid, which is Jesus Christ" (1 Cor. 3:11). Both spiritual houses may appear safe and livable. But when crisis situations come— sickness, family breakdown, death, loss of job—then our lives are tested. We either collapse or stand firm, depending on our foundation. When we hear Jesus' words and put them into practice, we rest on the unshakable foundation of Jesus' blood and righteousness.

Prayer

His oath, his covenant, his blood
Sustain me in the raging flood;
When all supports are washed away,
He then is all my hope and stay.
On Christ, the solid rock, I stand;
All other ground is sinking sand.

Put Your Hands Together

Reading: Philippians 2:1–4

Text: Philippians 2:4—"Each of you should look not only to your own interests, but also to the interests of others."

During the destructive flood of 1982, residents of Fort Wayne, Ind., faced a major crisis. Despite round-the-clock efforts of city workers, the waters continued to rise. Sandbags could not be filled and placed in position fast enough to hold back the waters. An emergency call went out to the citizens of Fort Wayne. And they responded in droves—men, women, and many high school students. They put their hands together and worked until their backs were weary and their hands bruised. The battle was finally won as the waters receded. Later city leaders used as a slogan to help economic recovery, "Put your hands together, Fort Wayne."

Paul in our text suggests that Christians need to work together within the fellowship of believers. Faced with persecution and ridicule for confessing Christ, the Philippian believers needed each other. Entrusted with Christ's command to be witnesses to the ends of the earth, they could succeed only by putting their hands together.

Put your hands together, Paul urges us—not to fight a flood for a few days but to witness to the Savior's love continually. Faced with ridicule, indifference, and anti-Christian values, we desperately need each other within the fellowship of believers.

Paul provides power for this cooperative venture by pointing to the One who put His hands to work for us. He took the nature of a servant, was made in human likeness, humbled Himself, and became obedient to death—even death on a cross. Because Jesus Christ completed His saving work for us, He joins us to the Christian community in our baptism and enables us to serve each other joyfully as we reach out to the world. Put your hands together!

Prayer

Stand up, stand up for Jesus; The trumpet call obey;
Stand forth in mighty conflict In this his glorious day.

Lenten Listening Posts:
With the Sanhedrin

Reading: John 11:45–53

Text: John 11:53—"So from that day on they plotted to take his life."

Preparing again to remember the death and resurrection of Jesus Christ, we station ourselves at various Lenten Listening Posts to see what we can learn.

The chief priests and Pharisees call a meeting of the Sanhedrin to discuss how to deal with Jesus of Nazareth. Sounds quite sinister to us, their scheming to kill Jesus. But from their point of view, they were developing a plan, not a plot. They loved the temple and the laws. They loved their nation with its heritage from the Old Testament. They wanted to protect that heritage and saw Jesus as a threat. The high priest's suggestion that one man die for the people provided them with a reasonable, though distasteful, way to solve their problem. Nevertheless, despite their rationalizations, these leaders were plotting, not planning, to get rid of the Son of God.

We develop our plans also. They seem quite reasonable to us. We love our heritage in home, church, and nation. We assume that what is good and right for us is good and right for everyone else. The Lord must be on our side. Nevertheless, like the Pharisees, our plans can easily turn into plots. Sin, rebellion, selfishness, and disobedience can easily lurk beneath the surface of our righteous-sounding plans. God exposes our plots as we examine ourselves with the searchlight of His Word.

Over our plots stands God's saving plan for the world. God took the plotting of the scribes and Pharisees and used it to make His Son the sacrificial Lamb. The high priest's words stand as a prophesy, "You do not realize that it is better for you that one man die for the people" (v. 50). And God works in us and through us despite our bungling. He forgives our plotting and transforms us into Gospel agents of His plan to save others.

Prayer

Father, forgive our plots and use us in Your saving plan. Amen.

Lenten Listening Posts:
In the Upper Room

Reading: John 13:1–17

Text: Luke 22:24—"Also a dispute arose among them as to which of them was considered to be greatest."

We listen to the disciples in the upper room on Thursday of Holy Week. What was their mood? We usually interpret the upper room in the light of Good Friday. Therefore we assume the disciples were somber and reflective. A better case could be made for linking Maundy Thursday with Palm Sunday. Jesus had entered Jerusalem triumphantly. The Messiah was coming into His own. Opposition, yes, but Jesus could win with His popular support. The disciples probably anticipated a great future for themselves. No doubt they relished the thought of a Passover meal with the soon-to-be-crowned Messiah.

They probably felt joyful, confident, and expectant. Internally they swelled with pride because of the good fortune they were experiencing. They disputed as to which of them should be considered the greatest.

How do you feel when everything seems to be going well? Your future looks bright. Externally you feel joyful, confident, and expectant. Internally you swell with pride and wonder whether you have received sufficient recognition for your accomplishments. At least in our minds, we join the dispute about who is the greatest.

But listening to Jesus produces a completely different result. He has come not to be served, but to serve. He washes the feet of the disciples, an act of lowly service. He tries to prepare them for the coming events. He goes as Suffering Servant to the cross, wearing a crown of thorns for us.

We look to Jesus. Confessing our pride, we rely on His service on our behalf. We cling to Him and rethink our values, placing our confidence not in our abilities or accomplishments but in His promises.

Prayer
Lord, replace our pride with Your humble service. Amen.

Lenten Listening Posts: In Gethsemane

Reading: Matthew 26:30–46

Text: Matthew 26:35—"But Peter declared, 'Even if I have to die with you, I will never disown you.' "

Our Lenten Listening Post moves to Gethsemane. Are the disciples in Gethsemane naive or realistic about evil?

As the story unfolds, we observe that the disciples seem incredibly naive about evil. Still expecting Jesus' popular triumph, they don't look ahead at the storm clouds on the horizon. Although warned repeatedly by Jesus about His imminent suffering and death, they continue hoping. They underestimate the forces of evil and overestimate themselves. They agree with Peter that they will never disown Jesus even if they have to die with Him. Offered the opportunity to pray with Jesus for strengthening, they fall asleep. Naive about evil.

How often we live with the same false optimism. We don't look ahead, though forewarned by Scripture about great evil in the end times. We underestimate the forces of evil—while the family unit is breaking down in society, human lives are snuffed out by abortions, and massive attacks are aimed at the church. We overestimate ourselves, especially when everything is going well. We believe our faith can withstand any tests, and we promise to remain faithful even unto death. Yet we avoid opportunities to pray and study the Word of God.

By contrast, Jesus faced His darkest hour realistically. Looking ahead with full knowledge of the cross, He accurately counted the cost and His own need for continuing communion with the Father. He prayed and was strengthened. He moved on to the Judgment Hall and Calvary, defeating evil with His sacrificial death. He died for the naive disciples and us.

He stands by us. Turning our naiveté into a realistic look at evil, we embrace Jesus Christ in faith and claim His victory. We come daily to His Word, live in our baptism, and go to the Holy Supper for strength and forgiveness.

Prayer

Lord, prepare us realistically to fight evil through Your shed blood. Amen.

Lenten Listening Posts: In the Council Room

Reading: Mark 14:53–65

Text: Mark 14:64—" 'You have heard the blasphemy. What do you think?' They all condemned him as worthy of death."

We set up our Lenten Listening Post in the council room where the Sanhedrin is trying Jesus. Do they praise or blaspheme God?

Some of Israel's worship leaders gather to uphold the honor of God by striking out against the "blasphemous" Jesus. Ostensibly they praise God by their actions. But in reality they blaspheme God for they are making mockery of God's Son. They meet illegally at the high priest's house instead of the temple, at a forbidden time—night, using false witnesses, without adequate time for the verdict to stand. They mock Jesus, slap Him, and treat Him roughly. Blasphemy on their part, not praise.

But surely we praise Jesus, while condemning the Sanhedrin! We believe in regular worship. We strike out against religious enthusiasm. Or is our intended praise really blasphemy? We limit Christ in our midst, restricting Him to our forms of worship. We don't want Jesus to rule our lives. In effect we place Him on trial for exceeding the bounds of religious traditions. Blasphemy on our part, not praise!

Jesus was accused of blasphemy. He dared to forgive the sins of the palsied man. He stated who He was as the Messiah and Son of God. Actually His life was filled with praise. He obeyed the Father at every point. He died for the blasphemers, praying "Father, forgive them, for they do not know what they are doing." His death and resurrection lifted praises to the Father.

Jesus turns our blasphemy to praise. He forgives our sin. He frees us to live as little Christs. By His grace we are sons and daughters of the living God. That's not blasphemy, but praise.

Prayer
Lord, fill us with Your praise. Amen.

Lenten Listening Posts: In the Courtyard

Reading: Matthew 26:69–75

Text: Matthew 26:75—"Then Peter remembered the word Jesus had spoken: 'Before the rooster crows, you will disown me three times.' "

Peter displays much courage in the courtyard, but he is relying on himself. We could call it self-courage. In the garden he draws his sword to protect Jesus, though hopelessly outnumbered by the temple guard. He follows Jesus to the courtyard at great personal risk. What courage! He loves Jesus and stands up for Him.

But we also know the inadequacy of Peter's self-courage. A servant girl comes and challenges him. Another does the same. Then others say, "Surely you are one of them, for your accent gives you away." Three challenges to his self-courage, three denials, the last one with curses. Then the remembrance and the remorse. Self-courage defeated.

What courage we sometimes display, self-courage. We handle household emergencies, deal with lingering illness, manage a change in job or school, and stand up to be counted for our faith. We love Jesus. But our courage also fails us. Like the cowardly lion in *The Wizard of Oz*, we often run and hide. We deny our Lord when pressed at home, on the job, and even in our church. We remember the words of Jesus and weep bitterly. Self-courage defeated.

Thank God for Christ-courage. He depended on the Father in the hour of trial. He moved unflinchingly to His arrest, trial, and crucifixion. He had the necessary courage to endure the taunts and jeers, the lashes and crown of thorns, all the brutal agony.

Christ looked at Peter with love. He forgave him and filled him, after the resurrection, with Christ-courage. Peter, repentant for his denial, became a bold spokesman for the Gospel. Christ fills also us with His courage. Forgiven, we can daily receive strength from God's Word to tackle our witness opportunities at home and in the community.

Prayer
Lord, give us Your courage in crisis. Amen.

Lenten Listening Posts:
In the Judgment Hall

Reading: Matthew 27:1–2, 11–31

Text: Matthew 27:24—"When Pilate saw that he was getting nowhere, but that instead an uproar was starting, he took water and washed his hands in front of the crowd."

Jesus' enemies seem to have Jesus on the defensive. They display such dignity! The scribes and Pharisees in their rich garments, Pontius Pilate, resplendent as Roman governor. These leaders possessed status and authority. Dignified, indeed!

But in reality they acted defensively. The leaders and the crowd had to cover up and prove their point. They had no clear case for the death penalty. Their trumped-up charges grasped at straws. They protested too much. Pilate too was defensive. His wife warned him not to prosecute. He tried to assuage the angry crowd in several ways. Ultimately, afraid of a riot, he washed his hands, hoping that would cover up his actions. Clearly defensive, not dignified!

We like to appear dignified as leaders at home, in the community, at work, and at church. But like Pilate and the Pharisees, we often live defensively. We make up excuses for our actions, why we don't attend church regularly or witness or love our relatives. We protest too much by asserting our innocence and blaming someone else. Inside, like Pilate, we are afraid to stand up against popular opinion. Undignified, which means unworthy, we are clearly defensive.

Only Jesus Christ, the defendant, displayed true dignity. He remained silent before His captors. He looked every inch the king, though suffering with a crown of thorns. He felt no need to defend Himself. "Worthy is the Lamb who was slain!"

And Jesus makes us worthy by His death and resurrection. We need not be defensive as we admit our sins. We can be dignified as we give ourselves for others, affirming their worth.

Prayer
Lord, give us Your dignity as we praise You. Amen.

TGIF

Reading: Romans 5:6–11

Text: Mark 15:20b—"Then they led him out to crucify him."

How often we use the expression TGIF—Thank God, It's Friday. Teachers sigh with relief as the weekend approaches. Factory workers seek a change of pace from the tiring routines of the assembly line. Wall Street traders leave the hectic noise of the exchange. TGIF—Thank God, It's Friday.

No such relief for the Son of God. Friday brought the greatest intensity of His suffering. Mark simply records, "Then they led him out to crucify him." Arrested, tried, flogged, sleepless, He stumbles on to Calvary, where six hours of agonizing pain await His weakened body. He bears our sins, the sins of the world on His shoulders, and fights the combined forces of Satan, sin, and death. Instead of saying, "TGIF," Jesus cries out, "My God, my God, why have you forsaken me?"

But in that death He wins the victory by His once-for-all sacrifice. "It is finished!" becomes His triumphant cry. Justified by His blood, we enjoy peace with God. That Friday in Holy Week becomes Good Friday year after year.

How much more pertinent to think of Jesus every Friday. TGIF—not mere relief from the week's work through a weekend of relaxation, but a reminder of Good Friday and eternal life through the death and resurrection of Jesus Christ. Thank God, it's Friday.

Prayer

Dear Lord, thank You for Your willing suffering on that first Good Friday to pay for our sins. Fill our hearts with joy each week as we complete our labors and rest in Your forgiveness. Amen.

Ministry Temptations Waiting

Reading: Luke 4:1–13

Text: Luke 4:1–2a—"Jesus, full of the Holy Spirit, returned from the Jordan and was led by the Spirit in the desert, where for forty days he was tempted by the devil."

Were Jesus' temptations in the wilderness merely *personal* temptations? Certainly He was personally attacked. Forty days without eating left Him terribly hungry and therefore vulnerable to Satan's appeal to change stones into bread. But Luke seems to indicate that these temptations were *ministry* temptations. God's plan for the world was at stake in Jesus' ministry. The wilderness temptation stands right between Jesus' baptism and the beginning of His public ministry in Galilee. If He succumbs to temptation here, His lifelong ministry is destroyed. Luke records the third temptation as occurring at the temple in Jerusalem, where Jesus' ministry will ultimately take Him. Furthermore, Luke indicates that "when the devil had finished all this tempting, he left him until an opportune time." In other words, Satan will continue threatening Jesus' ministry. How glorious that Jesus overcomes Satan's temptation and carries out his ministry of salvation!

When Satan tempts us, are they merely *personal* temptations? Certainly we sometimes think of temptations as threatening our salvation or happiness as believers. But in a broader view, are not our temptations also *ministry* temptations? God's plan for the world in Christ works through us. Jesus' ministry is our ministry. When we succumb to Satan's temptation, ministry damage is done.

Weak, often gullible and unsuspecting, we need the strong Son of God in this Lenten season. Victor over the wiles of Satan, crucified in payment for our sins, Jesus stands at our side with His Word to give us victory over temptation and encouragement for caring ministry during this Lenten season.

Prayer Thoughts

Reflect on your ministry during Lent. Consider specific temptations facing you right now. And claim the forgiveness of Christ for power over Satan's temptation.

The Temptation to Seek Bread

Reading: Luke 4:1–4

Text: Luke 4:3—"The devil said to him, 'If you are the Son of God, tell this stone to become bread.' "

Hungry? Indeed, Jesus needed bread. Forty days without food creates a gnawing hunger. The devil's temptation struck at this point of need. "Tell this stone to become bread." But more calculatingly, Satan raised the question of Jesus' purpose on earth. "If you are the Son of God . . ." Later the people would seek to make Jesus a bread king. Always He would be tempted to act as a wonder-working Messiah bringing worldly prosperity, rather than a Suffering Servant bringing forgiveness through a cruel cross.

Here as elsewhere, Jesus defeats the devil with the Word of God. "It is written, 'Man does not live on bread alone.' " Sustained by the Father's Word, Jesus moves on to a ministry in the shadow of the cross.

Hungry? Indeed, we need daily bread and desire much more. Life in a materialistic society creates a gnawing hunger for bread and cake and cars and boats and campers. The devil's temptation strikes at this point of need. "Turn this money into more goodies for yourself." He suggests that if we truly believe in Jesus, He will surely give us more and more prosperity. Always we are tempted to revere Jesus as a bread king who will provide for our worldly needs. Then our purpose is sabotaged. We seek to gain wealth rather than lose ourselves, to be served rather than to serve, to receive rather than to give.

As with Jesus, our antidote to Satan lies in the Word of God, "It is written, 'Man does not live on bread alone.' " Convicted of our insatiable hunger for more and more things, we turn in repentance to Jesus as Suffering Servant and receive His full forgiveness won on the cross. We feed on that forgiving Word, eat His body, drink His blood, and then rise to follow Him on a Lenten ministry in the shadow of the cross.

Prayer

Dear Lord, forgive me for seeking bread more than You. Amen.

The Temptation to Compromise

Reading: Luke 4:5–8

Text: Luke 4:7—"If you worship me, it will all be yours."

What an offer! The kingdoms of the world in exchange for simply worshiping the devil. All Jesus has to do is compromise, and He would have the world at His feet. "No one needs to know about the arrangement. Just think how much good You can accomplish—and without the cross!"

A recurring theme throughout history, not just in Luke's account of Jesus' temptation. *Faust, The Devil and Daniel Webster, The Year the Yankees Lost the Pennant* (on which the Broadway musical *Damn Yankees* is based)—all tell the dramatic story of some earthling tempted to sell his soul to the devil in exchange for some greatly desired success. Are we immune to this temptation?

"Sell my soul to the devil? Never. I'm loyal to God." But just a little compromise. Nothing so drastic. Sleep in this Sunday morning. You need the rest. Keep working those extra hours. Your family will understand your neglect of them. Just amend your income tax forms a little. Everyone does it. "So if you worship me, it will all be yours."

But Jesus sees the devil's temptation for what it is. He replies, "It is written: 'Worship the Lord your God and serve him only.' " No room for compromise. God or Satan. There is no in-between ground.

Our compromises abound. We divide our loyalties and our worship. Satan's offer appeals. Exposed, we repent and look to the One who alone makes our worship worthy. "Worthy is the Lamb who was slain." He forgives, heals, and fortifies us to live and worship without compromise. Victory in sight because of Jesus' victory in the desert and at Calvary.

Prayer Thoughts

Confess recent compromises at home, school, and on the job. Thank Jesus for His victory over Satan. Claim His victory for your own life.

The Temptation to Success

Reading: Luke 4:9–13

Text: Luke 4:9a—"The devil led him to Jerusalem and had him stand on the highest point of the temple."

The scene, Jerusalem, site of the holy temple, focal point for a nation looking for deliverance from Roman oppression. Jesus with the devil at the pinnacle of the temple looking down. Satan says, "Jump down," a sure path to spectacular success. If He lands safely in the temple courtyard, all Israel will be astir. The Messiah has come. Let's rally behind Him and win our independence. Jesus becomes hero of the hour. But at what cost? His only business in Jerusalem, a cross rather than a crown. Fully aware of His mission, Jesus answers Satan, "It says, 'Do not put the Lord your God to the test.' "

The scene, North America, site of prosperity, focal point for a culture based on spectacular success. The 1984 Olympics in Los Angeles captured our hearts as a glittering array of gold and silver medals were won by gymnasts, track stars, and swimmers. For months afterwards, Olympic stars were seen on television endorsing everything from cereals to shoes. Spectacular success—a key ingredient of our culture. Satan offers us the opportunity to achieve and gain a quick following. We teach our children early to succeed with an endless chain of Little League baseball, scouting, and beauty contests. We struggle to advance on the job, move to the right neighborhood, and belong to the proper social clubs.

The glory beckons in America. But our only business as the people of God is a cross, rather than a crown. He wants humble service to others, not spectacular success. Recognizing our misplaced priorities, we look to the One who willingly permitted Himself to be taken to a skull-shaped hill outside Jerusalem, where He died for our sins. His victory over Satan becomes the only victory we need for a life of service here and a life of praise hereafter.

Prayer

Dear Lord, by Your cross forgive me for my compulsion to succeed, and give me Your eyes to see the joys of serving others. Amen.

The Need for Cleansing

Reading: 2 Samuel 11:1–27

Text: Psalm 51:2—"Wash away all my iniquity and cleanse me from my sin."

Electric dishwashers painlessly produce sparkling plates, once dull and filmy. Electric washing machines with the right detergent turn soiled shirts and blouses into fresh, clean garments. And what of sin? A small problem? A slight stain?

Not so! Think of the sin of David. A king's prerogative to relieve tension? A one-night stand with a beautiful woman? A slight stain of conscience to be washed in the palace laundry? Bathsheba was bathing when he first saw her. And "she had purified herself from her uncleanness," 2 Samuel tells us. But ugly sin protruded. Adultery, the clear charge. Another man's wife was made pregnant by David. The need for cleansing was real. No easy solution. No human solution. The harder David tried to erase the stain, the more soiled the garment became. Uriah, home on leave at David's command, too much a loyal soldier to cover up David's foul deed. Front-line battle for Uriah, cold-blooded murder. The stain grows and grows. The need for cleansing is now desperate.

What sin stains your heart right now? Less dramatic perhaps than David's adultery and murder. Easy to explain away. Human solutions seem workable. Rationalization. Excuses. But the harder you try to erase the stain, the more soiled the garment becomes. Others probably know. Ugly sin protrudes. Certainly you know. And God knows. More than a ritual prayer, you speak with the agonized cry of a terrified sinner, "Wash away all my iniquity and cleanse me from my sin."

And God alone cleanses us from our sin. "The blood of Jesus, his Son, purifies us from all sin" (1 John 1:7b). "Though your sins are like scarlet, they shall be as white as snow" (Is. 1:18). With the need for cleansing so great, thank God for Lent and the Sunday liturgy and the daily reminder of a cleansing Baptism in the name of the Father and of the Son and of the Holy Spirit.

Prayer

Lord, cleanse me from my sin. Amen.

The Terrible Knowing

Reading: 2 Samuel 12:1–14

Text: Psalm 51:3—"For I know my transgressions, and my sin is always before me."

David knows the depth of his sin, a terrible knowing. He did not start with that knowledge. He knew that all people were sinners. He knew that adultery and murder were sins in the sight of God. He knew that he had committed both sins. But he does not "know" his transgressions until the Lord sends Nathan to him with a story about a rich man who takes for himself the only ewe lamb of a poor man. David still doesn't know his transgressions until Nathan says, "You are the man." Now David knows and tells Nathan, "I have sinned against the Lord." He acknowledges his sin, a terrible knowing.

Consider the case of a terminally ill woman, discovering the nature of her illness, a terrible knowing. She knew that everyone will die sometime. She knew that cancer is often incurable. She knew that she had not been feeling well lately. But she doesn't "know" her condition until the doctor announces that she has the terminal illness. Even then, she does not acknowledge her condition until she is able to accept the truth, a terrible knowing.

Jesus says, "I know my sheep and my sheep know me—just as the Father knows me and I know the Father—and I lay down my life for the sheep" (John 10:14b–15). Paul writes, "I want to know Christ and the power of his resurrection" (Phil. 3:10). He adds in his letter to Timothy, "The Lord knows those who are his" (2 Tim. 2:19b). God's terrible knowing of the world's sin is balanced by His Son's complete payment for that sin on our behalf.

Prayer

Lord, to you I make confession:
I have sinned and gone astray,
I have multiplied transgression,
Chosen for myself the way.
Led by you to see my errors,
Lord, I tremble at your terrors.

The Naked Confession

Reading: Genesis 2:15–3:7

Text: Psalm 51:4a—"Against you, you only, have I sinned and done what is evil in your sight."

Adam and Eve were naked and were not ashamed, according to the creation account in Genesis 2. But soon they were hiding among the trees of the garden and wearing fig leaves. Why the change? They had rebelled against the Lord God by disobeying His command. Adam replies to a questioning God, "I was afraid because I was naked; so I hid" (Gen. 3:10). They now also cover up with excuses and passing the blame.

David sinned in his nakedness with Bathsheba. And he started covering up with lies, deception, and murder. His guilt only grew within. But now, confronted by the prophet Nathan, he makes the naked confession, "I have sinned against the Lord." David has sinned against Bathsheba and against Uriah and against all of Israel. But in his naked confession David admits his sin against the Lord God. No place to hide. No excuses, no blaming others. God has seen David's naked sin all along. But now David makes a naked confession. Through Nathan, God can say to David, "The Lord has taken away your sin. You are not going to die." God accepts David and forgives him. He stands righteous before God because of the Son, the Descendant of David, who will someday, stripped of clothing, hang naked on a cross to pay for the world's sin.

Will you make a naked confession of your sin? Fig leaves and trees cannot cover you. Neither will sophistication and makeup. Excuses and blaming others cannot screen God's X-ray vision. We may well have sinned against the spouse or the children or the neighbor or the boss. But ultimately we need to make the naked confession to God, "Against you, you only, have I sinned and done what is evil in your sight." And God assures us that He has taken away our sins through the Son who died exposed upon the cross. We are clothed in His righteousness alone, faultless to stand before the throne.

Prayer
Lord, I have sinned against You. Forgive me. Amen.

Iniquity Blotted Out

Reading: Isaiah 1:18

Text: Psalm 51:9—"Hide your face from my sins and blot out all my iniquity."

Oh, the stains that mar our lives—red beet juice on the favorite tie, grease on the white skirt, coffee stains on the linen tablecloth, household pet stains on the family room carpet, grass stains on the new tennis shoes, mustard on the car upholstery. And the attempts to blot out those stains often meet with utter frustration. Home remedies, expensive solvents, powerful solutions, and elbow grease take their turn, usually making the stain worse. And for every successful stain removal, another stain takes its place.

That's how David must have felt about his sin-stained life. How could he blot out his adultery with Bathsheba and his murder of Uriah? Convicted of his sin by Nathan, David knows he is helpless to remove it. No ritual cleansing will work. Consequently, he cries out to God, "Blot out all my iniquity." Only God can blot out David's sin. God would later say through the prophet Jeremiah, "I will forgive their wickedness and will remember their sins no more" (Jer. 31:34b). Iniquity completely blotted out, stain removed, sin forgotten.

The stain of our sin proves far more troublesome than coffee on a tablecloth. We know the stain exists. Others may not notice. But we see the stains and so does God . . . unkind words, selfish actions, ugly thoughts, simmering resentment, green-eyed envy, bitter complaining, halfhearted worship. All our efforts to blot out these stains only seem to make them more obvious. We cry out to God, "Blot out all my iniquity."

God sent His Son to blot out our iniquities. "He was pierced for our transgressions, he was crushed for our iniquities . . . the Lord has laid on him the iniquity of us all" (Is. 53:5a–6b).

Prayer

O Lamb of God who takes away the sin of the world, grant us Thy peace. Amen.

Created and Renewed

Reading: 2 Corinthians 4:4–7

Text: Psalm 51:10—"Create in me a pure heart, O God, and renew a steadfast spirit within me."

Familiar words, part of the Sunday liturgy, prominent also during Lent. What do these words mean for self-sufficient, stylish, outwardly successful people today? We create jobs, ideas, leisure activities, dream homes, get-rich-quick schemes, and friendships. We make things happen and pull ourselves up by our own bootstraps. Or do we?

David used the word "create" to ask: "Create in me a pure heart, O God." Now on the other side of his tragic affair with Bathsheba, he recognizes his need for cleansing with a terrible knowing that leads to a naked confession. He wants a pure heart to proceed with his life of service as king! He knows the darkness, chaos, and confusion of his heart. He is nothing and can do nothing to make his heart pure. God needs to create in him that pure heart. God alone can make something out of nothing. He alone can bring renewal. "God, who said, 'Let light shine out of darkness,' made his light shine in our hearts to give us the light of the knowledge of the glory of God in the face of Christ" (2 Cor. 4:6). The Creator became a creature in the person of Jesus Christ, the second Adam. He lived with a pure heart and willingly died on a cross to bring light out of darkness. With the coming Messiah in view, God created a pure heart in David, granting full forgiveness. David's spirit was renewed for creative service.

"If anyone is in Christ, he is a new creation; the old has gone, the new has come!" (2 Cor. 5:17). Laying aside our confused darkness and our shabby attempts to create our own world, we turn to the Creator, who points us to Christ and grants us a pure heart. We let His creative Spirit renew us for service.

Prayer

Create in me a pure heart, O God. Amen.

Joy Restored

Reading: Psalm 30:8–12

Text: Psalm 51:12—"Restore to me the joy of your salvation and grant me a willing spirit, to sustain me."

Instant happiness. The goal of our age. Live life to the fullest. Grab what you want. Enjoy. Make big money. Above all, be happy. Appealing?

David grabbed for instant happiness, enjoyed a few fleeting moments with another man's wife, and then plunged into a nightmare of guilt, sorrow, and despair. He learned the difference between the "happiness" of the moment and God's kind of joy. Repentant, he prays, "Restore to me the joy of your salvation." Joy has its source outside of David, in God's salvation. God forgives David and preserves his life, even after his dreadful sin. The joy of God's salvation is restored.

And what of you? Do you seek that moment of exciting happiness, that forbidden pleasure—grabbing for the top job at any cost, golf on Sunday mornings, the occasional fling with someone else's spouse, the constant overindulging in food, alcohol, or drugs—fleeting happiness which can plunge you into a nightmare of guilt, sorrow, and despair?

"Restore to me the joy of your salvation." A fervent prayer to the God who can turn wailing into dancing and replace sackcloth with the clothing of joy. God's salvation makes the difference—the manger, the upper room, the cross, the empty tomb, the font, the altar with bread and wine, the circle of God's people, the reunion before the heavenly throne. Joy overflows from the saving acts of God to produce a peaceful mind, a clear conscience, a voice of praise, ready hands, a caring smile. Lasting joy instead of instant happiness for David and for us.

Prayer

Bane and blessing, pain and pleasure
By the cross are sanctified;
Peace is there that knows no measure,
Joys that through all time abide.

Lips Opened for Praise

Reading: James 3:9–12

Text: Psalm 51:15—"O Lord, open my lips, and my mouth will declare your praise."

Are you having trouble praising God? Do you find yourself going through the motions of worship? Perhaps you blame your lack of musical ability or knowledge of the liturgy. You are in for a surprise. The secret of praise lies with God.

Look at David. He was a master musician, often playing the harp to soothe Saul's fits of rage. He is credited with writing many psalms, a major part of the "hymnbook" of the Old Testament church. He obviously was gifted in speech as king and psalm writer. Yet he finds it necessary to ask God to open his lips so that he can praise the Lord. Why?

Could it be that David's lips had been sealed from praise because his heart had strayed from God? During the whole Bathsheba incident he had undoubtedly spoken and perhaps sung many words with his lips, but few words of praise to a God who disapproved of his sin. I can imagine David fumbling for words of praise and feeling dry in the mouth and empty in his heart. But having used words of confession to God for his sin, David prays for open lips, and God enables him to praise once again.

Forget about musical ability or a facile tongue. Look to your heart. Confess the wrong kinds of words springing from wrong thoughts and attitudes. Do you find selfishness, indifference, laziness, hardness, impatience, lust, or malice within your heart? With David pray, "O Lord, open my lips, and my mouth will declare your praise." He will hear. God sent His Son Jesus to begin a new song with His birth, life, death, and resurrection. His cries of loneliness, forgiveness, and completion signal victory over all evil. God places the new song in our hearts at Baptism and opens our lips each day to declare His praise in word and song. He accepts our praise because He has accepted Christ's sacrifice for us.

Prayer

"O Lord, open my lips, and my mouth will declare your praise." Amen.

The Sacrifice of Brokenness

Reading: Hebrews 10:1–10

Text: Psalm 51:17—"The sacrifices of God are a broken spirit; a broken and contrite heart, O God, you will not despise."

Formal sacrifices permeate the pages of the Old Testament, instituted by God with good purpose. But sacrifices sometimes became mere formalities without the worship of the heart.

David, a faithful proponent of formal sacrifices, has learned a lesson from his fall into the sins of adultery and murder. He writes, "The sacrifices of God are a broken spirit; a broken and contrite heart, O God, you will not despise." God has broken David's spirit by using the prophet Nathan to convince him of his sin. David has fully confessed his sin before God. In his brokenness David claims the mercy and promises of God. His broken spirit presents to God a pleasing sacrifice. Now the external sacrifices on the altar reflect the internal spirit of dependence on God for everything.

Are we not sometimes guilty of religious formalism? We think that our external acts—attending church, contributing financial resources, serving on church boards and committees, etc.—count before God as pleasing sacrifices. All the while we may have haughty, hardened spirits which harbor secret sins and unsavory motives. God knows our hearts and condemns our willful sin. He leads us to brokenness, where we recognize the inadequacy of our sacrifices both internally and externally.

We look to the once-for-all sacrifice of Jesus Christ as the spotless Lamb of God who takes away the sin of the world. God accepts Christ's sacrifice on our behalf. We respond by presenting our bodies as living sacrifices. The external acts remain as a testimony to Christ's sacrifice for us. We worship, give, serve, and love. But we start internally with the sacrifice of a broken spirit. Broken, we remember the One who was broken for us. We let the sweet savor of His sacrifice permeate our lives to the glory of God.

Prayer
Lord, break my heart so that I may serve You. Amen.

A Disciple Depends

Reading: Luke 22:31–34, 39–44

Text: John 15:5—"I am the vine; you are the branches . . . .
Apart from me you can do nothing."

The next eight devotions will focus on the word DISCIPLE. Each devotion will highlight one of the letters of that word to describe a characteristic of discipleship.

The first letter of DISCIPLE emphasizes that a disciple DEPENDS. In John 15 Jesus illustrates our relationship to Him with the imagery of the vine and branches. Detached branches can only wither and die. But attached branches, totally dependent on the vine, receive life and bear much fruit.

In the story of Holy Week we can see the contrasts. Simon Peter asserts his independence and falls short. He vows that he is ready to go with Jesus to prison and to death. He depends on himself and gets into trouble. True to Jesus' prediction, he denies his Lord three times.

Jesus, on the other hand, depends totally on the heavenly Father. He prays, "Not my will but yours be done." He receives strengthening and resolutely moves on to the arrest, trial, and crucifixion for us.

We have much to learn from this Biblical contrast. Like Peter we stress our independence. Disaster occurs. We make big promises but flee into the darkness and deny our Lord when the going gets rough. We need to confess our failure to depend on Him.

But Jesus, who depended on the Father, draws us to Him with His tender love and forgiveness. God attaches us to Christ, the Vine, by grace. His life flows through us and teaches us to depend on Him for everything. Like Jesus we can resolutely stand tall against the world and faithfully carry our crosses. Yes, a disciple DEPENDS!

Prayer

Faith clings to Jesus' cross alone
And rests in him unceasing;
And by its fruits true faith is known,
With love and hope increasing.

A Disciple Imitates

Reading: Romans 8:28–30

Text: Matthew 10:25—"It is enough for the student to be like his teacher, and the servant like his master."

Around the turn of the century a novel was written entitled *In His Steps*, which has exerted wide influence. In it a pastor challenges some parishioners to live with the constant question, "What would Jesus do?" As the novel unfolds, the question changes the lives of many people.

The second letter of the word "disciple" emphasizes that a disciple IMITATES. Jesus taught by example. For three years the disciples followed Him everywhere. In the upper room Jesus washed their feet and asked them to follow His example. The disciples could not imitate Jesus on their own. They faltered, stumbled, and fell. They needed His saving action on the cross to bring them new life, and the Spirit's outpouring at Pentecost to empower them. But by God's grace they later remembered His example and lived as He had taught them, also passing His example on to others.

How well do you imitate Jesus? During Lent you can retrace His steps to Jerusalem and Calvary. You can see His love, courage, obedience, and self-sacrifice. As a student and servant, you can carefully learn to know your Teacher and Master.

Like the disciples, we falter, stumble, and fall. We learn to depend totally on God's grace in the death and resurrection of Jesus Christ. Then we can follow *In His Steps*, living, in Luther's words, as "little Christs." We imitate Jesus in our words and actions. We disciple others to follow Jesus' example as well. Yes, a disciple IMITATES.

Prayer

"Come, follow me," said Christ, the Lord,
"All in my way abiding;
Your selfishness throw overboard,
Obey my call and guiding.
Oh, bear your crosses, and confide
In my example as your guide."

A Disciple Serves

Reading: John 13:1–17

Text: John 13:14—"Now that I, your Lord and Teacher, have washed your feet, you also should wash one another's feet."

An upper room in Jerusalem. The night on which Jesus is betrayed. Shadows of the cross fall on His face. Jesus takes a towel, pours water in a basin, stoops down, and begins to wash the dust-crusted feet of His disciples. Twelve times He stoops and washes feet.

The third letter of the word "disciple" emphasizes that a disciple SERVES. The disciples learned from Jesus to serve in little, distasteful ways. Many times a disciple thinks of service in dramatic terms—going to a foreign mission field or heading a major evangelism effort. But Jesus starts with dirty feet. The disciples learned to serve without glory or recognition. Belonging to community service organizations and church committees helps build a career. But Jesus washes feet in the privacy of an upper room. The disciples learned to serve simply because of love. Can we serve when there's nothing in it for us and when the act is not appreciated? Jesus loved His disciples and therefore washed their feet. We would rather be served than serve. We often avoid distasteful tasks and seek recognition for our service efforts. We confess our shabby discipleship before Almighty God.

But "the Son of Man did not come to be served, but to serve, and to give his life as a ransom for many" (Matt. 20:28). How else can you explain the bloody sweat, the stripes on His back, the crown of thorns, the weight of the cross on His shoulders, and the prayer, "Father, forgive them for they do not know what they are doing"? He served us by dying and in the process forgave our sins. He fills us with His love and motivates us to SERVE.

Prayer

In sickness, sorrow, want, or care,
Each other's burdens help us share;
May we, where help is needed, there
Give help as though to you.

A Disciple Commits

Reading: Matthew 8:18–22

Text: Matthew 16:24—"Then Jesus said to his disciples, 'If anyone would come after me, he must deny himself and take up his cross and follow me.' "

The fourth letter of the word "disciple" emphasizes that a disciple COMMITS. Jesus says, "Follow me." The disciple does not commit to a philosophy, a program, an organization, or a cause, but to a Person, namely, Jesus Christ. What a difference! Jesus committed Himself totally to His disciples. He called them. He trained them. He provided for their needs. He admonished them. He forgave them. He prayed for them. He suffered and died for them. That's commitment.

Commitment means suffering and a cross as Jesus said in our text. Peter resists the thought that Jesus, the Messiah, should have to suffer and die. By implication he doesn't want suffering and a cross for his own life either.

Suffering and a cross are not popular. We want status, success, wealth. We try to avoid suffering and live the good life. But Christ calls us to suffer for Him. Confessing our soft and easy Christianity, we turn to Jesus for forgiveness. He suffered and bore the cross for us so that we might be able to suffer and bear our crosses for Him.

Commitment brings life and joy to the disciple. Jesus says, "Whoever loses his life for me will find it." Strangely, in forgetting ourselves and reaching out to others we find new life and the joy of discipleship. God grants that life. Helpless, exhausted on our own, we discover His life flowing through us to others. Yes, by God's grace, a disciple COMMITS!

Prayer
Then let us follow Christ, our Lord,
And take the cross appointed
And, firmly clinging to his word,
In suff'ring be undaunted.
For those who bear the battle's strain
The crown of heav'nly life obtain.

A Disciple Instructs

Reading: 2 Timothy 2:1–2

Text: Matthew 28:19—"Therefore go and make disciples of all nations, baptizing them in the name of the Father and of the Son and of the Holy Spirit."

The fifth letter of the word "disciple" emphasizes that a disciple INSTRUCTS. Before ascending into heaven Jesus asked His disciples to make disciples of all nations by baptizing and teaching.

Disciples are first taught by the Master Teacher. Jesus instructed with words. Can you imagine listening in person to the Sermon on the Mount or hearing Jesus' parables day after day? Jesus shared intimate moments with His disciples when He prayed to the Father and prepared them for the time after His death and resurrection.

Jesus also instructed with His life. He lived in close relationship with the Father. He acted obediently in every situation. He demonstrated compassion for the multitudes and took little children in His arms.

He exposed the hypocrisy of the Pharisees. Most of all, Jesus went silently and willingly to His death on the cross and after His resurrection showed the disciples His hands and feet.

A disciple instructs. We speak words about Jesus as the only Savior from sin. We invite others to believe in Him. We teach the Word of God and continue to study it. We instruct our children and grandchildren in the commandments of God and assure them of His love.

We also instruct with our life. We set the example of regular church attendance, sacrificial firstfruits giving, study of the Word, and Christian witness. We treasure our family relationships and our opportunities for service. We also admit our sins, ask for forgiveness, and live in that forgiveness. We rejoice in God's free gift of eternal life. By word and example we INSTRUCT others so that they can pass it on.

Prayer

Lord, teach us Your saving truth so that we can disciple others. Amen

A Disciple Prays

Reading: John 17

Text: John 14:14—"You may ask me for anything in my name, and I will do it."

The sixth letter of the word "disciple" emphasizes that a disciple PRAYS. Jesus tells His disciples to pray. He promises them, "You may ask me for anything in my name, and I will do it." That same evening in the upper room Jesus prays His high priestly prayer (John 17) on behalf of the disciples and the world.

Think about Jesus' prayer life. He prayed on mountaintops and in the wilderness, alone and with His disciples, early in the morning and late at night. At the time of His suffering and death He prayed in the upper room, in Gethsemane, and on the cross. What an example for the disciples and for us. Certainly prayer strengthened Jesus for His saving mission.

As disciples we also need to pray. We are privileged to pray because Jesus has given us access to the heavenly Father. As God's dear children we can come freely into His presence. We praise God, confess our sins, thank Him for His many blessings, and pray for ourselves and others. We need God's strength to live the demanding lives of disciples. We come to Him in prayer, admitting our need for help and seeking answers in His Word.

Prayer takes discipline. Sometimes we run dry and feel removed from God. Trials come to test our faith and make prayer difficult. We often try regular prayer times but fail to sustain our efforts. Often we are distracted by busy schedules, interruptions, or wandering thoughts. But Jesus has paid for all our sins, including failure in prayer. We earn no merit because of our prayers. He forgives us in Word and sacrament and moves us to respond in prayer and thanksgiving. He promises to answer our prayers. Certainly we may ask Him for a stronger prayer life, and He will supply it. Yes, a disciple PRAYS!

Prayer

Lord, teach us to pray. Amen.

A Disciple Loves

Reading: 1 John 4:7–21

Text: John 15:12—"My command is this: Love each other as I have loved you."

What picture are you getting of a disciple so far? Certainly words like "committed" paint a portrait of a no-nonsense, steely, daring follower of Jesus. But the seventh letter of the word "disciple" emphasizes that a disciple LOVES. Without love all the other qualities mean nothing. In the upper room on Maundy Thursday Jesus tells His disciples, "My command is this: Love each other as I have loved you."

Note the source of a disciple's love—the Father and the Son. "As the Father has loved me, so have I loved you. Now remain in my love" (v. 9). We don't find our example of love in Hollywood or Valentine's cards or even in the sentiments of Mother's Day, but rather in the Father and the Son. In Pidgin English the word for love means "God hurts in His heart for us." That describes God's love beautifully. He hurts for us and sent His Son at great cost to die for us. That sturdy, enduring, self-giving love is the source of our love.

Jesus commands that we love each other as He has loved us. What a challenge! Not love because the other person loves us or if the other meets certain conditions, but love in spite of others' reactions. "While we were still sinners, Christ died for us" (Rom. 5:8).

We fall short. Our love flames up but then sputters and fizzles. Our love gets hurt so easily and withdraws into a shell. Our love reaches out and then, rejected, turns to hatred and disillusionment. We confess that of all the qualities of discipleship, love exposes our sin the most.

But the same Jesus who commands love promises His unending love for us. He comes to us in His Word and in the Holy Meal where we are united together around His table. Yes, forgiven and loved, a disciple LOVES!

Prayer

Father, help me to love others, based on the sacrificial love of Your Son Jesus. Amen.

A Disciple Enjoys

Reading: John 16:17–24

Text: John 15:11—"I have told you this so that my joy may
be in you and that your joy may be complete."

The final letter of the word "disciple" emphasizes that a disciple ENJOYS. In the upper room, on the night when He will say, "My soul is overwhelmed with sorrow to the point of death," Jesus tells the disciples, "I have told you this so that my joy may be in you and that your joy may be complete." How do you explain the contrast? In His hour of deepest sorrow Jesus talks about joy.

Jesus is the Source of the disciples' joy. He Himself is joyful. He rejoices in His relationship to the Father and in His fellowship with the disciples. The writer to the Hebrews states that Jesus "for the joy set before him endured the cross, scorning its shame" (Heb. 12:2).

In Jesus' joy we rejoice and therefore enjoy our discipleship. The disciples would sorrow, Jesus predicts, for a little while as they see Him arrested, tried, and crucified. They would sorrow also because of their sin in deserting Him at His time of need. But like a woman going through childbirth, their sorrow would be turned to joy. They would see Jesus risen from the dead and ruling the world. They would live as disciples in that Easter joy. Yes, hardship. Yes, cross-bearing. Yes, failure and sin. But always the joy of their salvation, the joy of His presence in the Holy Supper, and the joy of a promised reunion in heaven.

We can enjoy discipleship in a similar fashion as we confess our sins, look to Jesus, fellowship at His Table, obey His commands, and anticipate the heavenly celebration. Yes, a disciple ENJOYS.

We have considered the eight qualities of a disciple as action verbs: D-Depends, I-Imitates, S-Serves, C-Commits, I-Instructs, P-Prays, L-Loves, and E-Enjoys. May your Lenten observance focus your attention again on the Master, Jesus Christ crucified and risen, so that by His grace you will joyfully live as a DISCIPLE!

Prayer
Lord, make us faithful disciples. Amen.

Spring and Creation

Reading: Psalm 65:9–13

Text: Isaiah 45:8—"You heavens above, rain down righteousness . . . . Let salvation spring up."

Spring has officially arrived. In many areas of the country,
people are experiencing balmy breezes and soaring tempera-
tures. Everyone wants to get outside and breathe the fresh air,
to start thinking about gardening, golf, or fishing. Not only can
we say, "Spring is here," but also "God is here." For in the return
of greenery to the earth, the budding of trees, the warbling of
the birds, the warm sun, and the balmy breezes, God is announcing once more that He is alive.

In the words of Isaiah 45 the prophet is telling how God will
use Cyrus to bring His people back to their homeland. He uses
the language of creation to describe the salvation of His people.
In many ways we have tarnished God's creation by our sins. We
have turned against God and tried to use His creation for our
own glory rather than His. But God also makes possible a new
birth for us so that we can live for Him. He sent His only Son to
bear our sins by dying on the cross. He conquered death and
the devil and rose from the dead one spring Sunday morning to
prove His victory. All who believe in Jesus Christ have new life
and the promise of eternal life in heaven. "If anyone is in Christ,
he is a new creation; the old has gone, the new has come!"
(2 Cor. 5:17).

Think about these things as spring begins. Turn to Christ
for new life. And then ask God how you can best use the blessings
of creation to serve Him and to help those in need. He will give
you the life that is "springtime fresh."

Prayer

You forest leaves so green and tender
That dance for joy in summer air,
You meadow grasses, bright and slender,
You flow'rs so fragrant and so fair,
You live to show God's praise alone.
Join me to make his glory known.

Needing the Cross

Reading: Luke 23:39–43

Text: Luke 23:42—"Jesus, remember me when you come into your kingdom."

An assorted crowd stood beneath the cross, many of them hiding their need for Christ. Picture the arrogant scribes and Pharisees—their ornate clothing, superior bearing, words of contempt. Very much under control, they didn't need Jesus at all, except to get rid of Him as a threat to their religious standing. Picture the cocksure and hardened Roman soldiers—gambling in their spare time, accustomed to this gruesome sort of routine work, basically indifferent to the surroundings. Picture the cursing, mocking malefactors—guilty of some serious crime, using their dying hours to show their hardness and venom. All three groups, though externally hardened, were hiding their need for the cross.

Why have we come to the cross? What is our attitude? Sometimes we might appear arrogant. Properly dressed, duly religious, we have our life under control and pity all the others who struggle and lack what we have. Sometimes we come across as hardened. We are able to act worldly when in a certain crowd. We might even find ourselves cursing and mocking in order to hide our own guilt. Yes, like the Pharisees, Roman soldiers, and malefactors, we often hide our need for the cross.

But one of the malefactors at the cross brings his needs to Jesus. Observing His innocence, His dignity in death, His power, this man asks Jesus for mercy. He admits his own guilt, sin, and fears. Only the cross of Jesus can help him. Lonely, afraid, guilty, and helpless, we also need the cross of Jesus.

And we hear Jesus' answer. To the pleading malefactor He says, "I tell you the truth, today you will be with me in paradise." All pretense removed, his needs freely confessed, the dying thief receives eternal life, which flows from the cross of Christ. Jesus speaks the same life-giving words to us: I am dying for your sins. You are Mine. "Today you will be with me in paradise."

Prayer
Lord, I need You and Your cross. Amen.

Drawn to the Cross

Reading: Matthew 27:51–56

Text: John 6:44—"No one can come to me unless the Father who sent me draws him."

Powerful magnets attract metal, an almost irresistible attraction. Jesus talks about a drawing power which comes only from the Father, "No one can come to me unless the Father who sent me draws him." He is talking about how the heavenly Father draws us to the cross of Christ for salvation.

Unfortunately, we often follow the wrong attractions. The Pied Piper with his irresistible charm and pipe attracted the children of Hamelin. We revere magnetic personalities— professional athletes, entertainers, or political figures. Many times they draw us astray. In Jesus' day many forces drew people's attention and loyalty—the Maccabeans and zealots promoted political and military victory over the enemy, and the Pharisees and Sadducees convinced Judas to betray Jesus for money. These powerful forces which draw people to them will ultimately fail. They lead to slavery and destruction.

The only drawing power that works is the cross of Christ. We see it in the women who watched near the cross and later visited the tomb. We see it in John, the beloved disciple, who stood there with Jesus' mother. And a Roman centurion was transformed by the drawing power of that cross as he said, "Surely he was the Son of God."

Despairing of the phony magnetic attractions, we are drawn by the Father to the rugged cross where Jesus died to pay in full for the sins of the world. We are drawn to the cross, where we receive forgiveness and eternal life. Jesus gives us pardon, purpose, peace, and power—and our witness is used by God to draw others to that same saving cross.

Prayer

Drawn to the cross, which you have blessed
With healing gifts for souls distressed,
To find in you my life, my rest,
Christ Crucified, I come.

Nailed to the Cross

Reading: Romans 6:6–8

Text: Galatians 2:20—"I have been crucified with Christ and I no longer live, but Christ lives in me."

Hammerblows ring through the morning air as the Son of God is nailed to the cross. Nails through the hands or wrists to hold Him securely. Throbbing pain to an already pain-racked body. Later He would show those nail-pierced hands as proof of His physical resurrection from the grave.

But the nails have even more significance. Paul writes in Galatians, "I have been crucified with Christ . . . Christ lives in me." In a sense we have been nailed to that cross of Christ. Certainly our sins have been nailed to it. In Romans, Paul talks about the effect of our baptism: "We were therefore buried with him through baptism into death." We are in effect crucified, dead, and buried with Christ. Paul further writes in Romans, "Our old self was crucified with him so that the body of sin might be done away with." Yes, when we became children of God, we were nailed to the cross.

Not only does the cross have a one-time effect on us, but it makes a significant difference in our daily lives. In both Galatians and Romans, Paul tells us that our sins are nailed to the cross, thereby providing power for victorious living. "I no longer live, but Christ lives in me. The life I live in the body, I live by faith in the Son of God" (Gal. 2:20). "Now if we died with Christ, we believe that we will also live with him" (Rom. 6:8).

We live in our baptism, and Christ lives in us. We let the cross work in our lives. Nailed to the cross of Christ, we die to sin and live unto God. The hammerblows ring out in the morning air. The cross is lifted into its position. The Son of God dies once for all to pay for the world's sin. And we are reminded that those hammerblows ring for us as well—dead to sin, alive to God through Christ.

Prayer

O Lord, nailed to the cross, thank You for Your daily baptismal power in my life. Amen.

Wearing the Cross

Reading: 1 Corinthians 1:18–25

Text: 1 Corinthians 2:2—"For I resolved to know nothing while I was with you except Jesus Christ and him crucified."

What a common symbol the cross is today! We find crosses adorning church steeples, altars, homes, wedding cakes, caskets, and cemeteries. Crosses range from simple sticks or palm branches to heavily jewel-encrusted works of art.

This final devotion on the cross emphasizes *wearing the cross.* St. Paul in Corinthians recognizes the cross for what it is—foolishness to the Greeks and a stumbling block to the Jews. He knows that the cross does not bring popularity or acceptance or material wealth. Nevertheless, he also knows that, to those who believe, the message of the cross is "Christ the power of God and the wisdom of God."

Therefore Paul proudly "wears" the cross as a symbol of the Gospel. He says, "For I resolved to know nothing while I was with you except Jesus Christ and him crucified." He "wears" the cross with his words and his actions.

What does "wearing" the cross mean for you? Certainly you can give witness by wearing a lapel cross or a cross pin or necklace. Some carry pocket crosses which constantly remind us of the one who died for us. Labeling ourselves as Christians even today may mean ridicule or indifference.

But "wearing" the cross also means words, declaring "Jesus Christ and him crucified" not only in church but at home, in the neighborhood, in school, and on the job. And "wearing" the cross involves actions, a total life lived for Jesus. We care, reach out, counsel, console, challenge, and suffer for Him. The world may scoff or ignore. But we continue "wearing" the cross.

When we conceal the cross or wear it to our shame, God points us again to the simple message that Christ died on the cross for our sins. Bolstered by the power and wisdom of God, we begin anew *wearing the cross* for Jesus.

Prayer

Lord, help me to wear Your cross proudly because of Your death for me. Amen.

Jesus and Simon of Cyrene

Reading: Mark 15:20–24

Text: Mark 15:21—"A certain man from Cyrene, Simon . . . was passing by . . . and they forced him to carry the cross."

One of the more moving scenes from an Easter pageant sponsored by our church portrays Jesus carrying His cross with great difficulty and falling under its weight. A man is grabbed from the onlookers and forced to shoulder that cross. As Simon stoops to carry the cross, his eyes meet those of Jesus, and then the procession moves on to Calvary.

Jesus' journey to Calvary touches Simon of Cyrene. Simon meets Jesus unintentionally. He doesn't volunteer for cross-bearing. Yet, Jesus touches Simon. Luke records that he carried the cross behind Jesus. With eyes fixed on Jesus, Simon learns to know Him as Savior. At least his sons, Alexander and Rufus, are later listed as members of the early church.

Jesus' journey to Calvary also touches you. His willing obedience to the Father's plan, His suffering and death, stand as eloquent testimony of His saving love. More than words, His actions and His look of love reach out to us. We may have met Jesus unintentionally. But God draws our eyes to Jesus dying for our sins, and we believe.

Our journey to Calvary also touches others. Simon carried the cross for Jesus and helped Him. As we obey the Father's will, we can touch the lives of others. Our actions, our caring, as well as our words bear witness to the Christ who died for us. Jesus and Simon of Cyrene met one-on-one. We who know Jesus' personal love for us can also share Him with others one-on-one in the natural settings of daily life.

Prayer

Calv'ry's mournful mountain climb;
There, adoring at his feet,
Mark that miracle of time,
God's own sacrifice complete.
"It is finished!" hear him cry;
Learn from Jesus Christ to die.

Journey's End

Reading: John 19:16–18

Text: John 19:17—"Carrying his own cross, he went out to the place of the Skull."

The journey to Calvary started with His birth, when He was already "a sign that will be spoken against" (Luke 2:34). As the spiritual goes, "Jesus our Savior was born for to die." He began His public ministry with strong strides as He vigorously taught and healed. He covered the dusty roads of Palestine on a mission. From the Mount of Transfiguration in the north He "resolutely set out for Jerusalem" (Luke 9:51) on His final journey.

Triumphantly Jesus rode into Jerusalem with shouts of praise. But now He approaches journey's end—each small step agonizing until He falls and receives help. Yet His greatest hour is at hand. All depends on these last hours. Will He complete the journey? All the rest of the journey, magnificently handled, means nothing without a proper ending. A space shuttle may orbit the earth 36 times, flawlessly covering thousands of miles at tremendous speed, but without a safe landing it will be a disaster.

Jesus no longer has to walk. They lift Him up on the cross. Passively obedient, He continues to suffer. And—even here—He continues to care for others—for the criminal malefactors, for His mother, even for those who have crucified Him. All alone and rejected, He dies. But at journey's end, the victory has been won. "It is finished!" He proclaims. Paid in full. Complete.

We kneel with Jesus at journey's end and leave there our crippling sins and our weary efforts to save ourselves. We accept His "It is finished!" for ourselves. Dead to sin in Baptism, we rise with Him to a new life and a continuing journey. We press on toward journey's end in heaven with Him.

Prayer
Jesus, still lead on Till our rest be won;
Heav'nly leader, still direct us,
Still support, console, protect us,
Till we safely stand In our fatherland.

Craving Spiritual Milk

Reading: 1 Peter 1:22–2:3

Text: 1 Peter 2:2—"Like newborn babies, crave pure spiritual milk, so that by it you may grow up in your salvation."

People yawn in the pews waiting for the termination of the sermon. "Do we have to read family devotions again? I've got homework and a great television program to watch." "I wanted to read my Bible this morning, but I just couldn't get up." How can we persuade each other to read and hear the Word of God?

How much persuasion does a hungry baby need to drink milk? The crying baby grabs hold and eagerly drinks the milk until satisfied. Then contentedly the baby relaxes and goes to sleep. "Craving milk" is St. Peter's expression: He has already explained that we are born again through the living and enduring Word of God. Everything else withers and fades away, "but the word of the Lord stands forever" (1 Peter 1:25). That Word tells of the death and resurrection of Jesus Christ to bring us a living hope and a secure inheritance. Pure spiritual milk indeed!

Craving, you say? Not yawning, enduring, or complaining, but craving? Yes, craving pure spiritual milk. Hungry first. No pure spiritual milk in the world. Malice, deceit, hypocrisy, envy, and slander, but no spiritual milk. We try to make it on our own without drinking God's pure spiritual milk. But we only begin to fret and cry. Finally, we feel the gnawing of inner hunger. No one can hold us, cradle us, and rock us enough to satisfy that hunger. Close to the pure spiritual milk, we get all excited. We crave it. We grab hold and eagerly drink the Word of Christ's love for us and drink and drink and drink. Contentedly we fall asleep in the quiet confidence that more pure spiritual milk awaits us on the morrow.

Prayer

Lord, your words are waters living,
When my thirsting spirit pleads;
Lord, your words are bread life-giving,
On your words my spirit feeds.

Not Ready for Solid Food

Reading: 1 Corinthians 2:13–3:4

Text: 1 Corinthians 3:2—"I gave you milk, not solid food, for you were not ready for it. Indeed, you are still not ready."

Craving the pure spiritual milk. Contented babies nursing. Good imagery for seeking the Word of God, which helps us grow. But infants dare not remain babies if they are to survive. Drinking milk helps them grow, and growing bodies require the nourishment of solid food.

Paul writes in a scolding manner to the Corinthian Christians, who seem unable to grow up. Calling them "mere infants in Christ," he writes, "I gave you milk, not solid food, for you were not yet ready for it. Indeed, you are still not ready." He exposes the evidence of their spiritual immaturity. They live with jealousy and quarreling right within their church family. Therefore they continue to receive nourishment only in the form of milk. They need repentance for their worldly wisdom and sinful conduct. They need Jesus Christ crucified for their sins.

Content to be "mere infants in Christ"? We like to think of ourselves as worldly and sophisticated. We sometimes flaunt our educational degrees and our widespread experience. But Paul scolds also us for our immaturity. Too often we are not yet ready for the solid food that would give us spiritual growth. We still receive milk and even have difficulty digesting that!

Paul writes this letter to move those Corinthians toward maturity. He has confidence in God's Spirit to do His work, building on the Foundation, Jesus Christ. And he humbles us in our Christian walk so that we will confess our infantile behavior, turn again to the saving cross of Jesus Christ, and let the Holy Spirit move us from milk to solid food as we grow in His grace.

Prayer
Abide with us, our Helper,
Sustain us by your Word;
Let us and all your people
To living faith be stirred.

A Steady Diet of Solid Food

Reading: Hebrews 5:11–6:3

Text: Hebrews 5:14—"But solid food is for the mature, who by constant use have trained themselves to distinguish good from evil."

Craving the pure spiritual milk like newborn babies—a satisfying beginning to our spiritual growth. Not yet ready for solid food—the result of our worldly wisdom and selfish living. But God wants us to eat a steady diet of solid food with the same craving as babies have for milk.

The writer to the Hebrews admonishes believers to seek solid food. He writes, "Anyone who lives on milk, being still an infant, is not acquainted with the teaching about righteousness. But solid food is for the mature, who by constant use have trained themselves to distinguish good from evil." God wants to communicate the wonderful truth about Christ as the ultimate High Priest, who once and for all sacrificed Himself for the world. He wants to explain the implications of repentance, Baptism, and the resurrection of the dead for daily Christian life in a wicked world. But spiritual immaturity stands in the way.

How often do we fail to live boldly and faithfully for God with a clear testimony to the saving act of Jesus, our High Priest, because we refuse to grow up spiritually? We ignore our foundation of baptismal faith in Jesus Christ. Can we ever move beyond milk to solid food?

Hebrews suggests constant use of the solid food of God's Word as we train ourselves to distinguish good from evil. God sent His Son to die for our immaturities. He opens up the Word for us with its fresh forgiveness and nurturing power. As we attend to that Word, we receive the nourishment necessary for growth. That steady diet of solid food produces deeper insights and a dynamic life of service.

Prayer

Abiding, steadfast, firm, and sure
The teachings of the Word endure.
Blest he who trusts this steadfast Word;
His anchor holds in Christ, the Lord.

Why His Death?

Reading: Romans 5:6–11

Text: Romans 5:8b—"While we were still sinners, Christ died for us."

Recently a young seminary student was killed in a tragic accident. As we sat in a memorial service, we wondered, "Why his death?" He showed great promise for pastoral ministry, warmly related to fellow students and faculty alike, and demonstrated good ability as a theological student. Why his death?

I'm certain you can relate to similar deaths in your own experience—a child, a high school student, a young mother, or a dynamic church elder. The question pounds in our heads—Why his death? Why her death? No easy answer emerges, though we often try to rationalize. Gripped by grief and puzzled, we continue to search for God's answer.

Why His death? The right question when we refer to Jesus Christ. After all, He was and is God's only Son, who came into the flesh because He loved us so much. He lived a perfect life. He healed, helped, and served those around Him. Yet they arrested, tried, and convicted Him on trumped-up charges. And they killed Him by nailing Him to a cross with common criminals. Unfair? A life cut short? A promising career ended? Why His death?

St. Paul answers that question clearly: "But God demonstrates his own love for us in this: While we were still sinners, Christ died for us. Since we have now been justified by his blood, how much more shall we be saved from God's wrath through him!" He died for us so that we might live forever with Him.

I know that the young seminary student stands before God, washed clean in the blood of Christ. Though I don't understand God's timing, I know that this death gives witness to the resurrection of Christ and the sure hope of eternal life for all who believe in Christ crucified and risen from the dead. The right question—Why Christ's death?

Prayer

The sinless Son of God must die in sadness;
The sinful child of man may live in gladness;
We forfeited our lives yet are acquitted;
God is committed!

The Ability to Be Wrong

Reading: Psalm 51

Text: 1 John 1:9—"If we confess our sins, he is faithful and just and will forgive us our sins and purify us from all unrighteousness."

A few years ago the editor-in-chief of *Time* magazine gave a commencement address at New York University on a subject not taught at any American university: "The Ability to Be Wrong." How many domestic quarrels start and continue because neither husband nor wife has the ability to be wrong? The man of the house is accused of spending too much time away from home. The wife is chided for petty jealousy. Neither will budge. The barrier between teenagers and parents often is caused by the same inability to be wrong.

In the business world the ability to be wrong is also needed. The young junior executive, fresh out of college, offers a fistful of progressive ideas, challenging the traditional operation. The experienced senior executive disdains the cocky, know-it-all new-comer. They hold each other at arm's length, each convinced of the other's wrong position. Political viewpoints harden in a similar fashion, giving rise to bitter controversy and a reluctance to back down. All because of the inability to be wrong.

John clearly addresses this issue. "If we claim to be without sin, we deceive ourselves and the truth is not in us" (v. 8). Not one of us has the right to say that we are always right. The husband and wife, the teenager, the young or older executive, and the politician suffer from the same malady—sin. We need to get down on our knees daily and confess our wrongs, asking for God's forgiveness. Then, as John reminds us, "He will forgive and renew us." God sent His Son to suffer and die for our wrongs. God declares us righteous for Jesus' sake. Forgiven, we are free to admit our wrongs to our neighbor at home, at work, and in the community. Only God gives us the ability to be wrong. Think what a difference a good dose of that ability could make in our world today.

Prayer

Lord, help me to admit to others when I am wrong. Amen.

Lessons from a Storm

Reading: Psalm 107:23–32

Text: 1 Thessalonians 5:2—"For you know very well that the day of the Lord will come like a thief in the night."

I remember a Sunday evening storm that came without warning. Fear gripped us as the sky grew livid with flashes of lightning, the rain beat against the window of our apartment, and sirens screamed in the distance. Suddenly, a loud knock at the door urged us to join our neighbors in the basement apartment because tornadoes had been sighted nearby. Hastily gathering our sleeping one-year-old out of his crib, we hurried to the basement. As we rushed down the back stairs, we observed the back door torn off its hinges. Entering the basement apartment, we spotted our other neighbors sitting by candlelight holding their small children. We felt cut off from the rest of the city, wondering if others had suffered great damage or even loss of life. We prayed. Soon the worst was over, and we returned to our beds. But my thoughts continued.

How suddenly our sense of values can change. Normal events of importance—a relaxing weekend and getting to work on time—fade into the background when an emergency threatens. With the storm outside, we were concentrating on the essentials of life—surviving, protecting our children, providing our immediate needs. We felt very close to each other and to others in our community in similar danger.

The Bible tells us that the day of the Lord will come like a thief in the night—without warning, without time for special preparation. Who knows when our day will come and we will stand before God? But we can be ready for the Lord at all times. God sent His only Son Jesus Christ to die on the cross for our sins and to rise from the grave. God works faith in our hearts and makes us His own people in Holy Baptism. Trusting Christ alone for salvation, we develop different values. We are moved to love others and reach out to them while praising God for His mercy.

That Sunday evening storm moved us to turn to God and show concern for others. May God ever bring us closer to His Son Jesus Christ!

Prayer
Lord, thank You for lessons from a storm. Amen.

Gossip or Gospel?

Reading: 1 Peter 3:8–12

Text: Proverbs 11:13—"A gossip betrays a confidence, but a trustworthy man keeps a secret."

Gossip—what an ugly word! The dictionary defines it as "idle, often malicious talk, especially about others." The writer of Proverbs bluntly calls a gossip one who "betrays a confidence." The word has a disgusting ring.

Rarely do we think of ourselves as gossips. Others talk on the phone at length with the latest news about the new minister. Other enjoy scandalous celebrity newspapers in grocery checkout lines. Others regularly break confidences. But we join in the conversation only when we have the facts.

Could it be that we too are guilty of gossip? We permit others to talk in our presence. We find our own tongue slipping. We damage reputations. We strain friendships. That ugly word "gossip" comes home to roost, and we need to confess our sin.

Surprisingly enough, the word "gossip" comes from the Old English word "God-sibb," meaning baptismal sponsor or relative. To me God-sibb suggests the word "Gospel," the good news that God sent His only Son Jesus Christ to die on the cross for our sins. In Baptism that Gospel changes us into God's own special people. He gives us confidence or faith in Him as Savior and urges us to share that Gospel freely, no secrets reserved. That Gospel announces full forgiveness for our sins of gossip and gives us the power to hold our tongues when we should and to speak the Good News when we can. You see, Jesus Christ "was oppressed and afflicted, yet he did not open his mouth" (Is. 53:7), and when He spoke, many of His words were Gospel: "Father, forgive them, for they do not know what they are doing" (Luke 23:34).

By God's grace the ugly word "gossip" can be transformed into the beautiful word "Gospel." Which will it be for you?

Prayer
Father, forgive us for idle, malicious words. Fill our mouths with the good news of Your Son Jesus Christ. Amen.

Daily Burdens Transformed

Reading: Matthew 6:25–34

Text: Psalm 68:19—"Praise be to the Lord, to God our Savior, who daily bears our burdens."

Daily burdens mount. Strife in the family at breakfast. Angry words. Clutter left behind—dirty dishes, towels. Traffic heavy. Late arrival at work and school. Headache begins. Pressures increase. A pile of unfinished work. Decisions to be made. Rushed lunch break. Complaints. Traffic heavy. Home for rest. No quiet. More demands. Children's arguments. Telephone ringing during supper. Meetings to attend. Late to bed. Sleep and the thought of a new day. Daily burdens.

Do you experience daily burdens? When the harried days compound each other, the burdens seem unbearable. Our hectic, modern society is not the only one to claim daily burdens. Israel of old experienced similar problems, the result of sin and selfishness. Nations threatened destruction. Rulers made demands. Each family struggled for survival.

But in our text the psalmist brings a message of joyful praise. God, who brought Israel out of Egypt and into the Promised Land, would also lead Israel in triumphal procession back from captivity to Jerusalem. He who would send a Messiah also daily cared for the needs of His people.

Replay the daily burdens from breakfast to bed. Picture the Lord present to bear them. See Him as the great Burden-Bearer. See Him empowering us to praise Him in the midst of problems and troubles. See Him using us to bear the daily burdens of others. Begin the day with the sign of the cross. Remember your baptism. Fall asleep at day's end with the confidence that all your sins and shortcomings have been fully forgiven in His blood. Look forward with eagerness to the new day. Daily burdens become daily blessings.

Prayer

Let each day begin with prayer, Praise and adoration.
On the Lord cast every care; He is your salvation.
Morning, evening, and at night Jesus will be near you,
Save you from the tempter's might, With his presence cheer you.

God's Spacious Place

Reading: 2 Samuel 22

Text: Psalm 18:19—"He brought me out into a spacious place; he rescued me because he delighted in me."

Americans have traditionally loved the wide-open spaces. Much of the frontier push to occupy this spacious land was motivated by a desire to own a comfortable plot which could be called home. The move from crowded cities to gracious suburban living reveals the same desire for space. Yet we often feel crowded and limited. Cars jam the freeways. We often work among hundreds or thousands of people in a confined space. In short, we often live in narrow, confined prisons of human making.

David in the psalm verse describes God's spacious place. He reviews his life and the many harrowing escapes from his enemies. He knows the meaning of being cramped for space, hemmed in on every side. He was forced to flee home and hide from Saul in caves and behind rocks in the desert. No place to call his own. How confined and bottled up he had felt!

But David rejoices that God "brought me out into a spacious place; he rescued me because he delighted in me." Yes, God gave David and Israel the Promised Land and larger borders than at any other time in their history. But more important, David learned that God always provides a spacious place for us in the freedom of His promises. He rescues us in His Son, the promised Messiah.

Whether we live in a one-room apartment or a four-bedroom ranch, whether we work on a factory assembly line or as a farmer on a section of land, God brings us out into the spacious place of His love in Jesus Christ. Jesus narrowed His road to an appointment in Jerusalem. He was hemmed in by His accusers, confined to a cross between two thieves, and laid in a cave-like tomb behind a huge stone. But God rolled away the stone, and Jesus came out into a spacious place, where He rules the universe. We are free now to praise God wherever we are and can joyfully anticipate the spacious heavenly places forever.

Prayer

Dear Father, free me from the cramped quarters of my sin and bring me out into the spacious place of Your love in Jesus Christ, my Lord. Amen.

A Firm Place to Stand

Reading: Matthew 7:24–27

Text: Psalm 40:2b—"He set my feet on a rock and gave me a firm place to stand."

How shaky our world today! The dollar slips and slides on the world money market. Political leaders rise and fall. Solid jobs disappear with the rapid change from an industrial to an information society. Long-term marriages break up, with shattering consequences. Long-time church members fall away from the faith. Ministers drop out of their calling. Is there no rock, no security, no firm place to stand?

David in Psalm 40 faces the same uncertainties. He describes himself as being in a slimy pit. His situation is desperate. No strength to fight free from the mud and mire. Aware of his sin and the power of his enemies, he cries out to the Lord for help. Joyfully David proclaims the words of our text. God is his Rock, Redeemer, and Fortress. God lifts him out of the mud and mire. Now David has security. Problems and troubles remain. Sin still afflicts him. But God brings deliverance.

As we cry out to God from the mud and mire of our sinful lives, God rescues us as well. He has sent His Son Jesus Christ as the Rock of our salvation, the Rock upon which He builds the church. Jesus by virtue of His life, death, and resurrection stands firm and unshakable. When we build our house on this Rock, we have a firm foundation.

Problems and troubles remain. The world continues to wobble and totter. Sin still afflicts us. We may fall into other slimy pits. But God stands ready to set us again on the rock of Christ and His unfailing Word. Rejoice. Cling to the Rock. Bring others to the same sure footing.

Prayer
Rock of Ages, cleft for me,
Let me hide myself in thee;
Let the water and the blood,
From thy riven side which flowed,
Be of sin the double cure:
Cleanse me from its guilt and pow'r.

Unrestrained Joy

Reading: Psalm 47

Text: Psalm 47:1—"Clap your hands, all you nations; shout to God with cries of joy."

Joy is not always associated with Christianity. In fact, the stereotype of the New England Puritan gives quite the opposite impression. Cartoonists often picture the Puritan as an austere, gaunt, solemn-faced person dressed in black—in short, the caricature of a kill-joy. The pleasures of this world are rejected in favor of a disciplined, serious, frugal life with plenty of Bible reading and Sunday meetings for worship. The spirit of Puritanism is reflected in Sunday blue laws and an opposition to entertainment and the arts. In reality Puritans don't deserve the stereotype. They actually wore colorful clothes on occasion. But many people identify Christianity with the caricature of the kill-joy Puritan.

Nevertheless, joy constitutes a basic ingredient of the Christian life. God created the earth with its fields and streams, crops and animals. And He placed human beings on earth to enjoy these blessings with praise to Him. True, we turned against God and brought ugliness, hatred, and sorrow into the world through our sin. But God still bestows the gift of joy upon His people. He continues to shower His blessings on us. He enables us to laugh, sometimes in the face of life's disappointments.

The Christian rejoices for two reasons. First, we know that a loving God has reclaimed us by sending Jesus Christ to die on the cross, and He offers us forgiveness of sins for Jesus' sake. Second, because of this special relationship with God, we also see God's loving hand at work in creation. We rejoice at the goodness of God wherever we see it. The all-conquering power of God marches on to bring joy.

Prayer

Rejoice, the Lord is King! Your Lord and King adore;
Rejoice, give thanks and sing, And triumph evermore:
Lift up your heart, lift up your voice;
Rejoice; again I say, Rejoice!

Is Your House Divided?

Reading: Mark 3:22–27

Text: Mark 3:25—"If a house is divided against itself, that house cannot stand."

Abraham Lincoln once gave a famous "house divided" speech aimed at preserving and restoring the Union. Although his actual Biblical quote comes from a statement of Jesus that Satan cannot drive out Satan (therefore Jesus could not be possessed by Satan), it nevertheless raises the question: Is your house divided?

Is your life divided against itself? Are you sometimes Dr. Jekyll and sometimes Mr. Hyde? You want to live for Jesus, but often live for yourself. You want to go to church, but sometimes find it easier to stay in bed.

Is your family divided against itself? Jacob and Esau fought, although they were brothers. Absalom rebelled against his own father, David. In what ways does your family scrap, undermine, and shatter the unity which God intends?

Is your church divided against itself? Jews and Gentiles, with their differing cultural backgrounds and traditions, clashed in the early church. The congregation in ancient Corinth was plagued by factions. Similar conflicts can and do arise today.

The ultimate division pits Christ against Satan. Satan unites with the world and our sinful flesh to war against God. The battle rages fiercely and reveals itself in our divided lives. See the house divided for what it is—Satan versus God.

Who can unite our lives? Jesus Christ is united with the Father and the Holy Spirit. His life, death, and resurrection, united with the Father's will, works salvation and restores unity between God and humanity. The Spirit rules the flesh. We have power to fight Satan. Christ unites our families through His cross, giving us love to share and forgiveness to heal our divisions. He unites our churches through His pure, inspired Word and the unifying sacraments.

Prayer
Dear Lord, bring us together in Your love. Amen.

A Prophet without Honor

Reading: Mark 6:1–5

Text: Mark 6:4—"Jesus said to them, 'Only in his hometown, among his relatives and in his own house is a prophet without honor.' "

People love to honor heroes and celebrities. Astronauts. Presidents. Olympic athletes. We roll out the red carpet and strike up the brass bands.

Why then did Jesus, the Son of God and Savior of the world, receive such a cool reception in His hometown of Nazareth? He came fresh from several triumphs, stilling a tempest and raising Jairus' daughter from the dead. He taught powerfully in the synagogue. But the crowd raised serious questions about His authority. "Isn't this the carpenter? Isn't this Mary's son?" they asked. And they took offense at Him. No red carpet. No key to the city. No brass bands. In spite of all He had done, Jesus appeared commonplace to them.

We say: "How terrible! We would have given Him a hero's welcome. We would have honored Him!" Would we? Sometimes Jesus becomes commonplace also to us. We may fail to honor Him as we use the familiar liturgy, practice the traditional customs, and repeat the doctrinal formulations. We often live our lives as though He didn't exist. Sometimes our familiarity breeds skepticism and unbelief.

But God raised up people who honored Jesus even in His own country. John the Baptizer honored Him even to the death. The disciples, after His resurrection, obeyed and proclaimed His salvation. Paul asserted, "I resolved to know nothing while I was with you except Jesus Christ and him crucified." Why the difference? God changed their attitudes from dishonor to honor. He sent His Son to die and rise, worked faith in their hearts through the Word, and filled their hearts with praise.

In the same way Jesus reveals Himself to us as Savior. Sins of dishonoring Him forgiven, we honor Jesus with our lives. Sometimes we will be treated as prophets without honor, but Jesus moves us to keep on honoring Him every day.

Prayer
Lord, help us to honor You each day. Amen.

Is God's Kingdom Your Treasure?

Reading: Matthew 13:44–46

Text: Matthew 13:44—"The kingdom of heaven is like treasure hidden in a field."

Buried treasure always sparks intense interest—Spanish gold hidden in the Rockies or pirate loot buried on some deserted island. Men have invested great quantities of time and money and sacrificed their lives in pursuit of such treasure.

Matthew 13 contains a series of parables on the kingdom of heaven. One brief parable describes a man finding a treasure hidden in a field. You can almost picture his excitement as he uncovers the treasure and runs his hands through it with great joy. He buries the treasure again, rushes away to sell everything he owns, and then buys the field.

The parable identifies the treasure as God's kingdom. God rules the universe. He chooses a special people for His own. He redeems them through His Son's death. He calls them to serve in His kingdom. Belonging to that kingdom of God by grace represents a priceless treasure.

Is God's kingdom your treasure? Unfortunately, many glittering treasures beckon which detract from God's kingdom—success on the job, material wealth, family happiness. The demands of Kingdom service sometimes seem overwhelming. The root problem: We try to build our own selfish kingdoms. All kingdoms of this world crumble. Glittering treasures turn out to be fool's gold.

But God creates in our heart a burning desire for the treasure of His kingdom. Jesus ushered in the Kingdom with His message, His sinless life, and His sacrificial death on the cross. The cost to God was tremendous. God's Spirit has freely given us the treasure of His Son so that we might join Him in joyful Kingdom service. Valuing God's kingdom, we give all that we have and all that we are to the challenge of extending it to the ends of the earth.

Prayer
Hence, all earthly treasure!
Jesus is my pleasure, Jesus is my choice.

Hungry for the Bread of Life?

Reading: John 6:24–35

Text: John 6:35—"Then Jesus declared, 'I am the bread of life. He who comes to me will never go hungry.' "

How we hunger today for meaning and purpose in life—not just going through the motions and collecting the paychecks! How we hunger for love at a deep level—not just casual friendship or superficial romance but love! How we hunger for security—a job, a home, a lasting relationship, money in the bank! How we hunger for power—counting for something, having a voice, making some choices! How we hunger for peace—quiet privacy, no anxiety! How we hunger for joy—not just happiness, not just laughs and thrills, but deep, lasting joy! These hungers cause a constant craving for something more and better.

And, like the crowds following Jesus, we seek to satisfy our hunger with all sorts of foods. We seek physical and material goods—bread, cake, roast beef, and gourmet vegetables; high-paying jobs, luxurious houses, sleek cars, and recreational vehicles; exercise and physical fitness. But the basic hungers remain.

We pursue the food of education and science. Books, courses, degrees and advanced degrees, technical training, psychological counseling and group therapy. But our hungers remain.

Jesus describes for the crowds and for us the only food which satisfies our deepest hungers: "I am the bread of life." He came for us. Hungry in the wilderness, Jesus fed on God's Word. He gave His body on the cross. His flesh is the life of the world. He comes to us in the bread and wine with His body and blood.

He provides all that we will ever need. He gives us meaning and purpose, love, security, power, peace, and joy. He creates and then fills our hunger for Him.

Prayer

I come, O Savior, to your table,
For weak and weary is my soul;
You, Bread of Life, alone are able
To satisfy and make me whole.
Lord, may your body and your blood
Be for my soul the highest good!

Polite Welcome or Demonstrative Love?

Reading: Luke 7:36–50

Text: Luke 7:36–37—"Now one of the Pharisees invited Jesus to have dinner with him. . . . A woman who had lived a sinful life . . . brought an alabaster jar of perfume."

If Jesus came to town for a visit, how would you receive Him? A certain Pharisee gave Him a polite welcome. He provided a meal and a forum for conversation. Perhaps the man was a collector of celebrities or a curiosity seeker. On the outside he played a good host, but at best he gave Jesus a halfhearted welcome.

We might want Jesus in our home, too. He might be good for the business or contribute to our status in the community. Might we restrict ourselves to a polite welcome, not really listening to His Word except with a critical or patronizing air? Would we remain untouched by Him or His message, except when He approves of what we are already doing?

A notorious woman enters the house. She expresses demonstrative love toward Jesus. She wets His feet with her tears and wipes them with her hair. She kisses His feet and pours perfume on them. Jesus praises her act of love. He announces that her many sins have been forgiven. Her faith has saved her.

Polite welcome or demonstrative love? Do you love Jesus with a reckless abandon, sparing nothing in expense or open loyalty, not worrying about what others think? Demonstrative love means a deep caring and commitment 24 hours a day. The critical coldness of self-sufficiency permits at best a polite welcome. Unwilling to admit sin, the Pharisee thinks he needs no help—and therefore gives no love.

But the woman recognizes a tremendous need for help as a fallen sinner. She accepts Jesus in faith as her Savior from sin. She knows His full forgiveness. And she responds joyfully with actions of love. Admitting our need for a Savior—because of our cold, selfish hearts and many other sins—we turn to the Man who poured out unrestrained love on the cross. He forgives fully. Joyful beyond words for His forgiveness, we demonstrate a living, active love.

Prayer

Lord, move my heart to love You. Amen.

Through a Glass Window at Church

Reading: Psalm 119:81–88

Text: Psalm 119:81—"My soul faints with longing for your salvation, but I have put my hope in your word."

The other Sunday morning our family arrived late for the 9:15 service at church. Already somewhat in turmoil because of the last-minute rush, we found ourselves sitting on chairs in the overflow area looking through a glass window. The service proceeded. We strained to hear. We longed to participate and find nourishment in the Word of God. But only snatches of the readings and the sermon drifted through.

Growing frustration welled up within me. I needed God's peace and assurance, His guidance and direction. I needed to confess my animosity toward the family for making me late and to explain to them why the worship hour on Sunday meant so much to me. I realized how cut off I felt from the congregation at worship.

Perhaps the psalmist experienced similar feelings when he wrote, "My soul faints with longing for your salvation." He felt cut off from God's presence as others persecuted him and his suffering continued. But he added the words, "I have put my hope in your word." He knew that God had promised salvation through the coming of the Messiah.

Our family learned a lesson that Sunday through the glass window at church. We discovered how easily we can take hearing God's Word for granted. Distraught in our late arrival and frustrated by our straining to hear, we fainted with longing for God's salvation. But in the car on the way home and at the Sunday dinner table we put our hope in God's Word. We confessed to one another our wrong words and actions. We shared our need for regular growth in God's Word. And most of all, we looked to Jesus Christ, our Savior and friend, who graced our dinner and even our discouraging hour in the overflow area. We can always see and hear Him, even through a glass window at church.

Prayer

Lord, give me a longing for Your salvation. Open my ears to hear and my eyes to see you in Your Word. Amen.

Hearts Burning Within?

Reading: Luke 24:13–35

Text: Luke 24:32—"Were not our hearts burning within us while he talked with us on the road and opened the Scriptures to us?"

What impact does Easter have on your life? Is it a once-a-year festive celebration with bright-colored spring clothing and Easter lilies or a life-changing reality which motivates you all year long?

The excited declaration of the Emmaus disciples describes a lasting Easter effect: "Were not our hearts burning within us?" But on Easter Sunday afternoon they were walking home from Jerusalem to Emmaus with heavy hearts. No fire burned within. They were downcast. A stranger joined them, whom they did not recognize as the risen Christ. They were sad because they thought Jesus was still dead. They told the Stranger about the visit of the women and the message of the angels that Jesus was alive. They even knew about the visit of the disciples who found an empty tomb. Still, they hadn't seen Jesus personally and thus doubted His resurrection.

We know the story of Easter and may even accept Jesus' resurrection as a historical fact. But we don't always believe that He is alive today in our lives and for our problems. Like the Emmaus disciples, our hearts are cold.

Jesus makes the difference. He opens the Old Testament Scriptures to them about the Messiah's saving mission. While breaking bread with them in their home, Jesus reveals Himself. Now they joyfully speak the words of our text. They believe in the risen Christ and hurry to the city to bear witness.

Jesus kindles a flame also in our hearts. Sins exposed and confessed, we see Jesus as Savior, alive from the dead. The Scriptures come alive for us. Our hearts burn within, and we hurry to bear witness. Easter all year long. Burning hearts aglow with the risen Christ present in Word and sacraments!

Prayer
Risen Lord, kindle the fire of Your Word in our hearts. Amen.

Who Will Roll the Stone Away?

Reading: Mark 16:1–8

Text: Mark 16:3—"They asked each other, 'Who will roll the stone away from the entrance of the tomb?' "

The women journeyed sadly to the tomb on a mission of mercy to anoint Jesus' dead body. Then they remembered a problem—the stone. They were thinking of the literal stone, of course, but we could take the "stone" as symbolizing obstacles to faith.

As we recall the Easter story, do we come to the tomb with burdens or obstacles standing in the way of our relationship to God? Who will roll the stone away? Financial burdens—paying for the home, keeping a job, having enough money for the college education of our children. Personal burdens—guilt over past sins, loneliness, insecurity, uncertainty, no purpose in life. Family pressures—fights, disobedient children, impending separation and divorce. Who will roll the stone away?

We often try to devise our own solutions. We play politics on the job. We juggle our financial books. We try to make up for our guilt by putting more money in the offering envelope and coming to church more regularly. But we can't roll the stone away.

The text tells us, "When they looked up, they saw that the stone, which was very large, had been rolled away" (v. 4). God had already taken care of their problem and more. The angel told them that Jesus of Nazareth was risen from the dead. The women rejoiced and spread the good news: The risen Savior had lifted their burdens.

The stone has been rolled away from the tomb. Jesus, who died for our sins, has arisen from the grave. He brings peace and power. He forgives all our sins. He quells our fears. He stands beside us in our loneliness. Helpless on our own, we receive His undeserved love and power. We are free to serve Him.

Prayer
Vain the stone, the watch, the seal;
Christ has burst the gates of hell.
Death in vain forbids his rise;
Christ has opened paradise.

Is Your Christ Dead?

Reading: Luke 24:1–12

Text: 1 Corinthians 15:14—"If Christ has not been raised, our preaching is useless and so is your faith."

Has the Easter glow left you yet? Easter Sunday was a joyful day. In our church we proclaimed that Christ rose from the grave and still lives today. Do you believe that? Is the Christ who died on Good Friday still alive in your life a few days after Easter?

You may be familiar with an interesting anecdote about Martin Luther, the great leader of the 16th-century Reformation. He preached again and again that Christ is alive and at our side every day. But he was also subject to periods of depression and discouragement. On one such occasion his dear wife, Katie, came to his rescue in a rather unusual way. She dressed herself in mourning apparel and fixed a sorrowful expression on her face. When Luther returned from a walk, he saw Katie apparently overwhelmed with sorrow. He was startled and anxious. "What has happened?" he asked. "Alas," she replied to his question, "the dear Lord is dead." "What nonsense," he said. "You know that God lives and cannot die." "Is that possible?" she exclaimed. "I thought surely He must be dead since you seem so distressed." Then Luther smiled and said, "You are right. I should not be so sad, because God—who has been, is, and will be—is always the same, loving God."

The anecdote strikes home. We may believe that Jesus Christ rose from the grave, but often we don't act that way. For all practical purposes, He is dead in our life. We mope around, moaning about all the evils, troubles, and problems in the world. We develop ulcers and consume tranquilizers by the dozen. Selfishness dominates our thoughts and actions. How can we help others come alive in Christ when we act as though He were dead?

Katie Luther was wiser than many of us. In a comical way she reminded her husband that Christ does live, no matter how sad we may feel. He did rise from the grave, just as surely as He mounted the ugly cross to take away our sins. He is with us always, as He promised. That never changes.

Prayer

O risen Christ, live in my heart each day according to Your baptismal promise. Amen.

After Weeping, Rejoicing

Reading: John 16:19–24

Text: Psalm 30:5b—"Weeping may remain for a night, but rejoicing comes in the morning."

The sights and sounds of weeping: family members clinging to one another at the funeral of a loved one; husband and wife at the doctor's office after receiving word of serious illness; teenage daughter telling parents about breaking up with her boyfriend; employees learning about a plant closing; hot tears of guilt after ending a marriage relationship.

David weeps also, initially for some physical ailment (Ps. 30:1–5) and then for some spiritual problem which led to sackcloth (vv. 6–10). In both cases the weeping seems to endure for an endless night.

But David completes the picture: "Weeping may remain for a night, but rejoicing comes in the morning." God delivers David from the grave through physical healing and from sin through full forgiveness. Now David rejoices in the God of his salvation (vv. 11–12). After weeping, rejoicing!

Jesus describes a similar situation to His disciples in the upper room. They will weep while the world rejoices, He tells them. Jesus was to be arrested, convicted, beaten, and crucified. But their weeping would be turned to joy as they would see Him again, risen from the dead. Then they could live joyfully.

Because of our sin and a cruel world, we weep. We cry out to God for healing and forgiveness. We talk about leaving this "vale of tears." We don sackcloth and confess our sins. Like that of David and the disciples, our weeping remains for a night.

But "rejoicing comes in the morning." Jesus, who wept for Lazarus, has gone to the cross for us. The weeping women saw the empty tomb and met the risen Master. And Jesus Christ has clothed us with joy in our baptism so that we rejoice in forgiveness every morning and eagerly await that heavenly morning where there will be no more death or mourning or crying or pain.

Prayer
He lives to silence all my fears;
He lives to wipe away my tears;
He lives to calm my troubled heart;
He lives all blessings to impart

The Victory that Overcomes

Reading: 1 John 5:1–12

Text: 1 John 5:4b—"This is the victory that has overcome the world, even our faith."

We prize victory highly. Olympic competition stirs national pride. Children grow up in a world of highly competitive sports. That spirit translates into a lifelong pursuit of winning. We often hear that the self-made person wins the victory. If we try hard enough, overcome hardships, and build on achievements, we are told, we will gain victory. This philosophy sounds so American that we are tempted to follow it. But the unholy trinity of the devil, the world, and our sinful flesh cannot be defeated by our puny efforts.

John instead points outside ourselves to faith in Jesus, the Son of God, who died to save the world from sin. He grasps Him, clings to Him alone for salvation.

Victory for the individual comes only through believing in this same Jesus Christ. By the waters of Baptism the Christian is born anew into this victory. By receiving the body and blood of Jesus in Holy Communion, the victory is reinforced and celebrated. By feeding on the Word of the Savior, the Christian not only receives assurance of eternal life in heaven but also gains power for daily victorious living.

Yes, we need determination, discipline, and confidence for the daily struggle against the world, but our God-given faith in Jesus, the Son of God, supplies us with the power to win the victory. The Easter glow reminds us of Jesus' magnificent victory over death and assures us that the victory is ours for each day and for eternity.

Prayer

Jesus lives! For me he died,
Hence will I, to Jesus living,
Pure in heart and act abide,
Praise to him and glory giving.
All I need God will dispense;
This shall be my confidence

For the Flock: An Example of Suffering

Reading: 1 Peter 2:21–25

Text: 1 Peter 2:21—"To this you were called, because Christ suffered for you, leaving you an example, that you should follow in his steps."

When we think of the Good Shepherd, we often picture a peaceful pastoral scene with sheep contentedly grazing in green pastures by a gently flowing brook. In this section of 1 Peter, we are described as sheep gone astray, now returning to the Shepherd of our souls (v. 25). How wonderful to be sheep under the loving care of Jesus, our Good Shepherd!

But Peter jars us to attention when, in the words of our text, he speaks about suffering. The persecuted Christians of Asia Minor needed to hear these words because they wondered why they were enduring such persecution for the sake of the Gospel. Peter describes suffering as part of the Christian life.

How we need to hear the same message! Aware of suffering for Christ in the world, we often perceive the church as an escape from suffering. Peter tells us that God calls us to suffer as Jesus suffered.

Jesus, the Good Shepherd, suffered for us regardless of the consequences. He reached out for the lost sheep and silently went to the slaughter as the spotless Lamb of God. What an example of suffering! God wants us to follow that example.

But the same Good Shepherd who calls us to follow His example also provides His power for suffering. "He himself bore our sins in his body on the tree, so that we might die to sins and live for righteousness; by his wounds you have been healed" (1 Peter 2:24). He gathers us scattered sheep from the thickets, takes us in His arms, binds our wounds, and returns us to the flock. Christ's suffering helps us conquer fear and selfishness so that we can, if necessary, suffer for the Gospel. Belonging to Christ's flock doesn't mean grazing contentedly in green pastures but rather following our Good Shepherd on a path which may include suffering.

Prayer

Dear Jesus, help us to suffer for You, if You so will. Amen.

A Giver You Can Trust

Reading: James 1:16–21

Text: James 1:17—"Every good and perfect gift is from above, coming down from the Father of the heavenly lights."

We suspect people who give away free gifts. Who is the giver? What are the motives behind the offer? What is the catch or the gimmick? Experience tells us that you don't get something for nothing.

James tells us about a giver you can trust. Meet the Giver. God the Father created the world, including the heavenly lights. He loves us. You can count on Him. He does not have an angle or a pitch. He just gives freely and generously.

Receive His gift. He made us in His image as the crown of creation. He gave us a world to manage and enjoy. We rebelled and shattered the harmony of creation, but He never stopped giving. He sent His Son in the fullness of time as His greatest gift. He lived for us, died a cruel death for us, and rose from the dead. As Paul says, "The gift of God is eternal life in Christ Jesus our Lord" (Rom. 6:23). God gave us birth through the Word of truth so that we might live with Him forever.

Give His gift away. The Father gives to us by His grace. Now He wants us to give the gift to others. We give the gift by being "quick to listen, slow to speak and slow to become angry" (James 19). He wants us to "get rid of all moral filth and the evil that is so prevalent" (v. 21). By our life we point others to the Giver and therefore also to the free gift of eternal life.

All too often we hoard the gift and refuse to live it. But still He gives. He provides the Word planted in us, which can save. He exposes our sin. Humbly we come back to Him. We meet the Giver, our heavenly Father, and praise Him. We receive His many gifts, especially eternal life through His Son. And we eagerly give His gift away to others.

Prayer

Dear Father, thank You for Your faithful giving through Jesus Christ. Amen.

Mirror, Mirror on the Wall

Reading: James 1:22–27

Text: James 1:23b–24—". . . like a man who looks at his face in a mirror and . . . goes away and immediately forgets what he looks like."

You know the familiar story of Snow White, in which the vain queen looks at the talking mirror for confirmation that she is the fairest one of all. James uses the analogy of a mirror. He says that a person who looks into the mirror of God's Word with its description of the Christian life and then leaves the mirror to live otherwise has a worthless religion. Note several dishonest ways we look into the mirror of God's Word.

We sometimes use the self-righteous look. Like the queen in Snow White we puff ourselves up with pride, consider ourselves perfect, and use makeup to cover our moral blemishes.

At times we employ the judgmental look. We hold the mirror up to other people and let it expose all their sins and shortcomings. By comparison we decide that we live relatively decent lives.

On other occasions we give the mirror a religious look. We compartmentalize our life. We admit certain church sins, such as poor attendance, inadequate volunteer service or financial giving, but refuse to let the mirror show us any faults in the areas of our job and family life.

But James insists on an honest look into the mirror of God's Word. Confessing all the dishonest looks, we see ourselves in the light of God's law. The mirror exposes our sin and rebellion. Then we look again into the mirror and see Jesus Christ, who led a perfect life and died on the cross to pay for our sins. We look at the mirror a final time and see ourselves with Jesus Christ inside. God looks at us and sees Jesus. Therefore He declares us righteous.

Mirror, mirror on the wall, who's the fairest one of all? Jesus Christ—through Him we can live radiantly each day.

Prayer

Dear Jesus, help me to look honestly into the mirror of Your Word so that, repentant, I may see Your forgiveness and live obediently for You each day. Amen.

A Sunrise Encounter with the Risen Christ

Reading: John 21:1–14

Text: John 21:4—"Early in the morning, Jesus stood on the shore, but the disciples did not realize that it was Jesus."

Recently we celebrated an Easter sunrise visit at the empty tomb. But what happens after Easter on a regular day? John presents a dramatic story occurring at the Sea of Galilee. The disciples have returned to business as usual—fishing. When we return to business as usual, Easter often recedes into the background. The routine often discourages us. We may feel cut off from a close relationship with the risen Christ.

John describes a sunrise visitor who asks the disciples to throw their net on the right side of the boat. Amazingly, the net fills with large fish, 153 to be exact. The risen Christ appears at sunrise unrecognized, on a routine day to help with a routine problem. Note the response of two disciples. John has the spiritual insight to say, "It is the Lord!" Peter takes spiritual action by jumping into the water and heading for shore.

When the risen Christ appears to us on our ordinary days, God first gives us spiritual insight to see Him as our loving, powerful Lord and Savior. He also moves us to spiritual action by making us eager to respond to His call. Jesus helps us with our daily problems. Through regular worship, prayer, and study of the Word we recognize Him. Through attention to the needs of others we serve Him.

The risen Christ and the disciples then experienced a breakfast reunion, with a meal prepared by Him. How strengthened they felt! Our sunrise encounter with the risen Christ helps us remember our fellowship at the altar and anticipate the heavenly feast. Jesus fills our routine with the joy of Easter morning.

Prayer
Awake, my soul, and with the sun
Your daily stage of duty run. . . .

Twin Enemy of Easter: Fear

Reading: John 20:19–23

Text: John 20:19b—"The disciples were together, with the doors locked for fear of the Jews."

On Easter Sunday morning Christians boldly proclaim, "Christ is risen indeed!" They stand ready to confess the risen Christ and live for Him. But once the Easter glow fades, the twin enemies of Easter—fear and doubt—creep in to weaken that Easter faith.

At the time of our text Christ has risen. Mary of Magdala has seen Him alive and tells the disciples. Nevertheless, fear grips them in the upper room. They lock the doors for fear. No Easter for them. No joy. No hope. Only fear.

Does fear stand between you and the risen Christ—fear of death, fear of cancer or a heart attack, fear of loneliness, fear of failure, fear of financial problems, fear of the unknown? How do you lock the doors to protect yourself? Are you trying to hide, pretend, keep busy, or build false security in order to handle your fear? Nothing will work. At root, fear exposes our unbelief, which is sin. No Easter. No joy. No hope. Only fear.

In the John account, however, Jesus conquers fear. He comes right through the locked doors and says, "Peace be with you!" He shows the disciples His hands and side. Christ crucified lives and has forgiven their sins. The disciples, no longer afraid, rejoice and go on Christ's mission to forgive sins.

The same crucified and risen Christ comes to us also, through His Word. He breaks down our locked doors and conquers our crippling fears with the words, "Peace be with you!" He assures us in the water and Word of our baptism. He brings forgiveness in the bread and wine of Holy Communion. No longer afraid, we rejoice and go on Christ's mission to forgive sins.

Prayer

Dear Lord, I confess my unbelief when fear takes over as the enemy of Easter. Thank You for Your resurrection presence in my life through Word and sacrament. Amen.

Twin Enemy of Easter: Doubt

Reading: John 20:24–31

Text: John 20:27—"Then he said to Thomas . . .'Stop doubting and believe.' "

Easter has twin enemies: doubt and fear. Thomas misses the Easter appearance of Jesus. He hears from the disciples that Jesus has risen from the dead and appeared to them. But he declares, "Unless I see the nail marks in his hands and put my finger where the nails were, and put my hand into his side, I will not believe it." Thomas doubts. No Easter for him.

Doubt can destroy Easter for us. Satan raised doubts already in the Garden of Eden. Our modern age questions God, the Bible, the resurrection, and Christian values. We doubt God, ourselves, others, and our future. The twin enemies of Easter show their common birth. Fear traces to the root sin of unbelief, and so does doubt. "Unless . . . , I will not believe it." We want concrete proof or we will not believe.

Jesus conquers doubt as easily as fear. A week later He appears again in the upper room and says to Thomas, "Put your finger here; see my hands. Reach out your hand and put it into my side. Stop doubting and believe." All doubts melted, Thomas joyfully confesses, "My Lord and my God!"

To us Jesus says, "Blessed are those who have not seen and yet have believed." Jesus comes to us in our doubt with His peace. He shows us His hands and side as we read His Word. He gives us His real presence in the bread and wine of the Sacrament. He forgives our fear, doubt, and unbelief. He bestows faith in His death and resurrection as a free gift. With Thomas we confess, "My Lord and my God!" as we move into a bold new Easter world. The twin enemies of Easter defeated. The risen Christ victorious. Alleluia!

Prayer

Dear Lord, transform my doubt into sure confidence in You as my Savior, so that I may live boldly for You. Amen.

The Risen Christ for Your Trials of Faith

Reading: 1 Peter 1:3–9

Text: 1 Peter 1:6—"In this you greatly rejoice, though now for a little while you may have had to suffer grief in all kinds of trials."

The test of Easter. How well can you apply the power of Christ's resurrection to your daily life? St. Peter directs us to the trials of our faith.

Peter writes to Christians who face growing rejection, with more severe persecution on the way. Their faith is threatened. Peter understands their problem, for he painfully remembers promising to defend his Lord and then denying Him when under pressure.

We face trials of various kinds. Our Christian life-style faces the ridicule of a secular world bent on selfish living. We are pressed to abandon faithful marriages, concerned parenting, active church participation, and clean living. We also face the trial of faith in our failures. When we fall short in our Christian living, we often, like Peter, feel defeated. A third trial of faith comes to us by external circumstances such as the death of a loved one, illness, or financial reverses.

But Peter redirects his audience to the resurrection of Jesus Christ. "In his great mercy he has given us new birth into a living hope through the resurrection of Jesus Christ from the dead" (v. 3). Jesus reached out to Peter in the upper room and at the Sea of Galilee. Assured of forgiveness, Peter was able to live boldly amidst trials and feed the lambs and sheep of God.

Christ lives. Christ lives in us. He stands with us in our trials, forgiving, strengthening, and comforting us with His resurrection. Through Word and sacrament He fills us with a living hope.

Prayer

Should thy mercy send me Sorrow, toil, and woe,
Or should pain attend me On my path below,
Grant that I may never Fail thy hand to see;
Grant that I may ever Cast my care on thee.

The Easter Aftermath

Reading: Isaiah 29:19–24

Text: Isaiah 29:13—"These people come near to me with their mouth and honor me with their lips, but their hearts are far from me."

On Easter Sunday people flock to church in droves. Easter lilies grace the sanctuaries. Special music fills the air. Voices join in praise to the risen Christ. When ushers take down the extra chairs, the organ postlude ends, and worshipers have filed out of the churches with a "Happy Easter" greeting to all, life returns to normal. Empty pews greet the pastor on succeeding Sundays, and the spirit often seems lacking in worship.

The words of Isaiah aimed at a self-satisfied, hypocritical Israel seem appropriate: "These people come near to me with their mouth and honor me with their lips, but their hearts are far from me." How easy for us to worship only with our lips, halfheartedly. In the post-Easter season we do well to reflect on our relationship to God. Admitting that our hearts at times are far away from the risen Savior, we turn to Him for mercy. He offers us His nail-pierced hands of love and forgiveness.

Isaiah offers great hope for our ongoing worship from the heart: "Once more the humble will rejoice in the Lord . . . . Those who are wayward in spirit will gain understanding" (Is. 29:19a, 24a). Praise-filled worship awaits as we gather with God's people every Sunday. Moved by the crucified and risen Savior, our mouth and lips reflect the joy of our hearts.

Prayer

Alleluia! Now we cry
To our King immortal,
Who, triumphant, burst the bars
Of the tomb's dark portal.
Come, you faithful, raise the strain
Of triumphant gladness!
God has brought his Israel
Into joy from sadness!

Guile or Guilt?

Reading: Psalm 32:1–5

Text: Psalm 32:5b—"I said, 'I will confess my transgressions to the Lord'—and you forgave the guilt of my sin."

How do you deal with sin in your life, with guile or with guilt? We would much rather explain sin away. Like the serpent in the garden we learn to use guile in our relationships with others. In our marriages we often use our spouse to get what we want (the games people play). Guile. On the job we backbite against our employers and fellow workers, slow down deliberately in our work, and take company materials home with us for our own use. Guile. Children sneak a cookie when no one is looking, take something belonging to a brother or sister, and lie to Mom or Dad. Guile. In church we sometimes pretend piety toward God while blaming others for our wrong attitudes and bad example. Guile.

David tried to deal with sin by using guile or deceit—with miserable results. "When I kept silent, my bones wasted away through my groaning all day long. For day and night your hand was heavy upon me; my strength was sapped as in the heat of summer" (vv. 3–4). When he honestly admitted guilt, David experienced the beautiful forgiveness of God. "Then I acknowledged my sin to you and did not cover up my iniquity. I said, 'I will confess my transgressions to the Lord'—and you forgave the guilt of my sin" (v. 5).

We confess our guilt to God and to one another, "and the blood of Jesus, his Son, purifies us from all sin" (1 John 1:7). Jesus, who lived a sinless life, dealt with our guilt on the cross as He fully paid for the sins of the world. Children of God in Baptism, we regularly receive forgiveness in the Word and at the altar, where His body and blood await us. Ultimately, neither guile nor guilt avail, but grace and Gospel.

Prayer

I lay my sins on Jesus, The spotless Lamb of God;
He bears them all and frees us From the accursed load.
I bring my guilt to Jesus To wash my crimson stains
Clean in his blood most precious Till not a spot remains.

The One and Only You

Reading: Psalm 139:13–18

Text: Psalm 139:14—"I praise you because I am fearfully and wonderfully made."

Are you just a computer listing, a social security number, a face in a crowd? Images of conformity, anonymity. How easy to feel insignificant and unimportant!

But the psalmist describes you the way God views you—as fearfully and wonderfully made. God created you just right in every detail. He formed you in your mother's womb. That's why abortion represents such a heinous crime against God. No two people are exactly alike, not even identical twins.

In false humility we often deny that we are God's unique creation: "I could never do that." "I'm just average." Such denial, however, displays sin against the Creator, in effect accusing Him of doing a poor job when He made us.

God also has a special plan for our lives. The psalmist writes, "All the days ordained for me were written in your book before one of them came to be" (v. 16). God knows our sin and rebellion against Him. That's why He sent His Son Jesus Christ to save the world from sin. He went to the cross for us and rose from the dead so that we could be new creations. Forgiven and restored, we can now live for God uniquely, under His guidance, using the gifts and talents He has given us. Unique creation, special plan, personal attention. God alone by His grace makes you not a number or a carbon copy but *the one and only you.*

Prayer

All that my soul is needful
He with loving care provides,
Nor is he of that unheedful
Which my body needs besides.
When my strength cannot avail me
When my pow'rs can do no more,
Then will God his strength outpour;
In my need he will not fail me.
All things else have but their hour,
God's great love retains its pow'r.

Numbering Our Days

Reading: Psalm 90

Text: Psalm 90:12—"Teach us to number our days aright, that we may gain a heart of wisdom."

We live by clocks and calendars. Time to get up. Time for lunch. Time for a favorite television show. Time for bed. Marking off the days until school's out.

But the psalmist thinks in broader perspective about God's time, where a thousand years is like a day. We may live for 70 or 80 years, but they quickly pass and we fly away. In that context the psalmist prays, "Teach us to number our days aright, that we may gain a heart of wisdom." Often we don't number our days. We let them just drift along. We tell ourselves that there is always tomorrow. Then we realize that time is slipping by. We have failed to number our days.

Often we try to control our days. We make rigid plans. We try to control our future by disciplined diet and exercise and the careful accumulation of wealth. Then we learn that many things are beyond our control. Sickness comes. Business recession intrudes. Death comes to close family members and threatens us. Uneasy, we are afraid.

But God cares. The psalmist writes, "Satisfy us in the morning with your unfailing love, that we may sing for joy and be glad all our days" (v. 14). God numbers our days out of love. He sent His Son to live for us. Jesus carefully numbered His days in obedience to the Father. He died for us and rose again. He forgives our slipshod living and our feeble efforts at controlling time. He teaches us to look to His mercy. Each day, then, offers a fresh opportunity to live for Him, making the most of the time until eternity beckons. Clocks, watches, and calendars remain so that we may number our days by God's gracious time.

Prayer

Lord, give us wisdom to live our days in Your forgiving love. Amen.

Loneliness Lifted

Reading: Romans 8:31–39

Text: Psalm 102:7—"I lie awake; I have become like a bird alone on a roof."

Loneliness is one of the pervasive problems of 20th-century life. People live and work together in large cities. Thousands work side by side in factories. Large chain stores are jammed with shoppers coming from acres of cars in parking lots.

Yet we belong to the "lonely crowd." We often feel isolated, dehumanized, and computerized. We develop a hard shell of indifference and apathy. We fill our lives with whirlwind activities and material possessions. We bury our heads in color television and loud blaring music. But when the music dies down, we often experience a wave of loneliness sweeping over us. "Does anyone care? Will anyone reach out to me? If I were to die, would it make any difference?"

Loneliness is as old as the psalmist who in near despair cried out the words of our text. Tormented by his enemies, physically reduced to skin and bones, he felt desperately alone and even rejected by God. Can such intense loneliness be lifted?

Loneliness affected the Son of God, who was born in a barn, rejected by His hometown, deserted by His disciples when He most needed them, and even forsaken by God on the cross when He cried, "My God, my God, why have you forsaken me?"

By His loneliness Jesus made certain that we would always belong to Him and that nothing could ever separate us from His love. For He shouldered our sins and defeated our enemies on the cross. Before He ascended into heaven, Jesus promised that He would be with us always. God incorporates us into the fellowship of His church, where we continually meet Him in Word and sacrament and also meet loving, caring brothers and sisters. Loneliness is lifted.

Prayer

Dear Lord, thank You for enduring the loneliness of Calvary so that I might belong to You and to Your people. Amen.

An Every-Sunday Glad

Reading: Psalm 122

Text: Psalm 122:1—"I was glad when they said unto me, Let us go into the house of the Lord" (KJV).

How do you feel about going to church every Sunday? The psalmist indicates an enthusiasm for worship. Also the early Christians gladly met daily in homes and at least weekly to worship. An every-Sunday glad!

Unfortunately, we sometimes lack the joy of worship. Why? First of all, we may subconsciously say, "I was afraid when they said unto me, 'Let us go into the house of the Lord.' " We may be afraid to come because we haven't kept up with our church pledge. We feel unworthy. We come because we feel duty-bound. We want to avoid hell or excommunication from the church. No gladness in worship when we are afraid.

Second, we may be saying, "I was stubborn when they said unto me, 'Let us go into the house of the Lord.' No one can tell me what to do. I live in a free country. I'm not coming to church until I feel like it!" Or at church we may insist that we will not be able to worship unless they keep the traditional liturgy. No gladness in worship when we are stubborn.

Third, we could be saying, "I was bored when they said unto me, 'Let us go into the house of the Lord.' Other things excite me more, like golf, camping, or even sleeping. I'm bored at church—the same old service and same kind of sermons." No gladness in worship when we are bored.

Only God can give us an every-Sunday glad. He sent His Son for us with a life of glad worship. The temple of His body, though destroyed, was raised up on the third day. He stands at the center of His people with His blood-bought forgiveness. God transforms our hearts through faith in His promises. His Word and sacraments cleanse us of fear, stubbornness, and boredom. We come together into His presence with high expectations. Silent before Him, we hear again of His love. He fills our hearts with gladness that endures.

Prayer
Lord, fill my heart with gladness as I worship You. Amen.

Tarrying the Good News

Reading: Luke 24:44–53

Text: Luke 24:49—"Tarry ye in the city of Jerusalem, until ye be endued with power from on high" (KJV).

I was driving down Main Street one day and noticed the following sermon title on the bulletin board of a local church: TARRYING THE GOOD NEWS. I thought it rather unusual.

Turning to Luke 24 in the King James Version, I began to get the message. Jesus was preparing to ascend into heaven. He had personally made possible the Good News by coming to earth, announcing the kingdom of God, living the Gospel life, dying on the cross in full payment of sins, and rising from the dead. Yes, Jesus wanted the disciples to carry the Good News of His death and resurrection to the ends of the world.

But first He wanted them to "tarry" the Good News. He asked them to wait with prayer and the Scriptures until the Holy Spirit empowered them. During the 10-day period of waiting, they reflected on all that Jesus had done for them. They had been confused and afraid. Now "tarrying" the Good News for 10 days, they see that the Old Testament Scriptures explain Jesus as the crucified and risen Messiah. The Holy Spirit enables them to speak what they are learning and carry the Good News boldly to a world in need.

Have you been "tarrying" the Good News? Sometimes we fall short in carrying the Good News through our daily witness because we fail to spend adequate time in the Scriptures. Rather, through worship and group and individual Bible study we can reflect on all that Christ has done for us in His life, death, and resurrection. As His followers we tarry over that Good News, relish and savor it, discuss it with one another, and prayerfully praise God for it.

Then, empowered by the Holy Spirit, we faithfully carry the Good News to a world hungering and thirsting for it. We don't limit ourselves to 10 days of tarrying, but like the disciples develop an ongoing rhythm of tarrying and carrying the Good News.

Prayer

Father, help us to tarry for the Good News of Jesus Christ so that we may carry it to others. Amen.

"I Shall Return"

Reading: Acts 1:1–11

Text: Acts 1:11b—"This same Jesus, who has been taken from you into heaven, will come back in the same way you have seen him go into heaven."

In 1942 the Japanese were winning stunning victories in the Pacific. The Americans in the Philippines were forced to leave the islands. At that dark moment of history, General Douglas MacArthur firmly made a promise to the Philippine people, "I shall return."

Two years later, in October 1944, MacArthur's voice came on radio to the people of the Philippines with the electrifying news, "We have returned." A beachhead had been established in the Gulf of Leyte, and the Philippines would soon be liberated. MacArthur made good on his promise.

Forty days after His resurrection, Jesus gathers together His disciples for some final words about waiting for the Holy Spirit and witnessing to the world. They feel content in His presence, still basking in the glow of Easter. Suddenly He is taken up before their very eyes, and a cloud hides Him from their sight. Then comes a word of promise. Two men dressed in white tell them the words of our text. In effect, Jesus is saying to them, "I shall return."

We live in the period between the ascension of Jesus and His return at the Last Day. Even as the disciples received the Holy Spirit on Pentecost, we too through the Word of God know that the Holy Spirit has brought us to faith. Jesus has already won the victory over sin, death, and Satan. He died and rose again for us. He is with us through Word and sacraments.

We do struggle under occupation forces of evil as Satan directs a continual attack against the church. But we live with the promise that Jesus, who won the victory, will return at Judgment Day to liberate us forever. He will not fail us. One day Jesus will announce, "I have returned!"

Prayer
On Christ's ascension I now build
The hope of my ascension.

Elijah: Bold Spokesman of God

Reading: 1 Kings 18:16–46

Text: 1 Kings 18:18b—"You have abandoned the Lord's commands and have followed the Baals."

No backbone. Always compromising. Blending in with the world. Valid criticisms of modern Christianity. We often refuse to speak for God, to declare His unfailing Word no matter what the cost. We fail to confront abortion on demand, sexual immorality, injustice toward the have-nots, and abuse of the Word of God.

Elijah was not like that. Called by God in a wicked period of Israel's history, he accepted the challenge of being God's spokesman. Ahab and his evil wife Jezebel ruled over Israel and set up altars to Baal. But Elijah obeyed God and predicted a punishing drought. Then at the Lord's command he went to Ahab and dared to tell him the words of our text.

In a dramatic confrontation with the prophets of Baal on Mt. Carmel, Elijah said to Israel, "How long will you waver between two opinions? If the Lord is God, follow him; but if Baal is God, follow him" (v. 21). Then he called on God to light a fire on water-drenched wood. God, who had called Elijah, stood by him and brought the victory over the frantic prophets of Baal. The people cried out, "The Lord—he is God! The Lord—he is God!" (v. 39).

Despite our weakness and compromise, God calls us to speak for Him. In the midst of a wicked world He sent His own dear Son as the Word made flesh. He both spoke and acted on our behalf. His sacrifice on the cross won the Father's full approval. We cry out with Israel, "The Lord—he is God. The Lord—he is God!"

And forgiven, we speak His Word—His Word of judgment against sin and evil, His Word of love and mercy for that same world. Elijah's example points us to God's victory and fortifies us as bold spokesmen of God.

Prayer
We have a true prophetic Word
By inspiration of the Lord;
And though assailed on ev'ry hand,
Jehovah's Word shall ever stand.

Elijah: Self-Pitying Fugitive

Reading: 1 Kings 19:1–18

Text: 1 Kings 19:3a and 4c—"Elijah was afraid and ran for his life. . . . 'I have had enough, Lord,' he said. 'Take my life; I am no better than my ancestors.' "

Today we see another side of Elijah. Though a bold spokesman of God on Mt. Carmel, we find him running for his life. Threatened by Ahab and Jezebel, he reaches Beersheba, sits down under a broom tree, and wants to die. He engages in self-pity and despair. "I have been very zealous for the Lord God Almighty. The Israelites have rejected your covenant, broken down your altars, and put your prophets to death with the sword. I am the only one left, and now they are trying to kill me too" (v. 10).

Can you relate to Elijah? We, too, have times of victory when God seems so real and so powerful. But then come the discouraging moments when we feel surrounded by skeptics, cut off from believers, and scorned for our Christian commitment. Like Elijah we run away and wallow in self-pity. Lonely, afraid, discouraged, and depressed, we desperately need help.

God helped Elijah, but not in the way he expected. Instead of soothing him and reinforcing his self-pity, God takes him to the holy mount and speaks to him with "a gentle whisper." God's Word restores Elijah. He receives instructions for his ongoing ministry but is also assured that he is not alone in Israel. There are still 7,000 who have not gone over to Baal, and Elijah will have Elisha, his successor, to work with him. Elijah receives refreshment for ministry.

God also helps us. He doesn't encourage our self-pitying. He speaks also to us with the gentle whisper of His Word. He reminds us that the Savior has already come and endured the loneliness and rejection of death on a cross for us. He assures us that we are not alone but belong to the fellowship of His people gathered around Word and sacrament. Then He sends us back to serve Him each day.

Prayer

Father, free us from our self-pity to serve You joyfully. Amen.

Answers from Romans 5—No. 1

Reading: Ephesians 2:14–18

Text: Romans 5:1—"Therefore, since we have been justified through faith, we have peace with God through our Lord Jesus Christ."

Many people are asking, "How can I survive with all of the turmoil around me?" Life seems so hectic. Rapid change forces us to adjust when we can find no firm ground upon which to stand. Jobs change. Life-styles change. Values change. How can I survive? Pressures pound us and create migraine headaches. Conflicts arise both externally and internally. We feel dissatisfied with life and are troubled by inner guilt. How can I survive with all the turmoil around me?

Paul answers with the words of our text. Peace provides the answer to turmoil, God's peace. Not a subjective feeling of peace, but an objective peace established between God and humanity. He explains the basis for this peace.

"We have been justified through faith." The peace comes "through our Lord Jesus Christ." God's Son came to earth to restore peace. We had rebelled against God. Satan joined forces with the world to lead us astray. We were helpless to bring peace. But Jesus Christ lived a perfect life for us and died on the cross to atone for our sins. God declares the world righteous because of Christ. Through faith, God's gift, we receive God's peace which lasts forever.

Right with God, at peace with Him through Jesus Christ, we now face a world in turmoil. His peace frees us to experience inner peace with ourselves and to establish peace with others. We will not always feel peaceful, but God's peace remains. Looking to Him again and again in His Word and sacraments, we discover a growing peace.

Prayer

Through Jesus' blood and merit I am at peace with God;
What, then, can daunt my spirit, However dark my road?
My courage shall not fail me, For God is on my side;
Though hell itself assail me, Its rage I say deride.

Answers from Romans 5—No. 2

Reading: Ephesians 2:19–22

Text: Romans 5:2a—"Through whom we have gained access by faith into this grace in which we now stand."

Many people ask, "Why does God seem so far away? I pray, but He doesn't seem to hear me. It's the same everywhere. Government seems so big and bureaucracy so tangled that I can't get anyone to listen to me or help me. I have the same problem in the large company where I work. Everyone seems so inaccessible. Even God seems to fall into the same pattern."

Paul writes of Christ in Romans 5, "Through Him we have gained access." God is not far away. Jesus Christ came into this world and bridged the gap by His death on the cross. We have been brought near by the blood of Christ.

Through Christ we have immediate access to God. The Biblical word "access" describes a priest cleansed by sacrifice so he can go into God's presence, or a defendant brought before a judge and acquitted, or a subject brought directly into the presence of the king for a private audience. We have direct access to the Father. No red tape. No appointments necessary. No obstacles or delays. We have access by faith into this grace in which we now stand. Robed in Christ's righteousness, we stand before God every day with full and free access to His mercy and grace.

God may seem far away. Our prayers may seem to go unanswered. But Paul assures us that we have access and that God speaks to us through His Word and sacraments. Share God's gracious answer with those who are asking, "Why does God seem so far away?"

Prayer

With you, Lord, I have cast my lot;
O, faithful God, forsake me not,
To you my soul commending.
Lord, be my stay And lead the way
Now and when life is ending.

Answers from Romans 5—No. 3

Reading: Romans 8:18–25

Text: Romans 5:2b—"And we rejoice in the hope of the glory of God."

People commonly ask the question, "Does a person live after death?" Shakespeare describes life as a poor player who struts and frets his hour on the stage and then is heard no more. Thomas Gray writes pessimistically in his *Elegy Written in a Country Churchyard*: "The paths of glory lead but to the grave." How depressing. The daily struggles and the future planning have little meaning if no life exists after death. Paul writes, "If only for this life we have hope in Christ, we are to be pitied more than all men" (1 Cor. 15:19). No wonder many people desperately ask, "Does a person live after death?"

Paul gives a ringing answer in Romans 5, "And we rejoice in the hope of the glory of God." Not only does he affirm life after death, but he rejoices in the sure hope of eternal life with Christ in heaven. In Romans 8 Paul further explains the hope of the glory of God: "We wait eagerly for our adoption as sons, the redemption of our bodies. For in this hope we were saved" (Rom. 8:23b–24a). Because Jesus Christ died for us and rose again, we are justified through faith. Therefore we rejoice in the hope of the glory of God. Our bodies will be raised at the Last Day to live with God forever. A solid foundation for hope.

Share God's answer. No need for despair, gloom, and futility. True, the paths of human glory lead to the grave. But those of us who believe in Christ as Savior can rejoice in the hope of the glory of God. Daily life is worth living in praise to God, for eternal life beckons.

Prayer

I am flesh and must return
To the dust, whence I am taken;
But by faith I now discern
That from death I will awaken
With my Savior to abide
In his glory, at his side.

Answers from Romans 5—No. 4

Reading: 1 Peter 1:3–7

Text: Romans 5:3–4—"We also rejoice in our sufferings, because we know that suffering produces perseverance; perseverance, character; and character, hope."

A final question asked by many people is, "Why does God permit suffering?" We observe suffering all around us. Innocent people perish in terrorist attacks. Hurricanes and tornadoes claim lives. Diving accidents result in permanent paralysis. The list goes on. Why suffering? On a more personal level, we watch troubles come into our lives and ask, "Why is this happening to me? Doesn't God care? Why does He permit it?" Painful questions.

Paul answers stoutly. Rather than explain away suffering, he meets it head on: "We also rejoice in our sufferings . . . ." The Greek word for "rejoice" literally means "boast." Paul doesn't imply a boasting in self, but rather a boasting about God's works in our lives. Suffering causes us to despair of ourselves and look to God. We are then reminded that we have peace with God through our Lord Jesus Christ, an objective reality. God's peace in the midst of continued suffering produces perseverance in us, which in turn builds character. Ultimately suffering leads to the hope of God's glory. From start to finish, suffering immerses us in the loving God who sent His Suffering Servant Son to pay the price for us.

The suffering may continue. We may feel deserted by God. But He stands ready with His unfailing hope for today, tomorrow, and through eternity. Refined as gold and silver in the furnace, our faith continues to grasp the Savior. Share God's answers from Romans 5 about the joy of hope through suffering.

Prayer

In patient trust await his leisure
In cheerful hope, with heart content
To take whate'er your Father's pleasure
And all discerning love have sent;
Doubt not your inmost wants are known
To him who chose you for his own.

The Real Issue: Love

Reading: Matthew 22:34–40

Text: Matthew 22:37a, 39b—"Jesus replied, 'Love the Lord your God . . . . Love your neighbor as yourself.' "

What makes a truly alive church—sound doctrine? good organization? exciting programs? attractive facilities? meaningful worship services? a faithful pastor and capable lay leaders? When questioned by the critical Pharisees shortly before His passion, Jesus responds from the Old Testament that the real issue is love.

For the Pharisees the main issue was law. They prided themselves on knowing the details of rabbinic law. They considered themselves experts on all the legal exceptions. They fastidiously kept the rules. They tithed, observed Sabbath regulations, and performed ritual washings. But how far they were from God!

When asked which is the greatest commandment in the Law, Jesus replies, "Love the Lord your God . . . . Love your neighbor as yourself." For Jesus the real issue is love. Love God totally. As Luther writes, "We should fear, love, and trust God above all things." We are to love God, His name, His worship. With love flowing out of love for God, love your neighbor as yourself. The Law is kept only when love prevails.

We stand exposed. We don't always love God or what pertains to His worship and His house. Often we rebel or only comply dutifully. Repeatedly we fail to love our neighbor at home, in church, and elsewhere in the world. We confess our lovelessness.

Jesus not only talked love but lived love. He kept the law of love perfectly toward His Father and His neighbor. He also demonstrated His love by going to the cross for us. The real issue: His love for us, which frees us from the curse of the Law. He fills us with His love and forgiveness so that we can live for Him and others. Then they will know we are Christians by our love—His love.

Prayer
Dear Lord, thank You for making Your love the real issue for my salvation. Love others through me. Amen.

Will You Honor Jesus Today?

Reading: Luke 4:14–30

Text: Luke 4:22—" 'Isn't this Joseph's son?' they asked."

Jesus comes to the synagogue in His hometown of Nazareth to be honored as the Messiah. He reads the Word of God. He uses the reference from Isaiah about the coming Messiah to preach and point to Himself as the fulfillment of this prophecy. What an exciting event!

Jesus stands in your midst today waiting to be honored. He offers His life-changing Word in family devotions, personal meditation, and public worship. He comes in the waters of Baptism, daily remembered. He comes in the holy meal of His body and blood. He points to Himself crucified and risen for you. What an exciting event!

Yet the townspeople of Nazareth dishonored Jesus. He seemed too familiar. They even drove Him out of town and tried to kill Him. How rude and cold their welcome!

We often dishonor Jesus also. Often He seems all too familiar. We take Him for granted and even become antagonistic toward Him when He calls for our witness, service, and sacrificial giving. How rude and cold our welcome!

But Jesus also provides the power to honor Him in our lives. He preached good news to the Nazareth synagogue. He came to release the captives and forgive those who dishonor Him. He acted on their behalf by living a perfect life of honor to the Father and going willingly to a dishonorable death for us.

Jesus preaches Good News to us as well, so that we can honor Him. We confess our dishonoring and receive forgiveness. We worship, commune, and live in our Baptism so that our hearts overflow with praise and we bear joyful witness to Him. By God's grace, we honor Jesus today and always.

Prayer

Savior, again to your dear name we raise
With one accord our parting hymn of praise;
Once more we bless you ere our worship cease,
Then, lowly bending, wait your word of peace.

The Family Crisis in America

Reading: Joshua 24:14–24

Text: Joshua 24:15b—"But as for me and my household, we will serve the Lord."

During the month of May Americans celebrate Mother's Day. We can't afford to be too sentimental about it, because families in our society are under attack. The family of "Father Knows Best" and "Little House on the Prairie" has changed into the family of "Dallas" and "Dynasty." Marriages disintegrate, teenage pregnancies multiply, abortions increase, child abuse becomes more widespread, and all society suffers the consequences.

Joshua speaks out to Israel, poised to enter the Promised Land. He recognizes the temptations that will face families in Canaan, clearly labeling the problem as other gods. Our family crisis in America also traces to other gods—the gods of materialism, pleasure-seeking, and secularism. Values have eroded. The world appeals to our desires. The true God and His Word fade into the background. As a result, family transgressions multiply.

Joshua also presents a solution to the family crisis with the bold words: "But as for me and my household, we will serve the Lord." Trusting in God's promises of salvation through the Messiah, Joshua pledges obedience to God's commands. Aware of his own sin and the people's likely failure, he continues to trust God.

We face the family crisis by relying on God's mercy. He sent His Son, born in a family, to live and die for us in full payment for our family sins. We regularly feed on God's Word and sacraments so that He can build our trust in Him. Trusting His promises, we then recognize the family crisis for what it is, restore Biblical authority at home, and live in daily forgiveness with all of God's family. With Joshua we boldly assert: "We will serve the Lord."

Prayer

Gracious Father, as You have bound us to Your family through the death and resurrection of Your Son, so bind us to our family in faithful service and obedience. Amen.

Spirit-Filled Families Communicating

Reading: Ephesians 5:18–6:4

Text: Acts 2:6—"When they heard this sound, a crowd came together in bewilderment, because each one heard them speaking in his own language."

Which would be more difficult—sitting in the United Nations without earphones and hearing speakers from different nations talking in their own language or sitting around the supper table with your family in the midst of an argument, each person on a totally different wave length? Certainly good communication holds a key to Christian family living, and our sin disrupts communication.

The Pentecost story has something to say about this. After all, communication was a key to the Spirit's outpouring on that day. After the Fall, poor communication caused serious problems. The confusion of tongues at the Tower of Babel disrupted communication between people. The Pentecost account describes a restoration of good communication. Many believed in Jesus as Savior and formed a loving Christian fellowship.

Poor communication between family members often contributes to our problems. Husbands and wives often talk past each other. One tries to use logic while the other tries to communicate on a feeling level. One accuses while the other clams up and sulks. Parents and children struggle with communication. Parents promote high standards and want obedience from the children. Children feel misunderstood and unfairly judged.

The Spirit gently shows us our family communication problems. He points us to the crucified and risen Savior. He offers us a regular feeding on the Word and sacrament so that we listen caringly and speak honestly and lovingly to one another. What a testimony to Pentecost when we see Spirit-filled families communicating.

Prayer
Oh, blest that house where faith is found
And all in charity abound
To trust their God and serve him still
And do in all his holy will!

Tell Your Family

Reading: Mark 5:1–20

Text: Mark 5:19—"Go home to your family and tell them how much the Lord has done for you, and how he has had mercy on you."

A great miracle has occurred. A demon-possessed man, a maniac, has been healed by Jesus.

Now the grateful man pleads to go with Jesus and tell the world about God's great miracle. He wants to be an itinerant evangelist. But Jesus has other plans for him: "Go home to your family and tell them . . ." What a challenge, probably more difficult than going with Jesus, certainly a more effective form of witnessing. His family must have felt totally estranged by his madness. Would they now be able to accept him as a new person in Christ? Would they forget his past behavior? Would his new peace and sanity continue? The man obeyed Jesus and returned home. Apparently the miracle of readjustment to family and friends also worked, because we are told that the whole region was amazed at what Jesus had done.

Jesus Christ has also worked a great miracle within you. By nature estranged from God and controlled by selfish lusts, you have been cleansed by the blood of Jesus Christ, shed on the cross. In Baptism you have become a special child of God. Clothed in His righteousness, you are in your right mind, a mind new in Christ Jesus.

Grateful, you want to tell the world about Christ, but He has other plans for you: "Go home to your family and tell them . . ." What a challenge! Your family knows you, your shortcomings, your bad habits, your thoughtless, selfish words and actions. Will they accept your witness? Will they see Christ in you and rejoice at God's mercy? Jesus gives you the power to obey and return home. Just think how great a miracle would occur throughout our land if families everywhere would experience the healing of God and join in telling other families about God's mercy to them in Jesus Christ!

Prayer

Lord, make me a witness of Your love at home. Amen.

Are You Bearing Fruit?

Reading: John 15:1–8

Text: John 15:4c—"Neither can you bear fruit unless you remain in me."

Gardening time. Looking for produce and productivity, both quantity and quality. Last winter, from our freezer, we enjoyed home-grown peaches, blueberries, apples, and cherries for home-baked pies. Applied to the Christian life, the gardening question comes from John 15: "Are you bearing fruit?"

Scripture suggests the following fruit-bearing possibilities: (1) Bad fruit. Jesus says, "A bad tree bears bad fruit" (Matt. 7:17b). Backbiting, badmouthing, and gossip all evidence bad fruit in a life. Does bitterness not qualify as sour grapes? (2) No fruit. Jesus says, "He cuts off every branch in me that bears no fruit" (John 15:2a). If bad fruit represents sins of commission, no fruit describes sins of omission—a lack of love, joy, peace, and the other fruits of the Spirit. (3) Little fruit. "Every branch that does bear fruit he prunes so that it will be even more fruitful" (v. 2b). Sometimes unnecessary leaves and shoots drain off nourishment needed to produce fruit. The result—little fruit in both quantity and quality. We are bogged down by the world and its cares. (4) Good fruit. "If a man remains in me and I in him, he will bear much fruit" (v. 5b). The godly person is like a tree "which yields its fruit in season" (Ps. 1:3). The fruits of the Spirit are evident, and a life of witnessing brings many into the kingdom of God.

How can we bear much good fruit? Simply Jesus says, "I am the vine; you are the branches. If a man remains in me and I in him, he will bear much fruit; apart from me you can do nothing" (John 15:5). Jesus chose us. He died on the cross for us. He grafted us into Himself. His life flows through us as we feed on His Word, so that we bear much fruit.

Prayer

Dear Father, thank You for attaching me to Jesus Christ, the life-giving Vine. Help me to abide in the Vine through Your Word, so that I may bear much fruit. Amen.

Pentecost Power for Our Witness

Reading: Acts 2:1–14, 37–39

Text: Acts 1:8—"You will receive power when the Holy Spirit comes on you; and you will be my witnesses . . . ."

Yearly we observe Pentecost in the Christian church, 50 days after Easter. The story seems strange, with the crowded room, the rushing wind, the tongues of fire, people from many nations hearing the disciples speak in their native languages. What does it mean for us today?

Jesus' words give meaning to the event: "You will be my witnesses." Since Jesus will soon ascend into heaven, He intends for the apostles, witnesses of His resurrection, to proclaim the Good News in word and deed. They are to bear witness in Jerusalem, all Judea, Samaria, and to the ends of the earth. What a tremendous challenge! And the disciples stand there confused, weak, afraid—wavering in their witness.

The purpose of Pentecost remains for us. We are His witnesses—in our own homes, next door, at work, in our community, and throughout the world. What a task! And we hesitate, rationalize, stumble, fear—wavering in our witness.

For that reason God makes available to us the power of Pentecost. The disciples were emboldened to bear witness. Uneducated, sinful, afraid, the Holy Spirit transforms them into unashamed witnesses who cannot but speak the things that they have heard and seen—in the temple, before the council, in the synagogues. Pentecost power in the Word of God.

Wavering in our witness, we also receive God's Pentecost power. Peter points us to the crucified and risen One, Jesus Christ. Convicted of our witnessing sins, we repent and believe the Gospel—Jesus Christ fully paying for our sins on the cross. The Word works. The sacraments heal and empower. We cannot but speak and live the things that we have heard and seen through God's Word.

Prayer

Thank You, Father, for the outpouring of Your Holy Spirit in that first Pentecost. Pour out Your Spirit through the Word, so that we may witness to Your Son, Jesus Christ. Amen.

Your Body: A Temple

Reading: 1 Corinthians 6:12–20

Text: 1 Corinthians 6:19a—"Do you not know that your body is a temple of the Holy Spirit, who is in you?"

The human body receives major attention today. Scientists study it microscopically. Health magazines prescribe diet and exercise. Sunbathers try to tan the body. Movie magazines glorify fresh, young, appealing bodies. Pop philosophers urge unrestrained physical love between consenting adults and a "do whatever feels good" approach to the body.

But this attention actually devalues the human body. We look at people externally in terms of physical beauty and treat them as objects to be used and then discarded. Many dislike their bodies because they fail to measure up to a self-imposed standard of attractiveness. People corrupt their bodies with adultery, homosexuality, and other forms of sexual sin. The tragic number of abortions betrays a devaluing of human life.

Paul writes to Christians living in the sexually permissive city of Corinth. He condemns cohabiting with prostitutes and then raises the question asked in our text. Our bodies have great value to God. He created us in His image with a plan for our lives as sexual beings. He sent His Son to be born in human form. He went to the cross to pay for our sins, including the wrong use of our bodies. Paul writes, "You were bought at a price" (v. 20a). The Holy Spirit lives in our bodies because of our baptismal faith.

Therefore our bodies are temples of the Holy Spirit—special sanctified temples of God's grace. Paul concludes, "Therefore honor God with your body" (v. 20b). Your body—not a self-serving, throwaway object to be used for sinful pleasure, but a temple of God to show forth the saving love of Jesus Christ.

Prayer

Remove the pow'r of sin from me
And cleanse all my impurity
That I may have the strength and will
Temptations of the flesh to still.

Hope Beyond

Reading: 1 Corinthians 15:12–25

Text: 1 Corinthians 15:19—"If only for this life we have hope in Christ, we are to be pitied more than all men."

People often live only for this life. They deny any life beyond the grave. They hope and dream, make plans and carry them out, but only for this life. They may secure an outstanding education, succeed in business, gain great wealth, receive national honors, and help other people. But the hopes fade and the sand falls to the bottom of the hourglass.

Apparently some in Corinth were questioning whether there is such a thing as a resurrection from the dead. Paul points out that our very faith hangs in the balance on this question. With ringing certainty he declares, "But Christ has indeed been raised from the dead, the firstfruits of those who have fallen asleep" (v. 20). "Firstfruits" implies that more is to come. Because Christ, "the firstfruits," died for us and rose physically from the dead on the third day, we who believe in Him will also rise physically from the dead on Judgment Day—and thus complete the harvest, so to speak. We have hope not only here, but also beyond this life.

Hope beyond the grave through Christ's resurrection leads us to live hopefully here. We seek God's purpose for our lives, tell others about His resurrection, and live daily with the quiet assurance that He will take us to heaven. Easter lives on all year long. Eternity beckons with the open, inviting arms of our risen and ascended Lord. Thank God for the *hope beyond!*

Prayer

This is a sight that gladdens—What peace it does impart!
Now nothing ever saddens The joy within my heart.
No gloom shall ever shake, No foe shall ever take
The hope which God's own Son In love for me has won.

Dinner Talk

Reading: Luke 22:7–30

Text: Luke 22:15—"I have eagerly desired to eat this Passover with you before I suffer."

What do you talk about around the dinner table? Do you just sit there in silence surrounded only by the sounds of tinkling glass and fork hitting plate? "Pass the butter, please." "I'll take a little more gravy." Is your evening meal a race to see who finishes first? "May I be excused. My television program is starting." "I have to leave for bowling." "I'm going over to George's to do homework."

What do you talk about around the dinner table? Do you take out your frustrations from the day? "Mother, why did you have to make this same old hamburger dish again tonight? I'm tired of it." "I had a terrible day at the office. No one was willing to cooperate. I've got a splitting headache." "How was school today, Sue?" No answer. "How was school today, Sue?" No answer. "How was school today, Sue? Are you deaf?" "None of your business. You wouldn't be interested anyway. What's the matter? Are you afraid I got in trouble or something?"

How different that meal in the upper room when Jesus celebrated the Passover for the last time with His disciples. Yes, the disciples argued among themselves and accused each other. But Jesus focused their thoughts on the new covenant of His blood, to be sealed by His death.

The Lord Jesus hosts us in the upper room as He gives us His own body and blood. By grace He prepares for us the heavenly feast where we will dine with Him forever. And He is present with His forgiving love at every meal we eat, whether hamburger or T-bone steak. He makes it possible for us to care for each other and speak helpful, encouraging words and to gather around His Word together. What do you talk about around the dinner table?

Prayer

Come, Lord Jesus, be our guest and let Thy gifts to us be blessed. Amen.

More Dinner Talk

Reading: Ephesians 4:29–32

Text: Acts 2:46b—"They broke bread in their homes and ate together with glad and sincere hearts."

Jesus' last meal in the upper room with His disciples certainly stands in sharp contrast to our typical dinners together in the family. But you could argue that the upper room hardly provided a typical setting for a family. However, looking at the regular gathering of the early Christians for meals gives us reason to reflect further on our dinner talk.

What do you talk about around the dinner table? Sports, the weather, newspaper headlines about strikes or international tensions, parking problems downtown, your grocery list? Perhaps what you say is less important than how and why you say it. The evening meal may provide the only opportunity all day for your whole family to gather together. You can share with each other and show that you really care about one another and about the problems of each individual.

The meal can either draw you closer together or split you into warring factions. If you eat in silence, you may build a barrier of distrust and disinterest. If you make supper a gripe session, you gradually fray nerves and create tension. If you talk only about senseless, superficial things, you may never really get to know the members of your own family.

The early Christian community used to capitalize on meals together. They took the opportunity to build each other up. They could laugh together and talk about common problems. They could even talk freely about their faith in Jesus Christ, the crucified and risen One who had changed their lives. As Paul suggests, "Do not let any unwholesome talk come out of your mouths, but only what is helpful for building others up according to their needs, that it may benefit those who listen" (Eph. 4:29).

What will you talk about around the dinner table?

Prayer

Dear Lord, grace our table with Your holy presence. Amen.

Joy Is Like the Rain

Reading: Matthew 8:23–27

Text: John 16:22c—"No one will take away your joy."

After a rainy day in May, I've been thinking about a song entitled "Joy Is Like the Rain." These reflections give new meaning to Jesus' words regarding joy coming forth out of sorrow: "No one will take away your joy."

Just think about it. Joy is like the rain. Look at the raindrops on your window. Fresh, beautiful raindrops, bringing life to the soil, changing brown, dying grass to a healthy green, watering the parched earth. Watch those drops streaking your window and disappearing in a stream of water. Isn't joy like that? A moment of wonder and happiness—in your loved one's arms or at a candle-lit dinner table, at the lake or seashore, on a picnic with the delightful squeals of your laughing children, at peace with God. Then the moment fades; the laughter ceases; the bitterness comes; the loneliness, the boredom, the envy, the anger. But the joy comes again with the touch of the heavenly Father, a new burst of His love, the beauty of a sunset, the caring of a loved one, the understanding of a friend, the simplicity of a child's faith, the reassuring hand of the Master, Jesus, the Savior, the crucified, the risen One.

Just think about it. Joy is like a cloud. Sometimes silver, sometimes gray, always sun not far away. Are there clouds on the horizon of your life? Do you fret over financial problems, marital problems, labor-management quarrels, medical needs for your family, automobile insurance? Can you see the silver lining in your clouds? Are you looking for the Father's hand? Are you listening for His voice? Will you let the clouds deepen your life? Won't the sun seem all the brighter and more glorious when the clouds pass? Is Christ your Sun of righteousness? Yes, joy is like a cloud.

Prayer

Dear Lord, thank You for shining through the clouds with the sunshine of Your love. Help me to rejoice daily in the middle of rain and clouds. Amen.

More Thoughts on Rainy Joy

Reading: Luke 8:22–25

Text: John 16:24c—"Your joy will be complete."

Yesterday we looked at the song "Joy Is Like the Rain." Jesus really meant it when He said, "Your joy will be complete." My reflections continue.

Just think about it. Joy is tried by storm. Picture yourself on the troubled Sea of Galilee. The thunder rolls across the sky and whips the waves to a frothy and frightening intensity. Your life's boat is almost torn apart, and your heart is full of fear. All seems lost.

There is no joy. But then you remember. Christ is asleep in your boat—your Christ, your powerful, loving, living Christ. And your joyful, victorious shout cannot be silenced by the storms of life. You are whipped by wind, yet still afloat. And you live to see the calm. Yes, joy is tried by storm.

Just think about it. Joy is like the rain. The waters pound the earth, and the rivers, growing from a tiny rivulet to a mighty, roaring stream, rush through the valleys and plains to the vast oceans of the world. Joy in Christ starts small, but it can grow and grow as you experience the love of God. On and on it grows, bit by bit—the still, small voice of God within your soul; the daily yet timeless riches of His precious Word; the love of your brothers and sisters in Christ, understanding, accepting, forgiving, strengthening; the endless meetings with God, in a cloud, in a flower, in church, in a helpful stranger, in a friend, in a deep conversation which is honest and loving. Yes, joy is like the rain.

All this, and more, from a rainy day and a song about joy. God is alive. He speaks. He gives. He loves. He brings joy, complete joy, like the rain.

Prayer Thoughts

Describe specific examples of joy in your life and family. Thank God for filling you with joy even when tried by storm.

Our Nation's Peril

Reading: Ezekiel 36:16–21

Text: Proverbs 14:34—"Righteousness exalts a nation, but sin is a disgrace to any people."

Every May Americans observe Memorial Day, a time to reflect on the great blessings preserved for us by the sacrifice of those who fought and died in war. But the words of Proverbs suggest that our nation faces great peril: "Sin is a disgrace to any people."

We often forget those who fought for freedom. We forget the principles on which our nation was founded. Most of all, we forget what God has done for us in the death of His Son. We often disobey authority, ignoring the Fourth Commandment, fostering rebellion in our homes, our church, our place of employment, and our government. We grumble and complain. We often commit the sin of noninvolvement and irresponsibility. We stand by while wholesale abortion continues. We let crime increase. We contribute to increased deficit spending. We ignore the poor, the homeless, the handicapped, and the foreigners in our midst. Yes, our nation's peril stems from rebellion against God.

The writer of Proverbs says, "Righteousness exalts a nation." God provides a hope through His Son. We have been declared righteous by the life, death, and resurrection of Jesus Christ. Through faith we receive full forgiveness for all our sins. We receive God's power to live righteously as citizens of two kingdoms. As citizens of heaven, we live joyfully and productively as citizens of our country! Remembering God's mercy in Christ and His blessings on our land, we strive to obey legitimate authority and to involve ourselves responsibly in society. By God's grace we face our nation's peril—sin—and point to our nation's hope—salvation through Jesus Christ.

Prayer

Earth, hear your Maker's voice; Your great Redeemer own;
Believe, obey, rejoice, And worship him alone.
Cast down your pride, Your sin deplore,
And bow before The Crucified. Amen.

Does America Have a Reason to Boast?

Reading: Jeremiah 9:23–24

Text: Jeremiah 9:24a—"But let him who boasts boast about this: that he understands and knows me."

Every year near the end of May, Americans pause to remember those who died to keep us free. We reflect also on the character of our nation. Jeremiah challenges us to ask whether America has a reason to boast.

Can we boast of our wisdom? Certainly the founding fathers expressed great wisdom in writing the Constitution and structuring our government. But since then we have made our share of foolish choices. Jeremiah, aware of unwise decisions made by kings, boldly declares: "Let not the wise man boast of his wisdom."

Can we boast of our strength? We recall with pride how America rebounded from Pearl Harbor ignominy to build a mighty war machine in World War II. But today we are no longer unique in our military power. Furthermore, we often lack strength of character and commitment, which rank higher than military strength. Jeremiah, aware of Judah's hollow military boasts, asserts, "Let not . . . the strong man boast of his strength."

Can we boast of our riches? We have indeed been blessed with abundant wealth. But today we find ourselves struggling, with other nations growing in productivity. And our wealth doesn't bring happiness. Jeremiah, knowing the vanity of riches, cries out, "Let not . . . the rich man boast of his riches."

Jeremiah gives only one reason to boast, "that he understands and knows me, that I am the Lord, who exercises kindness, justice and righteousness on earth." America needs to confess sins of vain boasting and look to the Lord who came to die as a humble servant, paying fully for the world's sin. The Christians of America have only one reason to boast—that by God's grace they know the Lord!

Prayer
Till then—nor is my boasting vain—
Till then I boast a Savior slain;
And oh, may this my glory be,
That Christ is not ashamed of me!

From Downcast to Upraised

Reading: Psalm 43

Text: Psalm 43:5—"Why are you downcast, O my soul? Why so disturbed within me? Put your hope in God, for I will yet praise him, my Savior and my God."

Have you ever felt downcast? Head bowed. Eyes on the ground. Shoulders slumped. Sighs of heaviness. Everything wrong. The world against you. Circumstances hopeless. Trouble near. God so far away. You dread mornings and the pressures of a new day. You feel tired by mid-morning and exhausted by late afternoon. Thoughts race through your mind without focus and clarity. Gloom overwhelms you.

The psalmist feels cut off from God, longs for worship in the temple, and experiences the depression of emptiness. He cries out, "Why are you downcast, O my soul? Why so disturbed within me?" He answers his own question with a glance upward, "Put your hope in God." The human predicament provides no hope. Sin grips our hearts and makes us downcast. But God provides hope of forgiveness and salvation through the promised Messiah, Jesus Christ.

We need hope in God. He comes to us in our discouragement. He knows our depression. Jesus' shoulders were slumped with the weight of our sins. His head bowed in death. But by His death Jesus won the victory and brings hope through His resurrection. No longer do we need to be downcast.

Now the psalmist lifts upraised hands to God: "I will yet praise him, my Savior and my God." He longs for the temple worship and begins to praise with his lips. God lifts him up and empowers him for praise.

Similarly, God takes us where we are—downcast, hopeless, discouraged, afraid, uncertain, self-pitying—and lifts our hands to praise Him, our Savior and our God. Filled with the hope of Christ's resurrection, we long for regular worship in God's house and praise Him day by day. We have moved from downcast hearts to hands upraised in praise!

Prayer
In you is gladness Amid all sadness,
Jesus, sunshine of my heart.

The Ever-Present Mountains

Reading: Psalm 46

Text: Psalm 46:1—"God is our refuge and strength, an ever-present help in trouble."

Recently I taught a graduate course for pastors in the Denver area. My motel provided a breathtaking view of the mountains and the clear blue sky. Always the mountains. When I awakened and took a walk, I breathed in the clear air and gazed at the springtime Rockies—snowcapped, with patches of green in the foothills. Driving to class, the mountains were present. At twilight I paused again to look at their rugged strength and picture-postcard beauty. In some indefinable way I drew strength from the ever-present mountains.

The psalmist describes God that way. He even suggests that mountains might "fall into the heart of the sea," and still we need not fear. Life often brings problems and troubles. Threats of danger, destruction, and upheavals surround us constantly. We tremble. Dr. Martin Luther had this psalm in mind when he wrote his battle hymn of the Reformation, "A Mighty Fortress Is Our God." He was troubled by popes and rulers, attacked on every side. Yet he clung to God. In Jesus Christ he saw the Valiant One who holds the field forever.

In the midst of tumults and uncertainties we can look to an ever-present God. He sent His Son to do battle on a "mountain" called Calvary. His willing obedience unto death, "even death on a cross" (Phil. 2:8), won the victory over the old evil foe.

We may not be in a position to see the ever-present mountains and draw strength from them as evidence of God's matchless creation. But we can draw daily strength—morning, noon, and evening—from God, our ever-present help in trouble. As we fix our eyes constantly on His rugged strength, we receive power for victorious living and lead others to see Him too.

Prayer

May ev'ry mountain height, Each vale and forest green,
Shine in your Word's pure light, And its rich fruits be seen!
May ev'ry tongue Be tuned to praise
And join to raise A grateful song.

The Lord Is My Song!

Reading: Isaiah 12

Text: Isaiah 12:2—"The Lord, the Lord, is my strength and my song; he has become my salvation."

What kind of song do you sing with your life—dull, flat, off-key, halfhearted or enthusiastic, vibrant, melodious? Isaiah gives us a glimpse of the songs we sing.

We often sing a song of the world. In Isaiah's day the world was singing a very discordant song. Greed for wealth, vanity for clothes and jewelry, immorality and drunkenness, and exploitation of others blared loud and strident notes in the song of life. Our society, too, produces music which often jars the senses, splits the eardrums, and describes the very worst of life. We worship television, strive to keep up with the Joneses, drink excessively, take drugs, exploit others, and wallow in immorality.

We also sing a song of self. Our age capitalizes the "I." I want. I need. I think. I feel. Going far beyond a healthy self-image, we insist on our rights, satisfy our every desire, and live only for the moment. Children rebel. We work hard for the good life for ourselves and sometimes ignore God, country, and others. How enthusiastically we sing the song of the world and the song of self!

We need to sing a song of confession. Israel ultimately repented. In the Babylonian exile God's people sang a song of confession and looked to God for help with a humble desire to return home. We admit that worldly, selfish songs only lead to fear, defeat, guilt, and unhappiness. We sing a song of confession to God, admitting our sin and our need for Him.

Isaiah tells us that the Lord is our Song. God's people in their repentance looked to Him and His promised Messiah. He became their Strength and their Song. He gave them hope and filled them with joy, so that they could sing a different kind of song—a song of praise! Jesus, the crucified and risen Savior, is our song!

Prayer
Dear Lord, thank You for being my Song. Amen.

Singing His Song

Reading: Psalm 95:1–7

Text: Ephesians 5:19—"Speak to one another with psalms, hymns and spiritual songs. Sing and make music in your heart to the Lord."

Musical references fill the Bible. They speak of praise to God. In the next several devotions we look at the Christian life in terms of musical imagery. Yesterday we saw how we often sing a song of the world and a song of ourselves. Confessing our sin, we learn that the Lord is our Song.

God's song began with creation. He sang it from the mountains and valleys. Despite the discord and disharmony of sin, God kept singing His song with His merciful promises. He chose a people, preserved a remnant, and sent His Son to sing a song of love, peace, and victory on the cross. Risen and ascended, Jesus sings on in our world and into our hearts.

Because the Lord is our Song, He fills our life with singing. We respond joyfully to the words of Paul in our text. We join with God's people in regular worship and sing from our hearts in praise to the triune God. We continue singing in our hearts as we sit at the family dining table, drive in hectic rush hour traffic, and walk into our sometimes stressful place of employment. We join the psalmist, "Come, let us sing for joy to the Lord; let us shout aloud to the Rock of our salvation" (Ps. 95:1)—singing His song!

Prayer

Alleluia! Let praises ring!
Unto our triune God we sing;
Blest be his name forever!
With angel hosts let us adore
And sing his praises more and more
For all his grace and favor!
Singing, Ringing: Holy holy,
God is holy; Spread the story
Of our God, the Lord of glory!

Sounding the Trumpets

Reading: Psalm 98

Text: Psalm 98:5a–6a—"Make music to the Lord . . . with trumpets and the blast of the ram's horn."

Brass instruments always thrill me. Easter victory services with trumpets sounding forth fill my heart with praise that Jesus Christ is risen indeed. Purcell's "Trumpet Tune" and "Trumpet Voluntary" add celebration to wedding services. Bach and Handel also make such joyful use of trumpets!

The psalmist overflows with joyful praise to God: "Make music to the Lord . . . with trumpets and the blast of the ram's horn." Primitive ram's horns sounded the call to battle, the cry of warning, and the summons to worship. Along with the other instruments in the temple, the horns announced the presence of God in the midst of His people. The people were filled with both holy awe and great joy before the God who created them and brought them salvation.

Scripture knows of another use for trumpets, however. The trumpet sounds in Exodus 19, in 1 Corinthians 15, and in the Book of Revelation remind us of our sinfulness and of the end of the world with its final judgment. The Day of the Lord is indeed coming. We need to be prepared. Amidst the alluring and confusing sounds of our world, we need to hear the warning trumpet so that we can turn from our sins to God's love and mercy.

And then we hear the trumpet announcing that the Messiah has come. The heralds of good tidings summon us to the rooftops to see Jesus coming as crucified and risen Savior. Bowing down on adoring knees, we thrill to hear the joyful trumpet sounds before the throne of God. Sound the trumpets now! Make music in the congregation of God's people! Alleluia!

Prayer

Praise him who reigns on high, The Lord whom we adore:
The Father, Son, and Holy Ghost, One God forevermore.
Rejoice! Rejoice! Rejoice, give thanks and sing!

Clashing the Cymbals

Reading: 1 Corinthians 13:1–7

Text: Psalm 150:5—"Praise him with the clash of cymbals, praise him with resounding cymbals."

The music goes on. Singers sing a song of praise to the Lord. Trumpets sound forth God's glory. The psalmist pulls out all the stops and shouts, "Praise him with the clash of cymbals, praise him with resounding cymbals." Yes, loud clashing cymbals. Unrestrained praise to the God of our salvation.

But cymbals can also be loudly out of place. They are used in a negative way by Paul in 1 Corinthians 13:1 to describe a loveless Christian, "If I speak in the tongues of men and of angels, but have not love, I am only a resounding gong or a clanging cymbal." In other words, we may present ourselves to others in a showy fashion and worship in a form of high praise, but if we lack love we are no better than a loud cymbal. So often, instead of praising God, we make a discordant sound as people see our selfishness and lack of concern for others. We call attention negatively to ourselves and dishonor God.

God came into a discordant world in the person of His Son Jesus Christ. Good Friday resounded with the clanging cymbals of injustice, hatred, and prejudice. But Jesus endured the shame, and His cry of "My God, my God, why have you forsaken me?" was followed by the triumphant cry, "It is finished!" Clashing with evil, His love won the day.

His love frees us to love others. We are attuned to praise Him, and therefore we can joyfully worship Him with the clash of cymbals forever.

Prayer

Creator, humbly I implore you
To listen to my earthly song
Until that day when I adore you,
When I have joined the angel throng
And learned with choirs of heav'n to sing
Eternal anthems to my king.

Playing the Harps

Reading: Revelation 5:8–14

Text: Psalm 137:2—"There on the poplars we hung our harps."

Harps make beautiful music. We often associate them with angels making music in heaven. Certainly they make appropriate instruments of praise. But in Psalm 137 we find Israel's harps hung on trees, not being used. Why? God's people grieve in Babylonian exile. Gone the temple in Jerusalem. Far away their homeland. They don't want to accept the taunts of their captors to make music for them. They remain loyal to God. Repentant now, they long to return home and play their harps again in temple praise.

By contrast, Isaiah criticizes Israel for playing their harps at banquets with "no regard for the deeds of the Lord" (Is. 5:12). How easily we can be guilty of joining the world in loose living and disobedience against God. All the while we sing our songs and play our harps.

God wants us to repent and look to the Messiah for our deliverance. He came to make beautiful music in a dissonant world. He restored the harmony of creation by His death and resurrection. He brings us back home to Himself in our baptism. We dwell in the midst of His temple of living stones. Therefore we can take our harps off the poplars and play them beautifully in praise of Him. And someday we will join "the four living creatures and the twenty-four elders . . . before the Lamb" (Rev. 5:8) and use our harps to swell the new song eternally.

Prayer

Unnumbered choirs before the shining throne
Their joyful anthems raise
Till heaven's arches echo with the tone
Of that great hymn of praise.
And all its host rejoices,
And all its blessed throng
Unite their myriad voices
In one eternal song.

Praising with Full Orchestra

Reading: 2 Chronicles 29:25–30

Text: 2 Chronicles 29:26—"So the Levites stood ready with David's instruments, and the priests with their trumpets."

The last few days we have been looking at musical imagery in the Scriptures. Because the Lord is our Song, we sing a new song unto the Lord with our lives. Together as God's people we sound the trumpets, clash the cymbals, and pluck our harps in praise to the triune God—Father, Son, and Holy Ghost.

The Scripture text from 2 Chronicles describes praising God with full orchestra: "So the Levites stood ready with David's instruments, and the priests with their trumpets." Judah had lived wickedly under Ahaz, neglecting the temple and following false gods. When Hezekiah becomes king, he grieves over Judah's sin and orders temple repair. Now all is ready in the restored temple for a joyful celebration. Cymbals, harps, lyres, and trumpets stand ready for use by the Levites and priests. A burnt offering is presented to the Lord, followed by singing and praising God with full orchestra. God's people rededicate themselves to His service.

We recognize our neglect of worship and following after the false gods of secularism, materialism, and self-idolatry. Convicted of our sin, we work to restore true worship. Aware of God's Son going to Calvary for us and earning full forgiveness, we stand ready to praise Him each day. Singing and accompanied by a full orchestra, we worship Him as our Savior. We join with the psalmist in unfettered praise: "Praise him with the sounding of the trumpet, praise him with the harp and lyre, praise him with tambourine and dancing, praise him with the strings and flute, praise him with the clash of cymbals, praise him with resounding cymbals. Let everything that has breath praise the Lord. Praise the Lord" (Ps. 150:3–6).

Prayer
Now let all the heav'ns adore you,
Let saints and angels sing before you
With harp and cymbals' clearest tone.

The Side-by-Side Planting

Reading: Matthew 13:24–30, 36–43

Text: Matthew 13:26—"When the wheat sprouted and formed heads, then the weeds also appeared."

Jesus tells a parable about a man who sows wheat in his field. By night his enemy comes and sows weeds among the wheat. Not until the wheat sprouts do the servants realize that weeds stand side by side with the wheat. The bearded darnel weed or tare is deceptive. In the early stages it resembles wheat exactly. Its roots become intertwined with the wheat. When headed out, the darnel weed has a slightly poisonous effect, causing dizziness and sickness.

Satan, the enemy, still plants weeds today among the believers. He sows an evil influence in society. Side by side with believers live people who strive to undermine God's law. We often react naively in an undiscriminating fashion. We see people as "nice, beautiful, friendly." We begin to accept their values. We intermarry and choose close friends from among them. Before we recognize them as weeds, we discover intertwined roots and a tremendous weakening of our faith. Destruction threatens.

While we should oppose Satan's evil planting in society, we should not judge the individual plants or—as unfortunately happened in past centuries—urge the government to root them out. We must realize that only faith in Christ makes the difference. Some whom we consider our kind of people may in fact be weeds, and vice versa. Some make early mistakes and repent. Others begin in the faith and fall away. Only God can judge the heart.

Jesus cautions us to await God's judgment at harvest time. Then the weeds will be separated and receive eternal punishment in hell. The wheat will be harvested and gathered to eternal life in heaven. God alone makes us wheat by His grace in our baptism. He sent His Son to die for us. He keeps us growing to maturity.

Prayer
Lord of harvest, grant that we
Wholesome grain and pure may be.

Pierced Hands

Reading: John 20:24–29

Text: Luke 24:39—"Look at my hands and my feet. It is I myself! Touch me and see."

You can learn a great deal about a person by the hands—soft hands, callused hands, firm handshake, flabby handshake, smooth hands, wrinkled hands with brown spots. Today we begin a series of devotions on the Biblical significance of hands for our lives as Christians.

A good place to start is with a focus on the risen Christ appearing to His disciples on Easter Sunday evening with the exclamation, "Look at my hands and my feet. It is I myself! Touch me and see; a ghost does not have flesh and bones, as you see I have." Certainly He was calming their doubts and fears by showing that He was physically alive, not a ghost. But His hands! What kind of hands would the disciples see and touch?

Thomas frames the answer to that question when he sets his conditions for believing that Christ is risen: "Unless I see nail marks in his hands and put my finger where the nails were, and put my hand into his side, I will not believe it" (John 20:25b). Pierced hands! Pierced hands best characterize our Lord. We use our hands to grab things for ourselves, or to push people away. But Jesus permitted His hands to be pierced for us. They nailed Him to a cross and lifted Him off the ground. There, suspended between earth and heaven, He died for us in full payment for our sins. Laid in a tomb, He rose again triumphantly from the grave in physical form. Alive, He still bears the marks of the nails for Thomas and us to see and touch.

We look to His pierced hands every day. In them lie our salvation, our hope, and our power to use our hands in His service!

Prayer

Point us, Lord, to Your pierced hands so that we may see, touch, and believe! Amen.

Clean Hands

Reading: Psalm 24

Text: Psalm 24:3b–4a—"Who may stand in his holy place? He who has clean hands and a pure heart . . . ."

"Come in, Johnny. Supper is on the table. Wash those dirty hands before you eat." From little on, we learn the importance of clean hands—from the dinner table to the hospital operating room. But the difficulty of washing off the dirt accounts for the proliferation of soaps, cleansers, and even sterilization equipment for a germ-free environment.

The psalmist talks about clean hands in a spiritual sense: "Who may stand in his holy place? He who has clean hands and a pure heart . . . ." The holy Lord owns the earth and everything in it. The King of glory comes in. Who stands worthy in His presence? The one with clean hands, who does not worship idols or swear falsely. Who qualifies for that kind of cleanliness and purity? No one. "All of us have become like one who is unclean, and all our righteous acts are like filthy rags" (Is. 64:6).

Clean hands. How we need them to stand in God's presence. But how stained with sin our hands appear, and we can't find a cleanser of our own making to cover up the stains. That's precisely why the King of glory came in at Bethlehem, at the Jordan, and at Calvary. With clean hands of obedience He lived for us. With nail-pierced and bleeding hands He died for us, paying the price for our uncleanness. "And the blood of Jesus . . . cleanses us from all sin" (1 John 1:7).

Clean hands. Washed clean in the waters of Baptism, we approach the throne with Jesus' clean hands. He welcomes us and sends us out with clean hands to love, witness to, and serve others.

Prayer

Thank You, Lord, for giving me clean hands through Your death on the cross! Help me to participate in the daily cleansing of confession and absolution. Amen.

Strong Hands

Reading: Psalm 18:29–36

Text: 1 Kings 8:42—"For men will hear of your great name and your mighty hand and your outstretched arm."

We admire strong hands gripping a railroad tie, sculpting with hammer and chisel, lifting a child from danger, or defending helpless people from an attacker. Strong hands symbolize the hardy pioneer spirit that has made our country great. Despite the scientific sophistication of our age, we still sense the need for strong hands.

The Bible values strength for families and nations but names God as the Source of all strength. Solomon in his dedicatory prayer for the new temple in Jerusalem speaks of God's strong hands when he asks the Lord to answer the prayers of foreigners as well as those of the people of Israel. Both groups are to rely on God's strong help. God's mighty hand brought Israel out of Egypt, through the Red Sea and the wilderness, to the Promised Land. God's mighty hand brought victory after victory to Israel and made possible the completion of the temple. On her own, Israel stumbled and fell. By God's strength Israel could climb walls and storm fortresses.

You may feel weak and helpless, unable to continue making ends meet or holding your family together. You may have tried to succeed by your own strong hands, only to experience reverses and discouragements. Solomon points you to the mighty hand of God. He was willing to let His strong hands become tiny, helpless infant hands in the manger. Those strong carpenter hands later would be bound by captors and then stretched out on a cross. But the hands of the Savior, raised from the dead, are raised in blessing for you and the world. Strong hands to make you strong as you live for Him!

Prayer

Lord, in my weakness I seek the blessing of Your strong hands to forgive and sustain me. Amen.

Praying Hands

Reading: Matthew 7:7–11

Text: 1 Timothy 2:8—"I want men everywhere to lift up holy hands in prayer."

Before leaving one of our parishes for another call, we received a meaningful gift from a member, a brown ceramic sculpture of praying hands. The hands express an intensity of purpose. Those folded hands provided an important key to the new ministry as we frequently—pastor and laity together—went before the Lord in prayer.

That's what Paul intends for Timothy and his church as he writes, "I want men everywhere to lift up holy hands in prayer." Whether lifted up or folded, praying hands reveal a dependence on the Source of all life and strength—God the Father, Son, and Holy Spirit.

So often we first put our hands to work—baking, sewing, building, carrying. Only then do we ask why we are working or frantically playing. Restless hands. Selfish hands. Nervous hands. Hurting hands. Fearful hands. Repentance needed.

When we fold our hands in prayer, our thoughts turn to God. We admit our confusion and hyperactivity. He assures us of His love and forgiveness in Christ. We praise Him for being God. We thank Him for His countless blessings. We ask Him for help and direction in our lives. We pray for each other. We rest in His promises and expect His power. He speaks to us through His unfailing Word and nourishes us at His table.

Praying hands. The upper room. Gethsemane. Pentecost. Bedside. Dinner table. Living room. Sanctuary. Automobile. Hospital room. We rise refreshed to offer our hands in His service, but always also to pray again.

Prayer

Lord, we lift up our hands in prayer everywhere as we claim Your saving promises. Amen.

Open Hands

Reading: Acts 2:44—47

Text: Psalm 145:16—"You open your hand and satisfy the desires of every living thing."

The little child holds the quarter so tightly, you can't get it out of his grasp. Three shoppers grab a piece of sale clothing so firmly at the same time that the cloth tears. The robber clings so tenaciously to the valise of stolen jewelry that he fails to reach the getaway car in time. What do you refuse to release? How often do you grasp for yourself? Closed hands.

The psalmist describes the opposite, the God who gives freely, the God with open hands. "You open your hand and satisfy the desires of every living thing." He bountifully showers us with His blessings. Life, health, clothing, food, friends, family—the list goes on. He even opened His hand to send His only Son, Jesus Christ, into a selfish world of closed hands. Often rejected, Jesus nevertheless opened His hands to feed the multitudes and bless the children. He went to His capture, conviction, and cross with open hands of love. He reaches out to us as the risen and ascended Lord.

No wonder the early Christians after Pentecost "were together and had everything in common" and "selling their possessions and goods . . . gave to anyone as he had need." Forgiven and accepted as God's children, they opened their hands to each other and to a world in need.

Thanks to the God with open hands, we extend our hands to others. Received by Him because of Christ's death, we welcome others. We give. We touch. We comfort. We include. We heal. Open hands for others, an extension of His hands to "satisfy the desires of every living thing."

Prayer

O God of the open hands, use me to reach others for You. Amen.

Busy Hands

Reading: James 1:22–27

Text: Proverbs 10:4—"Lazy hands make a man poor, but diligent hands bring wealth."

Ultimately God gave us hands to work for Him. Idleness has no place in the Christian life. The proverb says it well, "Lazy hands make a man poor, but diligent hands bring wealth." Not diligent hands for selfish gain like the rich man who built bigger barns, but diligent hands for faithful stewardship of God's resources. Busy hands to work and build and help and produce.

How easy for us to sit back and watch television, to extend coffee breaks, work halfheartedly, and campaign for better working conditions. How prone we are to fill church pews, to hear, to talk, but never to do anything as a result. James questions such inactivity, "Do not merely listen to the word, and so deceive yourselves. Do what it says" (James 1:22). Busy hands are needed to work and to help those in need.

Because Jesus Christ's busy hands were pierced for us and He has made our hands clean by His shed blood, we offer Him our hands for His tasks. With praying hands we seek His will and His strength. From His open hands we receive both the opportunities and the ability to be busy. At home with dishes, garbage, and laundry; at work with wrench, word processor, and assembly line; in our community with food basket, paint brush, and snow shovel, we lend our busy hands to the ongoing opportunities for service. His saving hands. Our busy hands. A partnership of love.

Prayer

Lord, forgive us for idleness. By Your death on the cross, empower us with busy hands in Your service. Amen.

Blessing Hands

Reading: Psalm 115:12–15

Text: Mark 10:16—"And he took the children in his arms, put his hands on them and blessed them."

The series on "hands" from the Bible comes to a close today. We have looked at God's hands and our hands. His hands— pierced for us on the cross, clean because of His holiness and perfect life, strong as the Creator and Preserver of the universe, praying on mountains, in the wilderness, and in Gethsemane, open in abundant provision, busy in service. Our hands—bearing the imprint of His nails, clean because of His shed blood, strong from His saving strength, praying for His daily direction and empowering, open to share His bounties, busy for His purposes.

What better way to conclude than to picture Jesus' blessing hands. The disciples wanted to send the mothers away with their little children. But Jesus had time and energy to receive them. As Mark says, "And he took the children in his arms, put his hands on them and blessed them." Blessing hands. He loves the children. He accepts them in their humility. He saves them.

And those blessing hands stretch forth to us and through us to others. The pastor speaks the benediction, "The Lord bless you and keep you." God's people come to the baptismal font with their children and to the altar to receive Christ's body and blood. His blessing hands at work.

And we use our hands to bless our children and others in our lives as we tenderly share the saving death and resurrection of Jesus Christ.

Prayer

Lord, thank You for Your hand of blessing. We yield our hands to You so that through us the world may be blessed. Amen.

Lesson from a Robin

Reading: Matthew 23:37–39

Text: Matthew 23:37b—"How often I have longed to gather your children together, as a hen gathers her chicks under her wings . . . ."

Right outside our patio doors I see a robin sitting on her nest, warming two turquoise eggs. How protective the robins are against any intrusions! They guard their turf and fly away at the smallest noise to distract any threat to their young. How painstakingly the nest was built and how lovingly food is gathered!

Jesus on His way to the cross cries out pleading to Jerusalem, which has killed the prophets, "How often I have longed to gather your children together, as a hen gathers her chicks under her wings, but you were not willing." He loves like a hen and offers warmth, comfort, and protection under His sheltering wings. Jerusalem rejected Him and nailed Him to a cross. But He never stopped loving them.

He cries out to us as well. The world threatens to destroy us. Enemies lurk everywhere in the shadows. We live vulnerable lives, however self-sufficient we consider ourselves. Often we reject the advances of the mother hen. But God continues to love us. That death on the cross availed for our sins. Repentant, we find ourselves securely gathered under the protecting wings of the Savior. Nourished and cared for, we grow and gain strength to live for Him in a dangerous world.

Prayer
Lord Jesus, since you love me,
Now spread your wings above me
And shield me from alarm.
Though Satan would devour me,
Let angel guards sing o'er me;
This child of God shall meet no harm.

Transitions

Reading: Deuteronomy 31:1–8

Text: Deuteronomy 31:8a—"The Lord himself goes before you and will be with you; he will never leave you nor forsake you."

Each of us faces transition points in life. We graduate from high school or college. We begin married life. We give birth to the first child. We change jobs, move to a new community, form new friendships. Transitions often bring much pain, create anxiety, and disrupt our lives. They also present new challenges and opportunities for growth. How can we face transitions with confidence?

In Deuteronomy 31, Moses comes to the end of his life. Israel gathers at the Jordan River ready to enter the Promised Land. God taps Joshua as Moses' successor. Truly a time of transition. Joshua may have felt overwhelmed by the new responsibilities. But Moses gives these reassuring words: "The Lord himself goes before you and will be with you; he will never leave you nor forsake you."

God comes to each of us in our transitions. His Son moved from heaven to earth as a human being, began His ministry with His baptism in the Jordan, set His face toward Jerusalem, and went willingly from Gethsemane to Calvary. He faced each transition with confidence and made the transition from death to life to demonstrate His victory over sin. That saving and helping God now says to us, in the midst of our transition anxiety: "The Lord himself goes before you and will be with you; he will never leave you nor forsake you."

Prayer
God is my comfort and my trust,
My hope and life abiding;
And to his counsel, wise and just,
I yield, in him confiding.
The very hairs, His Word declares,
Upon my head he numbers.
By night and day God is my stay,
He never sleeps nor slumbers.

Changeless

Reading: Malachi 3:6–12

Text: Malachi 3:6—"I the Lord do not change. So you, O descendants of Jacob, are not destroyed."

We face many transitions in life and realize how rapidly our world changes. The book *Future Shock* details the enormous changes taking place both in number and in speed of change. We feel as though we are riding a merry-go-round that goes faster and faster until everything around us is blurry. What can we count on? What solid object can we grasp? Change can be positive or negative, but in either case we need to adjust to it.

In Malachi God says to Israel, "I the Lord do not change. So you, O descendants of Jacob, are not destroyed." He implies that Israel has turned from God and gone back on her covenant responsibilities. She has changed in her relationship to God. But God reaffirms His love. He does not go back on His covenant promises. He pleads, "Return to me, and I will return to you" (v. 7b).

In this changing world we often stand guilty of changing our loyalties from God to the enticements of worldly progress. But God, who sent His Son to fulfill His covenant promise by dying on the cross for our sins, declares to us, "I the Lord do not change." He provides solid ground for us as we come to Him in repentance. Indeed, we have "a changeless Christ for a changing world." We can see God's hand in change and turn to Him for strength until He calls us home eternally.

Prayer

Swift to its close ebbs out life's little day;
Earth's joys grow dim, its glories pass away;
Change and decay in all around I see;
O thou who changest not, abide with me.

Envy Rot

Reading: Philippians 4:10–13

Text: Proverbs 14:30—"A heart at peace gives life to the body, but envy rots the bones."

According to movie scripts, treasure hunters seeking pirate gold or jewels usually come upon hideous skeletons of greedy cutthroats who died in pursuit of ill-gotten wealth. The rotting bones bear mute testimony to the futility of greed.

Proverbs makes a similar point by saying, "Envy rots the bones." We always want what others possess—the fancier car, the more luxurious home, the high-paying job, the college scholarship, the attractive family. We daydream about enjoying these things, resenting those who prosper, and venting our frustrations on everyone around us. No wonder Proverbs describes envy as rotting the bones. The acid of envy eats away at our insides, rotting our peace, our purpose, and our hope. Purely and simply, we sin.

But the proverb also says, "A heart at peace gives life to the body." We look to the Prince of Peace, who came with a heart only for others. He knew who He was and why He had come. He gratefully accepted the Father's provision, renouncing the kingdoms of this world. At peace with the Father, He endured the storm of suffering and death for our sins. Though dead in the grave, His bones did not rot, for He rose on the third day to bring peace to the world.

Repenting of envy, we accept His forgiveness and receive His peace. "Godliness with contentment is great gain" (1 Tim. 6:6). We gratefully accept God's daily provision, rejoice in the blessings of our neighbor, and live like Jesus for others. God eliminates envy rot. Peaceful hearts give new life to our bodies.

Prayer

What is the world to me With all its vaunted pleasure
When you, and you alone, Lord Jesus, are my treasure!
You only, dearest Lord, My soul's delight shall be;
You are my peace, my rest. What is the world to me!

Promises in Peril

Reading: Isaiah 43:1–7

Text: Isaiah 43:1b—"Fear not, for I have redeemed you; I have summoned you by name; you are mine."

How often we live in fear of perils! Automobile accidents, tornadoes, floods, earthquakes, house fires, robbery, and the list goes on. Israel faced many perils as well, partly from foreign nations who threatened destruction. The individual traveler took life in his own hands by venturing forth on a journey to cross rivers and climb mountains.

Isaiah offers God's promises to a repentant people who look to the promised Messiah for salvation and deliverance. His words also provide real comfort to us as baptized Christians living each day for the Savior who paid for our sins. Let these vivid words of Isaiah strengthen you for the day: "Fear not, for I have redeemed you; I have summoned you by name; you are mine. When you pass through the waters, I will be with you; and when you pass through the rivers, they will not sweep over you. When you walk through the fire, you will not be burned; the flames will not set you ablaze. For I am the Lord, your God, the Holy One of Israel, your Savior" (vv. 1b–3b).

Promises in peril. God's promises, clearly stated in His Word, promises for the New Testament church as well as Israel, promises for you as an individual child of God. Redeemed, called by name, we belong to Him, now in the midst of our trials and forever in heaven. Thank God for His powerful promises.

Prayer
God is my comfort and my trust,
My hope and life abiding;
And to his counsel, wise and just,
I yield, in him confiding.
The very hairs, His Word declares,
Upon my head he numbers.
By night and day God is my stay,
He never sleeps nor slumbers.

Fishers of Men International

Reading: Luke 5:1–11

Text: Luke 5:10b—"Don't be afraid; from now on you will catch men."

Summer provides a good opportunity to go fishing. At the beginning of His public ministry Jesus met the disciples at their own lake and then used fishing imagery to call them into His service.

Jesus unveils His fishing plan. Starting with a miracle on the lake, He calls the disciples to follow Him. For three years He trains them. Then He goes to the cross to pay for their sins, rises from the dead, and commissions them for a worldwide fishing trip. He calls us to a similar fishing trip. Made His own in Baptism, we learn from Him, and we witness in family, community, nation, and world.

But we face obstacles to our fishing. The disciples struggled with catching men, because they were provincially bound to Galilee and constantly worried about unfavorable fishing conditions as opposition to Jesus mounted. We often live provincial lives as well. How difficult we find it to picture Christ coming for people of every city, state, tribe, and nation! We become so preoccupied with daily unfavorable fishing conditions that we lose sight of God's international plan.

The Lord reveals His fishing method. He saturates us with His powerful, life-changing Word. Peter heard that Word from the pulpit of his boat before launching on that Galilee fishing adventure. And we hear that Word in worship and Bible study. Jesus applied that Word to the daily experience of the disciples. How could they ever forget the miraculous catch of fish, the mountaintop transfiguration, the footwashing, the holy meal, the nail-pierced hands of the risen Lord? No wonder they responded to His call. We too respond to His ongoing call as *fishers of men international.*

Prayer
Raise up, O Lord the Holy Ghost,
From this broad land a mighty host;
Their war cry, "We will seek the lost
Where you, O Christ, will come."

Miracle of Birth

Reading: Psalm 100

Text: Psalm 139:13—"For you created my inmost being; you knit me together in my mother's womb."

Some notes on the birth of our middle child on Father's Day many years ago: The birth of a child is one of the miracles of life, even in a world which daily experiences the wonders of 20th-century technology. That truth becomes very personal when my wife is in the delivery room and I wait out the early morning hours in a father's room at the hospital.

I look out the window and see a beautiful day dawning, a fiery sun rising against a clear blue sky, and my thoughts turn to God. He is making the sun rise. He controls also the stillness and darkness of the night. And He is with my wife and the doctor and our baby in the delivery room. I don't know if our baby is a boy or a girl. Only God knows what abilities and potential are within the baby right now coming out of the womb. But our baby is in God's hands, and that means everything to me. He also cares for my wife. He is the God who loves us so much that He sent His own dear Son to be born just like our baby is being born. That Son was willing to die for me and my wife and that baby—so that all of us can be forgiven and free to serve Him.

Even before I know the results in the delivery room, I thank God for being God and for loving us. "Know that the Lord is God. It is he who made us, and we are his; we are his people, the sheep of his pasture" (Ps. 100:3).

Soon the waiting is over. At 5:49 a.m. our daughter is born. We rejoice together in the recovery room, anticipating her baptism in the name of the Father, the Son, and the Holy Spirit. We want her to know the God who brings the miracle of birth, who helps mothers in the delivery room, and who sent His Son to heal our broken, sick world by His death on the cross. It is a happy Father's Day for many reasons, but most of all because of God the Father, who makes it all possible.

Prayer

Dear Father, thank You for the miracles of birth and of rebirth through Your Son Jesus Christ our Lord. Amen.

God's Cookout

Reading: Isaiah 55:1–5

Text: Isaiah 25:6—"On this mountain the Lord Almighty will prepare a feast of rich food for all peoples, a banquet of aged wine—the best of meats and the finest of wines."

Cookouts are very popular in America these days. Almost every backyard has some sort of grill. Fathers bend over glowing charcoal as they wear a chef's hat and apron. Isaiah 25 describes heaven as a cookout on a mountain, with God spreading out a wondrous feast complete with the best of meats and the finest of wines. Do you have time for God's cookout?

The description of choice meats sounds inviting, but only if you are hungry. Many don't have time for God's cookout. They are busy tending to their jobs, getting promotions, paying bills, going on vacations, fishing, boating, and golfing. They just don't have time for heaven. Is that your problem? Could it be that you really aren't hungry enough for God? Full of hamburger, one doesn't have room for even the tastiest steak. Full of ourselves, we may not be hungry for God and His love.

When we live only to satisfy our whims, we discover that everything tastes flat. Even the finest wine and filet mignon fail to satisfy. Spacious swimming pools and growing bank accounts do not satisfy. Selfishness is sin, and the wages of sin is death. When we seriously probe our lives, we admit our growing hunger for God.

And He fills us. He sent His only Son to fast 40 days in the wilderness and to drink the bitter cup of suffering by dying on the cross. By His death Jesus invites us to attend God's great cookout in heaven, freely and without charge. He not only invites us but encourages us to invite others as well.

Think about these things the next time you are gathered with your family in the backyard for a cookout.

Prayer

Lord Jesus Christ, we humbly pray:
Oh, keep us steadfast till that day
When each will be your welcomed guest
In heaven's high and holy feast.

Flimsy Building

Reading: Ezekiel 13:10–16

Text: Ezekiel 13:10b–11—"Because, when a flimsy wall is built, they cover it with whitewash, therefore tell those who cover it with whitewash that it is going to fall."

We Americans love outward appearances. Homes are built quickly, with little concern for quality, but the paint and the trim look impressive. Automobiles feature fancy gadgets, plush seats, and racing stripes, but rattles and vibrations come early. Poor workmanship covered up to look good.

Unfortunately, we often build our lives in the same fashion. Not much attention to a solid foundation of Biblical truth. Not much character building. Not much painstaking attention to quality parenting. Instead, we concentrate on body building, social graces, fashion design, and cosmetics. Flimsy building covered up to look good.

Ezekiel uses similar imagery to describe the false prophets of Israel. They cry " 'peace' when there is no peace" and make Jerusalem falsely secure. In reality Jerusalem is like a flimsy wall built on a shaky foundation. The prophets merely cover that wall with whitewash to make it look good. But the Sovereign Lord will unleash a violent wind with hailstones and rain so that the wall collapses. Flimsy building exposed. No whitewash cover-up will help.

But God also brings hope. He sent His Son Jesus Christ as chief cornerstone of a new building. By His sin-atoning death on the cross and His resurrection, Jesus provides a solid base for the building of His church. By baptism we are "built on the foundation of the apostles and prophets, with Christ Jesus himself as the chief cornerstone" (Eph. 2:20). No flimsy building. No need for cover-up. We concentrate on inner growth in the Word, which keeps us strong.

Prayer

Christ is our cornerstone, On him alone we build;
With his true saints alone The courts of heav'n are filled.
On his great love Our hopes we place
Of present grace And joys above.

Foundational Building

Reading: 1 Corinthians 3:10–17

Text: 1 Corinthians 3:11—"For no one can lay any foundation other than the one already laid, which is Jesus Christ."

Covering up a flimsy building won't work, but how can we build solidly as individuals and as a church? Paul addresses this question as he writes to the church at Corinth. Troubles have developed in the church he founded. The Corinthian Christians have formed parties or factions loyal to Paul, Apollos, or Cephas (Peter). Paul points them to the true Foundation.

He writes, "By the grace God has given me, I laid a foundation as an expert builder, and someone else is building on it. But each should be careful how he builds" (v. 10). He refers positively to the various builders, but then adds that the only valid foundation is "the one already laid, which is Jesus Christ."

Jesus Christ, God's Son, by His saving death and resurrection laid the only foundation for our relationship to God and our relationships with one another. The church builds only on Christ crucified.

How do we build solidly? Will we use "gold, silver, costly stones, wood, hay or straw" (v. 11)? Only the Day of the Lord will reveal how solidly we have built. But all building needs to be foundational building, that is, building on Jesus Christ, the true Foundation. As we go again and again to Jesus in Word and sacraments, He will forgive us and lead us to choose only the finest of building materials. We will not act for self-glorification or out of party spirit, but will seek to honor Christ and share Him with others. Built solidly from the ground up, the church will stand and testify to the Savior before all the world.

Prayer

The Church's one foundation Is Jesus Christ, her Lord;
She is his new creation By water and the Word.
From heav'n he came and sought her To be his holy bride;
With his own blood he bought her, And for her life he died.

Surface Talk

Reading: Proverbs 20:5

Text: Proverbs 25:11—"A word aptly spoken is like apples of
gold in settings of silver."

Poor communication causes relationship problems. In the
next several devotions we will identify communication barriers
and seek ways to break them down.

A spouse comments, "We used to talk for hours about important things. We made so many exciting discoveries about each
other. Now all we ever talk about is the weather, the children's
runny noses, and what we will eat for supper. Or we just sit in
front of the television and never say anything."

Surface talk. A major problem in marriage and family relationships. How shallow, discouraging, and separating! We do the
same thing in offices, at social engagements, and in churches.
When surface talk serves to avoid more caring and honest communication, relationships deteriorate.

Our Bible reading from Proverbs suggests the wonderful potential for meaningful conversation: "The purposes of a man's
heart are deep waters, but a man of understanding draws them
out." Proverbs also describes how to break through the surface
talk: "A word aptly spoken is like apples of gold in settings of
silver." Speaking the caring word and listening to the heart
opens up new channels of communication.

Recognizing our selfish hearts and the rut of surface talk,
we turn in repentance to our Father, who speaks to us at the
deepest level of our being about the forgiving love of Jesus Christ,
His Son, who gave Himself for us on the cross. Listening to His
Word, we can listen to one another and speak words of deep
caring. Surface talk no more.

Prayer

Dear Lord, help me to move beyond surface talk to share
Your love with others in my life. Amen.

Nag, Nag, Nag

Reading: James 1:19–20

Text: Proverbs 13:3—"He who guards his lips guards his life, but he who speaks rashly will come to ruin."

A disgruntled husband complains, "I can't get a word in edgewise. All she does is nag, nag, nag. I can't take any more of the screaming. She criticizes everything I do or don't do. She remembers everything I have ever said and uses it against me."

If surface talk creates a communication barrier, then certainly nagging and constant criticism create an even more serious one. When one family member attacks, the others either lash back or tend to withdraw and sulk. Over a long period of time, nagging causes deep hurts and bitter resentments.

For this reason the writer of Proverbs asserts, "He who guards his lips guards his life, but he who speaks rashly will come to ruin." James in our Bible reading offers a practical way to break down this communication barrier: "Everyone should be quick to listen, slow to speak and slow to become angry." That listening ear helps us tune in to the other person's needs. Listening carefully will slow down our speaking and as a result keep our anger from rising to the surface. Good advice indeed.

But on our own, we stand helpless. Only One can forgive us our nagging and strengthen us to change long-established patterns of rash speech. He is the One who "was led like a lamb to the slaughter, and as a sheep before her shearers is silent, so he did not open his mouth" (Is. 53:7b). When He was being crucified, He spoke words of forgiveness. When He was suffering on the cross, He spoke words of comfort and concern for others. God's powerful remedy for nagging: quick to listen to Him and each other, slow to speak criticism, and slow to anger—because we have been forgiven for His sake.

Prayer

Dear Lord, forgive me for nagging and constant criticism. Fill me with love to listen carefully and speak words of healing, for Your sake. Amen.

The Silent Treatment

Reading: Ephesians 4:32; 5:19–21

Text: Proverbs 15:23—"A man finds joy in giving an apt reply—and how good is a timely word!"

Strange how communication barriers generate other barriers. You may have loved yesterday's devotion which exposed the sin of nagging, especially if that problem belongs to your spouse. But don't feel too smug because today God exposes as a serious sin "the silent treatment."

A frustrated wife says, "He won't say a word. I come to him with my hurts and disappointments. I need his support, but he clams up and refuses to answer me. He doesn't care about me at all. He just buries his head in the newspaper."

How devastating! Sometimes we nag because we want some reaction from our spouse. No answer. We beg and plead. No answer. We even try to compliment. No answer. The silent treatment often becomes a deliberate weapon to frustrate and repay the other person for verbal abuse. We may feel superior for holding our tongue, but often we stand guilty of lovelessness and thoughtlessness.

Proverbs states the positive value of speaking at the right time: "A man finds joy in giving an apt reply—and how good is a timely word!" Once again we come face to face with our need for forgiveness and our responsibility to forgive one another. Paul says it so well in our Bible reading: "Be kind and compassionate to one another, forgiving each other, just as in Christ God forgave you."

Yes, while Christ knew when to keep silent before His accusers, He also knew when to speak words of encouragement, caring, and forgiveness. His death on the cross and glorious resurrection makes us His own and frees us to "find joy in giving an apt reply." The silent treatment no longer.

Prayer

Dear Lord, open my mouth to sing Your praise and to speak the timely word of compassion and forgiveness, for Your sake. Amen.

Full-Scale War

Reading: Ephesians 4:26–27, 29–31

Text: Proverbs 17:14—"Starting a quarrel is like breaching a dam; so drop the matter before a dispute breaks out."

Sometimes marriages exist on noncommunication, whether surface talk or the silent treatment. But with equal frequency marriages feature full-scale war.

A spouse describes their sad relationship, "We manage to converse civilly when other people are around, but whenever we find ourselves alone, we seem to fight constantly. Even the most innocent remark leads to full-scale warfare." A well-known comedy recording introduces a couple named the Bickersons, who constantly shout at each other and outdo one another in taunts, put-downs, and insults. You laugh but wonder whether you should cry as this parody unfolds. Too true for comfort!

Again Proverbs brings wisdom about the lethal potential of quarreling: "Starting a quarrel is like breaching a dam; so drop the matter before a dispute breaks out." The imagery of a dam breaking and a deluge of water rolling over us accurately describes our full-scale warfare. Paul bluntly advises us in our Bible reading: "Get rid of all bitterness, rage and anger, brawling and slander, along with every form of malice."

Jesus had to deal with heated disputes among His disciples as well as the taunts, jeers, and accusations of His opponents. But He went to Calvary in full payment for our sins. Full-scale war raged between Christ and the combined forces of evil. He won the victory. Peace has been established between God and humanity. Jesus says, "Peace I leave with you; my peace I give you" (John 14:27). Living in that peace, we can avoid quarrels; and when full-scale war develops, we can seek His forgiveness and establish, on that basis, a loving, quarrel-free relationship with one another.

Prayer

Lord, give us Your peace so that we may live in peace together. Amen.

Empty Flattery

Reading: Matthew 23:23–28

Text: Proverbs 26:28—"A lying tongue hates those it hurts, and a flattering mouth works ruin."

Angry and cutting words certainly raise communication barriers, but seemingly positive words can also cause problems if they are insincere. A discouraged wife commented, "He talks a good game. When he is trying to get on my good side, he makes all kinds of promises and whispers sweet nothings into my ear. But I know he really doesn't care about me; he is simply not being sincere."

Empty flattery, we call it. Words abound, but they mean little because the heart lies elsewhere. Proverbs castigates such insincerity: "A lying tongue hates those it hurts, and a flattering mouth works ruin." How easily we slip into hollow words, flattering words, manipulative words which mask our selfish, scheming, and even vengeful hearts!

Paul describes the honest speech which God desires us to use: "Instead, speaking the truth in love, we will in all things grow up into him who is the Head, that is, Christ" (Eph. 4:15). As a result of our relationship to God in Christ, we speak from the heart. Sometimes we confront our loved one. Sometimes we register our concerns and problems. Sometimes we express our tender feelings. But always we speak the truth in love—honest, sincere, caring words. God speaks words of judgment against our sin, including empty flattery. He pulls no punches with us, because He loves us. But He also speaks His Word of mercy, most clearly spoken in His Son Jesus Christ, the Word-made-flesh. On Calvary, Jesus by His death spoke the truth in love for us. Cleansed by His blood, we lay aside flattery and speak honestly and lovingly from the heart.

Prayer

Dear Lord, purge my lips of empty flattery and strengthen me to speak the truth in love. Amen.

Cold Logic

Reading: James 3:3–8

Text: Proverbs 18:13—"He who answers before listening—that is his folly and his shame."

A final communication barrier deals with people according to cold logic and a clinical approach. A wife comments sadly, "I don't feel free to talk to him anymore. When I come with my problems, he is always giving me a quick answer that makes me feel stupid. I feel frustrated because he tries to be so logical and rational about everything. When he does listen, I think he is trying to play psychiatrist, and I serve as an interesting subject for analysis."

Even when we desire to help, quick answers, easy advice, and cold logic make the other person feel unimportant and un-cared-for. Often we use logic to avoid listening to the deeper feelings of our spouse. We remain detached and uninvolved. Proverbs tells us: "He who answers before listening—that is his folly and his shame." We fail to listen empathetically and speak caringly.

Communication barriers abound—surface talk, nagging, the silent treatment, full-scale war, empty flattery, and cold logic. At root, selfishness, jealousy, resentment, and indifference. We confess our sins toward family members and others whom we love. Paul states the goal of good communication: "Do not let any unwholesome talk come out of your mouths, but only what is helpful for building others up according to their needs, that it may benefit those who listen" (Eph. 4:29). Wholesome talk. Building others up. According to their needs. His words of life, of salvation through faith in Jesus Christ, of forgiveness, of healing. His words spoken to us, received in the water, the bread and the wine. His words spoken through us to the family because we have listened with love. Communication barriers broken down.

Prayer

Dear Lord, thank You for communicating with us through Your death and resurrection. Give us wholesome words to build up those in need. Amen.

Anniversary Thoughts: Companionship

Reading: Genesis 24:57–67

Text: Genesis 2:18—"The Lord God said, 'It is not good for the man to be alone. I will make a helper suitable for him.' "

I'm preparing to take my wife out for dinner on our wedding anniversary. Memories flood my mind as I treasure our time together. "It is not good for the man to be alone." I remember lonely nights before I met her, times when I wondered whether God would provide a wife for me.

"I will make a helper suitable for him." What a delight to meet her on that spring banquet weekend at college! Three years of daily letters followed, because we lived in different states. Communication flowed as we learned to know each other, our interests, values, common faith, family backgrounds, and dreams for the future. We rejoiced that by God's grace we completed each other.

We stood together at the altar and promised to be faithful. We began our journey together—new job, moving from school to church, the birth of children, more moves as pastor from church to church. Struggles. Challenges. Adjustments. Disagreements. But always companionship. Three children born. Ages and stages. Still companionship.

God deserves all praise and honor as we celebrate our anniversary together. He made us as unique individuals. He brought each of us into His kingdom through Holy Baptism. He brought us together. He forgives our sins when we strain the marriage relationship. He constantly reminds us of His Son Jesus Christ, who died for us. God is our Companion, though undeserved by us. Therefore we enjoy each other's companionship as we seek God's continuing purpose for our life together.

Prayer
Oh, blessed home where man and wife
Together lead a godly life,
By deeds their faith confessing!
There many happy days are spent,
There Jesus gladly will consent
To tarry with his blessing.

Anniversary Thoughts: One Flesh

Reading: Matthew 19:1–6

Text: Genesis 2:24—"For this reason a man will leave his father and mother and be united to his wife, and they will become one flesh."

The Hebrew word for "be united" or "cleave" to his wife means "stick together like glue." When a man and woman marry, God is joining them together in a permanent adhesive bond. He knows what is good for us. He promises to sustain us in our marriage bonds.

One could focus on the negative. If God joins man and woman together, why are so many marriages breaking up? As a society we have sown the wind and reaped the whirlwind. For generations couples have been divorcing and remarrying, and the children and grandchildren have followed suit in ever-increasing measure. Tremendous discord, emotional scars, and wounds of emptiness and bitterness have been the result. That's sin at work.

But I would much rather focus on the positive. God takes sinful people and forgives. He provided a third partner in our marriage, His Son Jesus Christ. I can love my wife because Christ loved the church and gave Himself for her. He has washed us with water through the Word and presents us to God without blemish, because He has paid the price for our sins.

With such cleaving, uniting, bonding on Christ's part, we can cleave to each other as one flesh. I love her and she loves me. Our lifelong commitment to each other flows from His unwavering commitment to us. From the solid "one flesh" foundation comes a delight in romance, wine and roses, intimate evenings together, and the prospect of delectable surprises and adventure in our future together.

Prayer
If they have given him their heart,
The place of honor set apart
For him each night and morrow,
Then he the storms of life will calm,
Will bring for ev'ry wound a balm,
And change to joy their sorrow.

Anniversary Thoughts: Children

Reading: Ephesians 6:1–4

Text: Genesis 1:28—"God blessed them and said to them, 'Be fruitful and increase in number; fill the earth and subdue it.' "

While my wife and I prepare to eat out for our anniversary, she is serving spaghetti to our three teenagers. It seems like just yesterday that they were infants. Who can forget the first shaky steps, the first children's Christmas service, the first day on the school bus? How many Halloween parties, Little League baseball games, school programs, and gymnastic meets have we attended over the years?

Oh, the joys of a family! Yes, God made Adam and Eve one flesh and so provided intimate companionship. But to many couples God also gives the gift of children. Children bring added responsibility, more than a few headaches, and an emptier pocketbook, but they also bring warmth, love, and joy.

Childbearing implies child-rearing. Parenting is an awesome task. No room for absentee parents. No room for permissiveness. No room for child abuse. Much need for time with the children, both quality and quantity. Much need for patience and a listening ear. Much need for firm discipline and Christian values. Much need for modeling worship, caring, and sharing.

I know that we have fallen short as parents in many ways over the years. We confess our sins as parents even as we commend our three to God's protective care. But we also recognize God's forgiveness in Jesus Christ and His gentle guiding of us in the parenting task. He lifts us up when we are discouraged, refreshes us with His good news, and shows us our children's potential.

Prayer
O Lord, we come before your face;
In ev'ry home bestow your grace
On children, father, mother.
Relieve their wants, their burdens ease,
Let them together dwell in peace
And love to one another.

Disneyland

Reading: 1 Peter 4:12–19

Text: 1 Peter 4:12—"Dear friends, do not be surprised at the painful trial you are suffering, as though something strange were happening to you."

When Walt Disney opened his theme park in Anaheim, a new era began in American entertainment. People flocked to the fantasy world of Mickey Mouse and the other Disney characters. Similar parks have sprung up in Florida and in various countries of the world. Disneyland offers wholesome fun for children and grownups alike. But unfortunately we sometimes expect that real life will feature a Disneyland-type experience, with no major problems and constant pleasure.

St. Peter tells a quite different story to the persecuted Christians in Asia Minor. He writes, "Dear friends, do not be surprised at the painful trial you are suffering, as though something strange were happening to you." He goes on to suggest that they are participating in the sufferings of Christ. Living a clear Christian witness will bring insults and persecution at times. Peter tells them that they can praise God though they're suffering.

Christ has suffered and died for us to make us His own dear children. He indeed promises us joy and an abundant life as Christians. But we may end up suffering for our faith in Christ. The Christian life is not a spiritual Disneyland, but an opportunity to praise God as we bear His name, no matter what the cost. He strengthens us in and through suffering and promises us eternal glory in heaven.

Prayer
Then let us follow Christ, our Lord,
And take the cross appointed
And, firmly clinging to his word,
In suff'ring be undaunted.
For those who bear the battle's strain
The crown of heav'nly life obtain.

Heat and Humidity

Reading: John 15:18–25

Text: John 16:33b—"In this world you will have trouble. But take heart! I have overcome the world."

In many parts of the country, summer brings sweltering heat and high humidity. One walks out of an air-conditioned building and faces a blast furnace of hot, humid air. Soon the sweat begins to pour out. We hurry to complete our business so we can again seek air-conditioned shelter. Heat and humidity create an environment that controls our life.

Christians face the "heat and humidity" of a hostile world. Our Lord repeatedly warned His disciples to expect persecution. St. Peter speaks of a "fiery trial" the early Christians could expect (1 Peter 4:12 KJV). We too face a culture that causes us as much trouble as heat and humidity. But within the fellowship of God's people we gather around Word and sacrament, experiencing God's cool refreshment before we walk out into the hostile world. As Jesus tells His disciples in John's gospel, "In this world you will have trouble. But take heart! I have overcome the world."

When faced with the blast furnace of temptation and ridicule, we begin to sweat. But Jesus, who resolutely faced the world's hatred and went to the cross in payment for our sins, offers us strength to face the world's heat and humidity. He has overcome. We can live boldly in the midst of the world's anti-Christian culture as He continues to refresh us in the air-conditioning of worship with God's people.

Prayer

The world seeks to be praised And honored by the mighty
Yet never once reflects That they are frail and flighty.
But what I truly prize Above all things is he,
My Jesus, he alone. What is the world to me!

Moving

Reading: Hebrews 11:8–10

Text: Hebrews 11:8—"By faith Abraham, when called to go to a place he would later receive as his inheritance, obeyed and went, even though he did not know where he was going."

Oh, the headaches of moving to a new home! A house to sell. Endless house showings, with a scurry each time to make the home presentable. Moving arrangements, complete with sorting, garage sales, packing, and leaving. A house to purchase in the new community. Thousands of little details concerning utilities, doctors, services, church and school choices, and adjustment to a new job. Not to mention the emotional turmoil of leaving good friends and reestablishing roots! And yet God leads us into new situations as part of His plan for our lives.

God similarly came to Abraham with a call to leave his homeland and travel long miles to a promised land. God was establishing special people who would carry out His promises for the world. Out of that special nation would come the Messiah, the Savior of the world.

No doubt Abraham must have faced major obstacles and the wrenching experience of leaving his homeland. Nevertheless, the writer to the Hebrews tells us, "By faith Abraham . . . obeyed and went, even though he did not know where he was going." He lived in tents, as did Isaac and Jacob, and "was looking forward to the city with foundations, whose architect and builder is God" (Heb. 11:10).

We gain a new perspective on moving. God calls us to live for Him in a new land. By faith we obey. His promise, fulfilled in Christ's death and resurrection, stands sure for us. We live as pilgrims in this world and will someday experience the joys of living in the heavenly "city with foundations, whose architect and builder is God."

Prayer

Therefore I murmur not, Heav'n is my home;
Whate'er my earthly lot, Heav'n is my home;
And I shall surely stand There at my Lord's right hand.
Heav'n is my fatherland, Heav'n is my home.

Unity and Power

Reading: Acts 2:42–47

Text: Acts 4:32a—"All the believers were one in heart and mind."

Peru, Ind., annually hosts an amateur circus of dazzling proportions. Formerly the winter home of a major professional circus, Peru involves the youth of the community to produce "the greatest amateur show on earth." High wire and trapeze acts, jugglers, tumblers, clowns, and a circus band delight audiences from far and wide. Townspeople work closely together with the youthful performers for at least four months of the year to make this July event possible. What unity of heart and mind displayed by this circus community!

How much greater the unity and power of the early believing community in Jerusalem, as stated in our text! Persecuted by the religious leaders in Jerusalem, these believers nevertheless stood firm in the confession of their faith and cared deeply for one another. With great power the apostles continued to testify to the resurrection of Jesus Christ. The believers shared their possessions with one another. Only the Spirit of God, by His grace, created this unity and this witnessing power.

God established the early Christian church, and He also sustains us. As we devote ourselves "to the apostles' teaching and to the fellowship, to the breaking of bread and to prayer," God assures us of our salvation through faith in Jesus Christ and empowers us to live in harmony and work together as witnesses of His love.

Prayer
Come, Holy Ghost, God and Lord,
With all your graces now outpoured
On each believer's mind and heart;
Your fervent love to them impart.
Lord, by the brightness of your light
In holy faith your Church unite;
From ev'ry land and every tongue
This to your praise, O Lord and God, be sung.
Alleluia, Alleluia!

America: Lost and Found

Reading: Luke 15:1–10

Text: Luke 15:6b—"Rejoice with me; I have found my lost sheep."

The well-known parable about the lost sheep provides a different perspective on our country as we prepare to celebrate Independence Day. Where does America stand today?

Like the Pharisees and teachers of the law in the Bible reading, we often think we have arrived. We fancy our supremacy in the world and our high standard of living. We may even look down upon less fortunate peoples of the world. The Pharisees murmured that Jesus ate with tax collectors and sinners.

In reality America is lost whenever we attempt to succeed on our own power. We have chinks in our armor. We no longer control everything in world affairs. Other nations sometimes outstrip us in industrial productivity. We struggle with moral corruption and the breakdown of our families. Personally we fall short of God's glory. We often live selfishly instead of serving God. The Pharisees were lost but refused to admit their condition. Could we be more like the lost sheep than the ninety-nine?

But God wants to find America. The Shepherd goes out of His way to seek us. He finds us confused and lost, bruised and bleeding, tired and forlorn. He takes us in His arms and brings us home. He has given His life for the sheep. America is found. God restores us to our heritage as a nation under Him. He forgives our arrogance and helps us share our bounty. He turns the Christians of America from self to His love. Once lost and now found, we rejoice in finding the lost. God bless America!

Where does America stand? Wrong question. We kneel before God in confession and let God find us in Jesus Christ.

Prayer

Dear Father, thank You for finding us lost sheep and restoring us to the fold. Help us to seek the lost at home and abroad, for Jesus' sake. Amen.

A Beacon in the Harbor

Reading: Psalm 137

Text: Proverbs 14:34—"Righteousness exalts a nation, but sin is a disgrace to any people."

Recently our nation celebrated the centennial of the Statue of Liberty in New York Harbor. A gift of France and the brilliant work of sculptor Frederic Auguste Bartholdi, the Lady symbolizes basic American values of liberty and an opportunity for immigrants from many lands. Even as ordinary citizens in the United States and France had contributed their pennies, nickels, and dimes in the 1880s to make the Statue of Liberty a reality, so in the 1980s many across America contributed to refurbish and repair the statue. The festivities of Liberty Weekend in 1986 properly crowned this renewal project and reaffirmed the American dream of liberty for all. The Lady continues as a beacon in the harbor for all to see.

Our text speaks of national righteousness and sin. Certainly God has blessed America and we have much we can be happy about. Nevertheless, America also reveals a record of sin. Selfishness, greed, prejudice, manipulation, corruption, and lovelessness have reared their heads in politics, business, labor, and even in the church. We need to search our hearts and confess our sins as American citizens. Like the Lady in need of repairs, our values have been tarnished and our ideals corroded.

But righteousness is ultimately God's doing, not ours. Despite our sin, He declared the world righteous, based on the death and resurrection of Jesus Christ, who fully paid for our sins. By His Spirit God makes us righteous through faith in Jesus Christ as Savior and Lord, and we are empowered to live righteously as citizens of our land.

When we see the Lady, renewed and shining in the sun, we are reminded to let God cleanse us of our sins and renew us to live righteously for Him and for our fellow citizens. God bless America!

Prayer

Dear Father, help us to shine as beacons of Your love. Amen.

Fireworks or Handiwork?

Reading: Psalm 104

Text: Psalm 19:1—"The heavens declare the glory of God; the skies proclaim the work of his hands."

Fireworks go hand in hand with the fourth of July. Large fireworks displays bring people flocking to parks, city squares, and drive-in theaters. Gigantic firework shows fill the sky in large cities and at major theme parks. Sitting and watching an unfolding fireworks show from a blanket, lawn chair, or bleacher with thousands of spectators elicits awe-inspired oohs and aahs of appreciation as one burst of rockets follows another—towering Roman candles, multiple explosions of many-colored starbursts, pinwheels, and trailing comet tails. Everything breaks loose in a spectacular finale, with the sky full of reds, greens, blues, and golds. But the spectacle is short-lived, and life goes on as usual.

Our text and our Bible reading speak of something far more spectacular and enduring than the most dazzling fireworks—the handiwork of God. The heavens and all of creation provide a permanent display of the power and love of Almighty God—the sun traveling across the sky daily, the moon and the stars, the clouds as God's chariot, the winds as His messengers, springs pouring water into ravines, birds nesting by the waters and singing among the branches of well-watered trees.

We stand in awe of God's spectacular display —the mountains, the plains, the rivers, the oceans, the sky with its infinite stars, and the seashore with unlimited grains of sand. We look with new eyes of wonder. Instead of taking this world for granted and thinking only of ourselves, we realize that God's handiwork surpasses everything made by human hands. We praise the God who not only created the world but sent His own Son to die on the cross and to bring about a new creation of forgiven humanity.

Prayer

"I will sing to the Lord all my life; I will sing praise to my God as long as I live. May my meditation be pleasing to him, as I rejoice in the Lord" (Ps. 104:33–34).

An Unlikely Champion

Reading: 1 Samuel 17:1–51

Text: Psalm 18:29—"With your help I can advance against a troop; with my God I can scale a wall."

David describes facing an enemy with super strength. He felt overwhelmed by the challenge. One could think either of David's encounter with Goliath or later with Saul, who marshaled all his official troop strength against a fleeing David with a ragtag band of followers. But David had a secret weapon which he mentions in our text—God's help. With God's strength behind him, David knew he could win the victory. Ultimately this unlikely champion was crowned king of Israel.

How often we feel like underdogs. The opponents look tall and strong. The troops lined up against us are hardened fighting men with superior equipment. In front of us looms a huge wall blocking our road. We lack money, degrees, intelligence, physical ability, or the courage to speak the right words. We want to witness to our faith, demonstrate love to others, work for the Kingdom, but we feel overwhelmed by the challenges.

Then we remember that God sent His Son Jesus to face the old evil foe. He appeared to be the underdog. Born in a manger, growing up in the obscure provincial town of Nazareth, sentenced to an ignominious death on the cross, Jesus nevertheless emerged the victor. He conquered Satan, death, and the world's sin by His death and resurrection. The underdog was crowned King of kings and Lord of lords.

He lives in us by virtue of our baptism. He forgives us our doubts, builds up our faltering confidence, shows us the way, and goes with us into battle. We can advance against the troop and scale the insurmountable wall. By His grace, we too are crowned as champions—unlikely champions—in His service.

Prayer

Fight the good fight with all your might;
Christ is your strength, and Christ your right.
Lay hold on life, and it shall be
Your joy and crown eternally.

Memories

Reading: Psalm 25:6–7

Text: Luke 22:19c—"Do this in remembrance of me."

A popular song of recent years bears the title "Memories." America seems caught in a wave of nostalgia in which "the good old days" are remembered as bright and untarnished. Antique cars, painted milk cans, barn wood, old movies, and baseball trading cards attract keen interest and stir memories in our mind. But nostalgia and history sometimes come into conflict. History records the problems and pain, the failures and disasters, as well as the successes and blessings.

The psalmist covers both kinds of memories when he asks God, "Remember, O Lord, your great mercy and love, for they are from of old" and then adds, "Remember not the sins of my youth and my rebellious ways" (Ps. 25:6–7). He recognizes that because of sin our past record needs to be forgotten. Repentant, he depends on God to remember His steadfast love and forget those sins. God sent His Son to pay for them so that He could say, "I will . . . remember their sins no more" (Jer. 31:34c).

In our text we hear Jesus in the upper room instituting the Supper of His body and blood. He says to the disciples and to us, "Do this in remembrance of me." We remember Him regularly as we go to the Sacrament. What a great focus for our memories— regular worship in God's house, hearing His unchanging Word and receiving His body and blood for the forgiveness of our sins!

Prayer

All honor, thanks, and praise to you,
O Father, God of heaven,
For mercies ev'ry morning new,
Which you have freely given.
Inscribe this on my memory:
My Lord has done great things for me;
To this day he has helped me.

Oaks of Righteousness

Reading: Isaiah 61:1–6

Text: Isaiah 61:3e—"They will be called oaks of righteousness, a planting of the Lord for the display of his splendor."

Few people stand tall today against the evils of our age. People talk resolutely but soon bend like a willow in the wind when compromise seems the better course. When forests covered the land in America, sturdy leaders pioneered the way for a fledgling nation. Now strong leaders seem harder to find.

Isaiah in a time of disobedience and compromise points ahead to the Messiah who will one day step into the synagogue at Nazareth and apply these words of Isaiah 61 to Himself as Savior. Isaiah prophesies the results of the death and resurrection of Jesus Christ for believers: "They will be called oaks of righteousness, a planting of the Lord for the display of his splendor." Oaks of righteousness—sturdy, unbending, enduring, solid, towering oaks.

God makes us "oaks of righteousness," beginning in our baptism. Our weakness and compromise forgiven in the blood of Christ, we stand tall with His strength. As a planting of the Lord, we display His splendor, witness to His love, and speak out for Him against evil in its many forms. When the storms come and the winds blow, we can by God's grace stand tall and firm in His strength, so that others can find their strength in us, to the glory of His name.

Prayer

Fear not, I am with you, oh, be not dismayed,
For I am your God and will still give you aid;
I'll strengthen you, help you, and cause you to stand,
Upheld by my righteous, omnipotent hand.

Pain

Reading: Psalm 6

Text: Psalm 6:2b—"O Lord, heal me, for my bones are in agony."

The pain strikes suddenly and sharply. The lower back aches. The pain spreads up the spine. Movement increases the discomfort. Lying down helps, but even sleep becomes difficult. Day after day the pain continues. No relief in sight. Why is this happening? Who can help? We often live with pain—if not in the back, then the head or the chest or the stomach. When pain leaves, we often forget, but when chronic symptoms persist, we quickly wilt and lie helpless.

The psalmist struggles under affliction and cries out, "O Lord, heal me!" He adds, "I am worn out from groaning; all night long I flood my bed with weeping and drench my couch with tears" (v. 6). No easy, pat answers for the problem of pain. No help from philosophical answers about the inevitability of pain or the beneficial results of maturing through pain. Like the psalmist, we turn to God in our despair. We ask for healing, for relief, for strength. God understands and can help. Later the psalmist exclaims, "The Lord has heard my cry for mercy; the Lord accepts my prayer" (v. 9).

But most of all, we focus on God's Son, who took on flesh and therefore experienced pain for us. He hurt when roughly handled and scourged. The nails through His hands and feet sent pain stabbing through His nervous system. And the hours of tortured breathing on the cross took their toll. In the process, He conquered sin and death. Pain continues now, but God heals, soothes, and strengthens. Risen and ascended, Jesus will come again to take us to eternal life with Him, where there will be no more pain. He stands with us.

Prayer
But the pains which he endured, Alleluia!
Our salvation have procured; Alleluia!
Now above the sky he's king, Alleluia!
Where the angels ever sing. Alleluia!

Failure

Reading: Psalm 73:1–5, 21–28

Text: Psalm 73:26—"My flesh and my heart may fail, but God is the strength of my heart and my portion forever."

In our success-oriented society no word conjures up more dread than the word "failure." Students fear to take home a report card with an F. Aspiring athletes hang their heads when cut from a team. Unfortunately, high achievers condemn themselves as failures when falling short of the first prize or the highest office or the million dollar bonus. Failures abound, with divorces, bankruptcies, prison terms, unemployment, and alcoholism. In short, every one of us lives with the reality of failure, either real or imagined.

The psalmist has been struggling with failure because he looks enviously at the prosperity of the wicked. He sees them with healthy and strong bodies, free from human burdens, and fabulously wealthy. He bemoans his own struggles and ill-treatment by these wicked people. Then he realizes his own foolishness and stupidity. He has failed to see God's love for him.

Failures? Not in God's eyes. He created us in His image. Despite the failure of our sinful rebellion, God sent His own Son into the world. Living faithfully in love, obedience, and service, Jesus was rated a failure in the eyes of the world. His crucifixion appeared to signal a final humiliating defeat. But in that sin-atoning act, Jesus won the victory. Because of Jesus' death and resurrection for us, God accepts us as His special people, headed for eternal life in heaven. Yes, God is the Strength of our hearts and our Portion forever. Failures no more.

Prayer

Jesus, all our ransom paid, All your Father's will obeyed;
By your suff'rings perfect made: Hear us, holy Jesus.
Save us in our soul's distress; Be our help to cheer and bless
While we grow in holiness: Hear us, holy Jesus.

Obstacles

Reading: Isaiah 49:8–13

Text: Isaiah 49:11—"I will turn all my mountains into roads, and my highways will be raised up."

Obstacles in the way everywhere—mountains of bills, family problems and challenges, pressures and demands at work, struggles with personal identity and purpose. We confidently start out toward our goals. An obstacle looms large in front of us. We fight our way over, around, or through it and continue on with less energy. Another obstacle appears. We scratch and claw our way through to the other side, this time with less enthusiasm. Plodding on, we reach a third obstacle and sit down, exhausted and discouraged. How can we keep on going?

Judah faced similar obstacles because of powerful surrounding nations and her own rebellion against God. She tried to face the obstacles all alone through alliances and military might. Ultimately, Judah and Jerusalem were destroyed and the nation herded into exile.

Isaiah writes to people like us, overwhelmed by obstacles and deeply conscious of sin and helplessness. But God reassures us by handling the obstacles and turning them into roads. He prepared the way by sending His own dear Son. Jesus walked straight toward His goal of a cross outside Jerusalem. Obstacles loomed ahead everywhere—crowds who sought to make Him king, disciples who failed to understand His purpose, enemies around every bend in the road. But He persisted. God turned the greatest obstacle of all, the cross, into the road to eternal life. In death Jesus brought life to the world through the forgiveness of sins.

The risen Christ goes before us as we face innumerable obstacles in life. Sometimes we circumvent them, and sometimes we plow through them. But always the forgiving Christ provides the way, the strength, and the support to move on toward the goal of eternal life.

Prayer

In God, my faithful God, I trust when dark my road;
Great woes may overtake me, Yet he will not forsake me.
It is his love that sends them; At his best time he ends them.

Backbone

Reading: Acts 5:25–42

Text: Acts 5:29—"Peter and the other apostles replied: 'We must obey God rather than men!' "

We lack backbone. We bend, compromise, give ground, sell out, and look the other direction. Society preaches a new morality, abandons long-held standards, and lives permissively. Abortions on demand, pornography, corruption in high places, and ruthless business practices abound in our country. We lack the courage to stand up and be counted. Spineless wonders!

In the first days after Pentecost the disciples of Jesus faced stiff opposition from the religious establishment. Peter and John were arrested, brought before the Sanhedrin, and told to keep quiet about their faith in Jesus Christ. They could have played it safe and gone underground. They could have compromised their convictions. But by God's grace these apostles displayed backbone. Arrested again for preaching Christ crucified, they replied, "We must obey God rather than men!" They continued boldly proclaiming the good news of Jesus. Ultimately their confession of faith cost most of them their lives as martyrs. But God used their testimony to build the church on the solid foundation of the apostles and prophets, with Jesus Christ as the Chief Cornerstone. No spineless wonders, the apostles!

We confess our lack of backbone because of our weak, sinful flesh. He points us to His courageous Son, who endured the cross, despising the shame. With backbone He drove the money-changers out of the temple and exposed the sham of the Pharisees. Risen, He offers us forgiveness and strength to stand up for Him and obey God rather than men. Reinforced by regular use of Word and sacraments, we step forward with backbone to proclaim Jesus as Savior and Lord in today's society. No longer spineless wonders!

Prayer

Stand up, stand up for Jesus; The trumpet call obey;
Stand forth in mighty conflict In this his glorious day.
Let all his faithful serve him Against unnumbered foes;
Let courage rise with danger And strength to strength oppose.

Complacent?

Reading: Amos 6:1–7

Text: Amos 6:1a—"Woe to you who are complacent in Zion,
and to you who feel secure on Mount Samaria."

Last year's World Series champion often struggles to win again. So easy to rest on past accomplishments! Complacency. Top management sometimes relaxes after climbing the corporate ladder and coasts toward retirement. Disastrous results. Complacency. Confirmed Christians frequently take it easy in worship attendance, Bible study, witness, and service. Their relationship with God and with other believers begins to slip. Complacency.

The prophet Amos writes to both Judah and Israel with a bold message against complacency. He describes their lives of ease—lying on beds inlaid with ivory, dining on choice lambs and fattened calves, strumming away on harps, and drinking wine by the bowlful while both countries, wicked and rebellious, are headed for destruction. Amos condemns their pride and self-satisfaction. He calls them to repentance and trust in the promised Messiah.

Amos' words rock our complacency as well. We drift away from God and His Word, filling our lives with trivialities and selfish pursuits. We forget about God's plan for the world and our key missionary role in that plan. Complacency shattered by the reality of God's judgment, we turn to the One who came for us, always intent on His saving mission. Never complacent about the Father's plan or the opposition of Satan, He went to the cross and finished the work of paying for our sins. Even now He hears and forgives. And we, complacent no more, live for His purposes.

Prayer
Rise, my soul, to watch and pray;
From your sleep awaken;
Be not by the evil day
Unawares o'ertaken.
Satan's prey Oft are they
Who secure are sleeping
And no watch are keeping.

Complaining?

Reading: Job 10:1–7

Text: Job 10:1—"I loathe my very life; therefore I will give free rein to my complaint and speak out in the bitterness of my soul."

How common our complaining! The weather always seems too hot or too cold, too wet or too dry. We always need more money and more time. We complain about sickness, job stress, family conflict, church coldness, and garbage collection. Then when serious problems of an extended duration arise, we complain on a deeper level.

You know the serious plight of Job, who suddenly lost his possessions, his children, and his health. Sitting in rags on a dung heap, he faced stark reality and cried out in the words of our text. He did not understand, and asked God why he was suffering. He tried to maintain his own innocence and wondered when God would vindicate him.

Ultimately Job learned not to complain but to accept God's authority as Creator. He also learned to trust in God's love for him. No human arguments can suffice. We sin and deserve nothing but punishment. Like Job, we voice our complaints against God and others. We despair of ourselves and wish to place the blame on someone else. God silences also our complaints. We realize that we are sinful and that God is holy. But with our complaints silenced, we listen to His voice and hear a word of love. His Son endured all the pain, injustice, and punishment of a sinful world. No complaints from His lips. Silent before His tormentors, He went willingly to death on the cross for us. He lives, and so shall we. Complaints transformed to thanksgiving and praise!

Prayer

My heart is rich in lowliness;
My soul with love is glowing;
My lips the words of grace express,
Their tones all gently flowing.
My heart, my mind, my strength, my all
To God I yield; on him I call.

Confused?

Reading: Luke 18:31–34

Text: Luke 18:34—"The disciples did not understand any of this. Its meaning was hidden from them, and they did not know what he was talking about."

Confusion reigns. So many words bombard us. So many conflicting facts are reported. So many contradictory ideas are expressed in politics and religion. So many life-styles surround us.

Are you confused also about your faith? Do you wonder why we have so many different world religions and denominations within Christianity? Do you struggle as to whom to believe? Do you have difficulty understanding God's will for your life?

The disciples also got confused. Jesus had just told them that He was going to Jerusalem, where He would be arrested, beaten, and killed, and then would rise again. Luke tells us, "The disciples did not understand any of this." Why the confusion? They had been walking with Jesus for an extended period. He had communicated quite clearly about Himself and His purpose for coming. But still they were confused. Why? As sinners, their minds were clouded. They could not grasp that Jesus must suffer and die to save them. Thank God that Jesus journeyed to the cross and saved them anyway! Then they began to understand the Scriptures correctly.

We often don't understand either, despite the fact that as baptized Christians we hear His Word on a regular basis. We, too, are sinners with clouded minds, preoccupied with a selfish way of thinking. Thank God that Jesus still died for us! Now He opens also our minds to understand the Scriptures as we gather around Word and sacraments. The more we look to Jesus and absorb His Word, the more the confused, contradictory ideas of the world fade away and we clearly see our Savior. Confused no more!

Prayer

Restrain, O Lord, the human pride
That seeks to thrust your truth aside
Or with some man-made thoughts or things
Would dim the words your Spirit sings.

A Well-Watered Garden

Reading: Isaiah 58:11–12

Text: Isaiah 58:11b—"You will be like a well-watered garden, like a spring whose waters never fail."

Summer gardens take much work before yielding good produce. Gardeners plow, plant, hoe, and weed to prepare for harvest. But the garden needs adequate water to grow. A well-watered garden produces an abundance of beautiful vegetables.

Isaiah describes Israel as a well-watered garden. What great promise! She would first become a dry desert because of her rebellion. But then God would bring deliverance and supply the water of life to His people by bringing them back from captivity. By making them a well-watered garden, He would enable them to produce much fruit as they rebuilt the walls of Jerusalem.

In our sun-scorched world of sin, we are helpless to produce an abundant crop. But God sent His own Son as the water of life to die for our sins. Through our baptism God has made us a well-watered garden so that we might produce a bountiful harvest of souls won for the Savior. We receive His watering regularly as we worship with Word and sacrament. We depend on Christ for life and respond with a joyful, caring, witnessing life-style. A well-watered garden indeed!

Prayer

I heard the voice of Jesus say,
"Behold I freely give
The living water, thirsty one;
Stoop down and drink and live."
I came to Jesus, and I drank
Of that life-giving stream;
My thirst was quenched, my soul revived,
And now I live in him.

Trophies

Reading: 1 Corinthians 9:24–27

Text: 1 Corinthians 9:25b—"They do it to get a crown that will not last; but we do it to get a crown that will last forever."

I just glanced at some trophies on my bookshelves, probably in need of dusting. So many have been discarded over the years with broken arms or heads or misplaced identification plates. But a few remain to remind me of tennis victories or basketball participation. I remember once working hard to win them and then displaying them proudly. Now they seem forgotten except for an occasional glance and the fleeting memory of a triumphant hour.

How avidly we collect trophies, not just the kind that stand on bookshelves but houses, cars, jewelry, club memberships, and perhaps even church memberships. We work hard, look for opportunities, meet the right people, take risks, and then savor the victories. Very impressive.

But then we hear Paul writing to the Corinthians about dedicated athletes training rigorously for the Isthmian games to win a coveted garland crown. "They do it," he says, "to get a crown that will not last." And only one gets the prize. How futile the pursuit of fading crowns or trophies that will gather dust.

Paul goes on to describe a much more worthwhile pursuit. "But we do it to get a crown that will last forever." He describes the Christian life as a race or a boxing competition. Rugged training and great self-discipline are needed for a life of service to God. But the crown of eternal life comes only from God by His grace. God's Son came to earth for us, obeyed the Father's will, endured suffering, pain, and death on the cross to pay for our sins. Risen from the grave, He freely offers us the crown of life. We respond by living for Him with single-minded purpose, never taking our eyes off Jesus Christ and our crown of life. Our trophies gather dust. His trophy shines forever.

Prayer
Sinners, whose love can ne'er forget
The wormwood and the gall,
Go, spread your trophies at his feet
And crown him Lord of all.

205

Humble or Harried?

Reading: 1 Peter 5:6–11

Text:. 1 Peter 5:6—"Humble yourselves, therefore, under God's mighty hand, that he may lift you up in due time."

Americans often make a virtue of rushing around and leading hectic lives. Full calendars, frequent business trips, and endless meetings are considered marks of success. Is it any wonder that we often feel harried?

St. Peter sounds a warning that living harried lives, trying to do it all on our own, may signal a lack of humility. Are you humble or harried? Peter refers to anxiety as one source of harassment. We worry about money, health, family, job. Peter adds that we are harried by the devil, who "prowls around . . . looking for someone to devour" (v. 8). Finally, Peter suggests that harassment takes the form of suffering for Christ. Persecutions came to the early Christians because of their faith. We also may suffer when we stand up for the faith in family and community.

Peter in our text suggests that we humble ourselves. Admitting our need for help, we turn to Christ, who "humbled himself and became obedient to death—even death on a cross" (Phil. 2:8b). We humble ourselves by casting all our anxieties on Him, for He cares for us (1 Peter 5:7). He bears the burden. We rest in Him. We humble ourselves by resisting the devil (v. 9). We know that God has caged Satan, the roaring lion, in the death of Jesus. We humble ourselves by seeing God's hand in suffering. He makes us "strong, firm and steadfast" after we "have suffered a little while" (v. 10).

Are you humble or harried? By God's grace you can humbly rest in Him.

Prayer

Rely on God your Savior And find your life secure.
Make his work your foundation That your work may endure.
No anxious thought, no worry, No self-tormenting care
Can win your Father's favor; His heart is moved by prayer.

In the Wilderness

Reading: 1 Corinthians 10:6–13

Text: 1 Corinthians 10:13b—"God is faithful; he will not let
you be tempted beyond what you can bear."

I'm free from Egypt. What a great miracle at the Red Sea! I
walk into the wilderness with a spring in my step. We're headed
for the Promised Land! God is wonderful!

Wait a minute. I'm hungry and thirsty. How long will we
have to walk? My feet hurt. Why did God bring us here to die?

Where is Moses anyway? The clouds and fire from Mount
Sinai were impressive. But now with Moses gone, I'm ready for
that golden calf they're making, a chance for some joyful celebration in this dreadful place.

You say we are near the Promised Land? Spies are returning.
"A land flowing with milk and honey." Sounds great! Giants?
Fierce warriors? Why did God bring us here? We can't risk en-
tering the land. Forty more years of wandering! What a blow!

I'm grumbling again. What a horrible life here in the wilderness! Food the same. Water scarce. Rebellion. I'm ready. Oh,
no, fiery serpents! We'll all perish! I'm looking at the serpent of
brass. Thanks, God, for saving me!

I can't believe it. The Promised Land at last! God is faithful
to His promises. We have arrived at our destination.

So it is with us. We journey with high hopes. The hopes are
shattered. Weary trudging sets in. We grumble and complain.
We seek religious thrills outside the church. We're afraid to risk
discipleship. But a faithful God leads us from slavery to eternity
along a wilderness road marked with the sure promises of salvation and lighted by the cross of our Lord Jesus Christ.

Prayer

Guide me ever, great Redeemer,
Pilgrim through this barren land.
I am weak, but you are mighty;
Hold me with your pow'rful hand.
Bread of heaven, bread of heaven,
Feed me now and evermore;
Feed me now and evermore.

Passing By on the Other Side

Reading: Luke 10:25–37

Text: Luke 10:31b—"When he saw the man, he passed by on the other side."

You know the story. Too bad about a negative title, but it labels a serious problem. Man in need. Fallen among thieves. Left half dead. Two people in a position to help—a priest and a Levite, both tied to the temple and the worship conducted there. Result: Both passed by on the other side, leaving him to die.

Can you relate their inaction to your life? Wife in need of caring time with you. Newspaper and television sports take precedence. You pass by on the other side. People hurting and struggling at work or school. Business comes first. Tasks pile up. Promotion needs to be considered. No time. You pass by on the other side. National and local issues scream for your attention. Abortions increase. Teenage pregnancies rise. Refugees need help. But yardwork beckons. Vacations are needed. Making money takes precedence. You pass by on the other side.

The story, though, doesn't end with the priest and Levite passing by. It goes on to describe the grace of stopping to help. A despised Samaritan cares enough to risk his safety and attend to the man's wounds. We all recognize him as the Good Samaritan. We could think of him as a type of Jesus, the One who endured suffering, pain, and death for us to save us. His stopping to help us, "God's enemies" (Rom. 5:10), demonstrates pure grace and forgiveness.

And helped, we learn to stop for others. Forgiven, we receive the grace to help. Not "Who is my neighbor?" (v. 29) but "To whom can I be a neighbor?" becomes our question. The answer comes back: "Go and do likewise" (v. 37). With God's help, no more passing by on the other side!

Prayer

In sickness, sorrow, want, or care,
Each other's burdens help us share;
May we, where help is needed, there
Give help as though to you.

Sitting at the Lord's Feet

Reading: Luke 10:38–42

Text: Luke 10:39—"She had a sister called Mary, who sat at the Lord's feet listening to what he said."

In the Good Samaritan story, the priest and Levite are criticized for passing by on the other side instead of helping the injured man. In the well-known story of Mary and Martha, Martha is criticized for helping prepare food for Jesus instead of sitting at His feet like Mary. How do you explain the difference?

Martha serves without sitting at Jesus' feet. Perhaps she serves selfishly, wanting to be recognized as a good hostess. Certainly she serves anxiously. Jesus chides her gently, "Martha, Martha . . . you are worried and upset about many things" (v. 41). Caring for Jesus, wanting genuinely to serve Him, she grows fretful and troubled, showing open irritation toward her sister.

Are we sometimes guilty of trying to serve without sitting at Jesus' feet? We may be serving for selfish reasons—looking good in people's eyes, trying to soothe our conscience. Certainly we often serve anxiously. We push ourselves, rush around, worry and fret as we do the Lord's work. Like Martha we don't sit enough at the Lord's feet listening to His Word.

Mary sits at Jesus' feet and learns to serve. The rabbis had students "sitting at their feet." Only men were allowed, no women. Mary finds it a great joy to be included by Jesus. She knows the value of not living "on bread alone, but on every word that comes from the mouth of God" (Matt. 4:4). She no doubt hears about her sin, God's forgiving love in the Messiah, and the joy of serving God every day. She sits so that she may serve.

We also need to sit at Jesus' feet, listening to His Word. All distractions put aside, we worship, commune, and study the Word. We see Jesus as the One who became a servant for us, fully paying for our sins on the cross. Thus we let Him prepare us for joyful, genuine service.

Prayer

Dear Lord, make us Marys sitting at Your feet so that we can serve generously, as Martha wanted to serve. Amen.

Spiritual Aerobics

Reading: Romans 8:1–17

Text: Romans 8:6—"The mind of sinful man is death, but the mind controlled by the Spirit is life and peace."

Physical fitness rates as a much higher priority in America today than in the past. Along with greater attention to nutrition and diet, aerobic exercise has received widespread endorsement. Such exercise demands careful discipline in order to bring results.

St. Paul in Romans 8, his great chapter on the Holy Spirit, stresses the importance of what we might call spiritual aerobics. By nature we live the wrong kind of life-style—selfish, rebellious, disobedient. But God sent His Son in the likeness of sinful humanity to be a sin offering. He fed on the Word of God, obeyed the Father, exercised spiritually in prayer and worship, and went to the cross for us. The Spirit of God brought Jesus into our hearts in our baptism and nurtured our spiritual life through whatever Christian education we received. The Spirit of life has set us free from sin and death.

We are now free in Christ to choose a life-style of spiritual aerobics. We put to death the old nature every day and let the Spirit control our minds. We come to God in prayer. We read and study His Word. We worship with fellow believers. We confess our sins, breathing out the stale air of sin and breathing in the fresh air of God's forgiveness in Christ. As Paul puts it, "the mind controlled by the Spirit is life and peace."

We need careful planning, discipline, regularity, and positive motivation in order to grow in God's peace and joy. But the Spirit testifies with our spirit that we are God's children. Jesus Christ has won the victory for us. Spiritual aerobics, letting Christ live in us and through us, works to the glory of God.

Prayer

Dear Father, discipline my spiritual life so that I may serve You freely and joyfully. Let Your Spirit fill my mind with life and peace through Jesus Christ. Amen.

Walking

Reading: 1 John 1:5–7

Text: Micah 6:8b—"What does the Lord require of you? . . . to walk humbly with your God."

Spiritual aerobics suggests the importance of exercise in the Christian's life. The next five devotions will apply physical activities associated with exercise to the spiritual disciplines of the life in Christ. We start with walking. Most fitness manuals recognize the value of regular, brisk walking for good health. I personally derive great pleasure from lengthy walks during the various seasons of the year, combining wholesome exercise with an enjoyment of God's creation.

Scripture uses the walking imagery to describe the believer's relationship to God. Micah, for example, condemns superficial sacrifices of burnt offerings, hiding wickedness and the exploitation of people. Instead, he tells us "to walk humbly with . . . God." John communicates the same truth when he contrasts walking in darkness with walking in the light: "If we . . . walk in the darkness, we lie and do not live by the truth. But if we walk in the light, as he is in the light, we have fellowship with one another, and the blood of Jesus, his Son, purifies us from all sin" (1 John 1:6–7).

Jesus walked the road that led to Calvary because we had stumbled in sin and could go no farther. He completed His walk by dying for our sins and rising again from the dead. Made His children through faith, we now receive His power to walk humbly with our God in service to others. Proverbs tells us, "I . . . lead you along straight paths. When you walk, your steps will not be hampered" (Prov. 4:11–12a).

Prayer

I am the light; I light the way,
A godly life displaying;
I help you walk as in the day;
I keep your feet from straying.
I am the way, and well I show
How you should journey here below.

Running

Reading: Hebrews 12:1–3

Text: Hebrews 12:1c—". . . let us run with perseverance the race marked out for us."

Running always gets high marks as a vigorous form of physical exercise. Jogging has both zealous advocates and detractors, but millions purchase jogging equipment and pursue a rigorous program of regular exercise. Long-distance running seems to provide more aerobic value than sprinting.

The writer to the Hebrews uses the running imagery as a key to spiritual aerobics. Having reviewed for us the great heroes of faith in chapter 11, he calls for a lifelong race with the necessary quality of perseverance. Paul echoes the same thought when he writes, "Run in such a way as to get the prize" (1 Cor. 9:24b). Hebrews further points to the only One who can save us, "Jesus, the author and perfecter of our faith, who for the joy set before him endured the cross, scorning its shame, and sat down at the right hand of the throne of God" (v. 2). He ran the race for us and won the victory. On our own we grow weary and lose heart. We cannot continue. We sin daily. But God supplies the strength, through Christ's death and resurrection, so that we can "run with perseverance the race marked out for us." Proverbs assures us, "When you run, you will not stumble" (Prov. 4:12b). And Isaiah beautifully promises, "Those who hope in the Lord will renew their strength . . . they will run and not grow weary" (Is. 40:31a, c).

And so we run for physical exercise, disciplining our bodies for good health. And we run spiritually with eyes fixed on the cross of Christ which alone saves us and the world. Spiritual aerobics at work in the body of Christ.

Prayer

Run the straight race through God's good grace;
Lift up your eyes, and seek his face.
Life with its way before us lies;
Christ is the path, and Christ the prize.

Leaping

Reading: Luke 6:22–26

Text: Luke 6:23—"Rejoice in that day and leap for joy, because great is your reward in heaven. For that is how their fathers treated the prophets."

Leaping provides a more strenuous form of physical exercise. Aerobic dancing features leaps into the air along with stretching and jogging in place. Long jumping, high jumping, and pole vaulting take great conditioning and muscles in the legs like coiled springs. Leaping ability helps greatly in basketball, football, and baseball.

The spiritual aerobics parallel to leaping with joy connotes a somewhat different imagery, though difficult to achieve. We think of happy reunions or jubilant football or basketball players after a victory leaping for joy. What makes Jesus' words so difficult is His point of reference. He has been describing the inevitable persecutions which will come to faithful believers. "Blessed are you when men hate you, when they exclude you and insult you and reject your name as evil, because of the Son of Man" (Luke 6:22).

What a challenge—to leap for joy when we are being hated and rejected because of our faith in Jesus. On our own, we cannot leap in such circumstances. We have no spring in our step or joy in our heart. But Jesus "for the joy set before him endured the cross, scorning its shame" (Heb. 12:2). He brings forgiveness and new life to us with the promised great reward in heaven by His grace alone. We can join the lame man healed by Peter and John outside the temple, "walking and jumping, and praising God" (Acts 3:8). We can exclaim with the psalmist, "My heart leaps for joy and I will give thanks to him in song" (Ps. 28:7c).

Prayer
Zion hears the watchmen singing,
And in her heart new joy is springing.
She wakes, she rises from her gloom.

Climbing

Reading: Luke 19:1–10

Text: Luke 19:4—"So he ran ahead and climbed a sycamore-fig tree to see him, since Jesus was coming that way."

Climbing fits well as a physical exercise. Children's monkey bars and swing sets provide opportunities for using many different muscles and developing coordination. Public parks provide ingenious equipment designed to encourage safe climbing. High school gymnasiums often feature a climbing rope. Military basic training usually features obstacle courses requiring superb conditioning and climbing skills.

Spiritual aerobics also include climbing imagery to describe the disciplines of the Christian life. Think of all the mountains in the Bible, and Moses, Abraham, Elijah, and Jesus Himself climbing mountains in obedience to God.

Luke, though, describes a memorable climbing incident. Zacchaeus the tax collector, an outcast and a sinner, wants to see Jesus. No doubt he feels a need for rescue from his predicament. Since he is a short man, he runs ahead and then climbs a sycamore tree for a better glimpse of the Man from Galilee. Jesus then seeks him out and brings salvation to his house. Repentant, Zacchaeus believes in Jesus as his Savior.

What a marvelous example! Are we willing to climb for a glimpse of Jesus? Do we sense our own helplessness and need for His grace? He freely offers us the salvation won for us as He climbed Mount Calvary and was lifted on the cross. Through regular Word-and-sacrament communion with Him, He supplies the strength for us to climb every mountain in our lives and scale every wall as we serve Him and witness to others regarding our Savior.

Prayer

Calv'ry's mournful mountain climb;
There, adoring at his feet,
Mark that miracle of time,
God's own sacrifice complete.
"It is finished!" hear him cry;
Learn from Jesus Christ to die.

Sitting

Reading: Deuteronomy 6:4–9

Text: Deuteronomy 6:7b—"Talk about them when you sit at home . . . ."

Walking, running, leaping, and climbing obviously qualify as physical exercises leading to better health and an aerobic life-style. Sitting at first glance doesn't seem to fit. It suggests a sedentary life and spectatoritis rather than participation. In the exercise cycle, however, sitting could suggest needed rest between active exercises. We all need a breather before resuming exercise.

The psalmist talks about refusing to sit with the wicked (Ps. 26:5) and describes the man as blessed who does not "sit in the seat of mockers" (Ps. 1:1c). Amos criticizes a self-serving elite who lounge on couches to dine on fattened calves (Amos 6:4).

But Moses gives important advice to Israel ready to enter the Promised Land. He asks them to worship the Lord our God as one Lord and to love Him with heart, soul, and strength. He then instructs them to share God's teaching with their children in every aspect of life. Moses tells Israel, "Talk about them when you sit at home." Sitting at home provides a needed opportunity to study the Word of God and teach the whole family about God's love in Jesus Christ for lost sinners.

We remember Jesus commending Mary for sitting at His feet and hearing the one thing needful. We sit to rest and let God refresh us through worship and study of the Word so that we can rise to serve Him through walking, running, leaping, and climbing. Through Christ we can anticipate the promise of Revelation, "To him who overcomes, I will give the right to sit with me on my throne, just as I overcame and sat down with my Father on his throne" (Rev. 3:21).

Prayer

New graces ever gaining From this our day of rest,
We reach the rest remaining To spirits of the blest.
To Holy Ghost be praises, To Father, and to Son;
The Church its voice upraises To you, blest Three in One.

215

Before They Call . . .

Reading: Isaiah 65:21–25

Text: Isaiah 65:24—"Before they call I will answer; while they are still speaking I will hear."

Sometimes when we make a telephone call the other person says, "I was about to call you!" Always surprising. But God says something far more surprising through the prophet Isaiah: "Before they call I will answer; while they are still speaking I will hear."

Israel would go through great trouble because of rebellion against God. In captivity far away from home, they would cry out in anguish. Now God is making the tremendous promise that He will answer Israel's prayer even before they call. He was already planning to send His Son as the promised Messiah to save the world from sin.

How often we wonder whether our prayers will be answered. We struggle because of our sins. We feel overwhelmed by circumstances. We cry out in despair. But even before we call, God has already answered by sending His Son, who is with us always, "to the very end of the age" (Matt. 28:20).

Jesus says, "Ask and it will be given to you; seek and you will find; knock and the door will be opened to you" (Matt. 7:7). We can go to God regularly with all our needs, small or large, and we can be certain that He will hear our prayer and answer in His own way and at His own time. How comforting to know about God's personal, immediate attention!

Prayer
Christians, while on earth abiding,
Let us never cease to pray,
Firmly in the Lord confiding
As our parents in their day.
Be the children's voices raised
To the God their parents praised.
May his blessing, failing never,
Rest upon his people ever.

When I Called . . .

Reading: Isaiah 66:1–4

Text: Isaiah 66:4b—"For when I called, no one answered, when I spoke, no one listened."

Yesterday we heard about God's great care for us: "Before they call I will answer." In the very next chapter of Isaiah, from which today's text comes, we learn of how people despise the love of God: "When I called, no one answered, when I spoke, no one listened."

God details the disobedience of His people. Their sacrifices do not come from the heart but only display an external obedience. They choose to go their own way and delight in abominations. They do evil and choose what displeases God. In these ways they refused to answer when God called to them and failed to listen when He spoke His Word.

How tragic that we often fail to listen and refuse to answer the God who calls us with His love! Like Israel we sometimes go through the motions of worship while inwardly pursuing our own selfish agenda. But God's Word has a way of hitting us like a hammer, and He calls us again to repentance and faith in His Son, the Crucified One. Then by His grace we rewrite the verse of our text: "When I called, they answered in faith, when I spoke, they listened with thanksgiving."

Prayer
Today your mercy calls us
To wash away our sin.
However great our trespass,
Whatever we have been,
However long from mercy
Our hearts have turned away,
Your precious blood can wash us
And make us clean today.

Earthquake

Reading: Matthew 24:3–14

Text: Matthew 24:7b—"There will be famines and earthquakes in various places."

The other day my wife and I were upstairs soon after supper and noticed everything shaking on the dresser top. Unusual in the Midwest, the shaking turned out to be tremors from a moderate earthquake centered in southern Illinois. While for the world as a whole such tremors are not that unusual, they gave us pause for reflection. How easily and unexpectedly nature can unleash destruction upon thousands of people!

Jesus describes signs of his second coming in Matthew 24 and includes this reference: "There will be famines and earthquakes in various places." He refers to such signs as "the beginning of birth pains" (v. 8). We can easily live for the moment, forgetting about the second coming of Christ. Even a slight earth tremor calls us to account as we look away from ourselves to the One who lived, died, and rose again for us and will come again in glory at any moment.

While earthquakes can strike fear into the hearts of people, we also recall the solid foundation of God, our Refuge and Strength, who dwells in the midst of all the turmoil. Thank God for His control of nature and for His redemptive plan, which will soon bring the whole creation "into the glorious freedom of the children of God" (Rom. 8:21).

Prayer

The seas shall waste, the skies in smoke decay,
Rocks fall to dust, and mountains melt away;
But fixed this Word, this saving pow'r, remains;
Thy realms shall last, thine own Messiah reigns.

Painful or Painless?

Reading: Jeremiah 15:15–21

Text: Jeremiah 15:18a—"Why is my pain unending and my wound grievous and incurable?"

I sit in the dentist's office getting two teeth filled. Is it painful or painless? Thanks to modern dentistry, the affected areas are numbed once the needle penetrates the gums with the anesthetic. But few people enjoy the process. This minor procedure causes me to reflect on the purpose of pain in our lives.

Jeremiah, rejected and discouraged in his ministry, cries out to God, "Why is my pain unending and my wound grievous and incurable?" He compares his discouragements with a terminal illness, bringing unending pain. God answers him, "If you repent, I will restore you that you may serve me" (v. 19b). God doesn't promise an easy, pain-free life. He doesn't let Jeremiah engage in self-pity. He simply promises to be with Jeremiah as he speaks the Word of God.

To understand the purpose of pain, look to Jesus, who endured untold pain and suffering. He suffered physically, emotionally, and spiritually. But through it all, God the Father made His Son the instrument of salvation for the world. Saved by Christ's painful death, we begin to see the value of pain in our lives. Pain turns us to God for help. Forgiven and restored, we then serve Him as we reach out to others. He promises to be with us in the midst of pain. And He understands our pain, because He Himself suffered for us.

With Him at our side, trusting in His promises, we find it easier to endure the pain that comes to us in this fallen world.

Prayer
When I suffer pain and losses,
Lord, be near, Let me hear
Comfort under crosses.
Point me, Father, to the heaven
Which your Son For me won
When his life was given.

© CPH

The Sower and His Powerful Seed

Reading: Matthew 13:1–9

Text: Matthew 13:3b—"A farmer went out to sow his seed."

Many gardens dot the backyards of our land. If you have planted a garden, by now you are harvesting or anticipating the harvest. But it all begins with sowing the seed. Jesus knew that also, as He told the familiar parable of the sower. Over the next several days we focus on the parable and its meaning for our lives. Ask yourself the question, "Is my soil receptive to God's seed?"

Jesus moves from the synagogue to the seashore, where large crowds gather to hear Him. He teaches about the Kingdom by using several parables, all down-to-earth examples with immediate application to the people who hear and understand.

He begins with the parable of the sower. Two common methods of sowing were employed. In the broadcasting method, the farmer would simply throw the seed to either side of him and let the wind carry the seed. Or sometimes a sack of seed was placed on a donkey. A hole cut in the corner of the bag permitted the seed to fall to the ground as the donkey meandered through the field. Either method would account for the kinds of soil described in the parable.

Clearly the seed represents the Word of God, described by Jesus as "the message about the kingdom" (v. 19). That Word is powerful and effective, always producing a harvest. God, the Sower, provides the good news that the Kingdom comes in Jesus Christ, who suffers and dies to pay for the world's sin.

We now enter the parable. The Sower wants to sow the good seed of the Word on our soil so that He can produce an abundant harvest in us. Will we be receptive soil? What a joy to receive that seed of the Kingdom in action! Thank God for His powerful Word and His victorious Son! Tomorrow we begin to consider the kinds of soil upon which the seed falls.

Prayer

Almighty God, your Word is cast
Like seed into the ground;
Now let the dew of heav'n descend
And righteous fruits abound.

The Wayside Soil of a Closed Mind

Reading: Matthew 13:18–19

Text: Matthew 13:4—"As he was scattering the seed, some fell along the path, and the birds came and ate it up."

The parable of the sower continues. God, the Sower, sows the powerful seed of His Word, with some falling by the wayside. This wayside or path probably refers to a narrow strip of land used as a common walking ground between the fields. This path was trampled down by many feet and therefore totally hardened against the penetration of any seed. Birds could easily see and take the seed for themselves.

Jesus identifies the wayside soil as follows: "When anyone hears the message about the kingdom and does not understand it, the evil one comes and snatches away what was sown in his heart" (v. 19). The wayside soil tells a grim story. Some hearers of the Word do not understand, because they have a hardened, unteachable spirit.

Pride rears its ugly head: "I don't need to study the Word. I feel quite satisfied spiritually. I'm not like the heathen. I come from a long line of church people, so I heard all of it years ago!" Fear may also intervene: "I don't want to hear anything new that will challenge my way of life. I'm quite content with my current life-style. Certainly I'm no worse than others I know. Frankly, I'm afraid the Word might upset me, so I'd rather not have anything to do with it." Both pride and fear spring from hardened hearts, and the evil one easily sees and takes the seed away.

Do I ever hear like seed sown on wayside soil, rejecting the Word of God? Or is my soil receptive to that seed? Thank God for Jesus Christ, who died also for those with hardened hearts. Thank God for sending His Holy Spirit to break down my stubborn refusal and my hardened spirit.

Prayer

O Lord, help me to listen with an open mind so that Your Word can take root in my heart as I trust in You alone for salvation. Amen.

The Rocky Soil of Shallow Faith

Reading: Matthew 13:5–6, 20–21

Text: Matthew 13:5a—"Some fell on rocky places, where it did not have much soil."

God, the Sower, sows the powerful seed of His Word. Some of that seed, according to the parable, falls on rocky soil. In parts of Palestinian fields a thin skin of earth only a few inches deep lies on top of an underlying shelf of limestone rock. The seed falling on this rocky soil would quickly germinate because of the warmth of the soil, but no roots would be able to penetrate the limestone shelf. The promising young plant, however, quickly withers and dies when the hot sun scorches it.

Jesus describes the rocky soil as follows: "The one who received the seed that fell on rocky places is the man who hears the Word and at once receives it with joy. But since he has no root, he lasts only a short time. When trouble or persecution comes because of the Word, he quickly falls away" (Matt. 13:20–21).

This description of seed on rocky soil strikes right at the heart of much modern religious life. We often grow tremendously excited over fads and new trends. We respond to religion as an emotional high. We make a faith commitment with good intentions. But then the good beginning quickly fades away; we lose our initial enthusiasm. We have experienced only a shallow and emotional faith, with no lasting roots in the promises of God.

Am I ever like seed on rocky soil, or is my soil receptive to the seed? Thank God that the powerful seed of His Word produces roots that go deep into the soil of His love. Thank God that Jesus Christ heard the Father's Word and obeyed, lived in a world of rocky soil, yet committed Himself to death on a cross and offers forgiveness of sins also to those hearers who, at least at times, resemble rocky soil. Thank God for His gift of deep and solid faith in Jesus Christ as Savior.

Prayer

O Lord, strengthen my shallow and emotional faith by pointing me to the sure promise of salvation through Your death and resurrection. Ground me solidly in Your saving Word. Amen.

The Thorny Soil of Conflicting Interests

Reading: Matthew 13:22

Text: Matthew 13:7—"Other seed fell among thorns, which grew up and choked the plants."

God, the Sower, sows the powerful seed of His Word. Some of the seed falls on soil with thorns. This soil looks clean at the outset but is deceptive. When one turns over a garden with fibrous roots still in the ground, similar trouble lies ahead. When the seed germinates and the young plant begins to grow, thorns and weeds grow up right alongside the plant and choke the life out of it.

Jesus describes the thorny soil as follows: "The one who received the seed that fell among the thorns is the man who hears the Word, but the worries of this life and the deceitfulness of wealth choke it, making it unfruitful" (Matt. 13:22).

How devastating to us the thorny soil! We grow as young plants in good soil but all the while permit the many conflicting interests of our life to grow beside us. We lead busy lives filled with activities. We make money. We buy appliances, gadgets, and recreational equipment. We plunge our children into activities. We build a social life—all alongside our hearing the Word of God. Most of these interests need not be wrong in themselves, but the second best is always the enemy of the best. Gradually the thorns begin to choke off the life of God in us.

Do I hear like thorny soil or is my soil receptive to the powerful seed of God's Word? Thank God that Jesus of Nazareth was not distracted by conflicting interests but shunned Satan's temptation to material wealth and went to the cross. In His death He won life for a sinful world attracted by thorns and weeds. Thank God for showing us the priceless value of His life and His Word for us.

Prayer

Lord, forgive me for letting the thorns of conflicting interests sap my strength. Restore to me the saving life that flows from Your Word. Amen.

The Good Soil of a Receptive Heart

Reading: Matthew 13:23

Text: Matthew 13:8—"Still other seed fell on good soil, where it produced a crop—a hundred, sixty or thirty times what was sown."

Jesus is teaching by the seashore. In the background a sower is sowing seed in the fields. The people gather to hear, but with different attitudes and motivations. They listen spellbound to His parable taken from a familiar scene in their lives. As He describes each kind of soil—the wayside soil of a closed mind, the rocky soil of a shallow faith, and the thorny soil of conflicting interests, the Spirit of God convicts them of sin—poor hearing and false understanding. Now comes the fourth kind of soil.

"Still other seed fell on good soil, where it produced a crop—a hundred, sixty or thirty times what was sown." Good soil. Deep, clean, soft soil. Nourishment for the germinating seed. An abundant harvest.

God's grace at work. He sent His Son to live and die for a world which represented all the wrong kinds of soils. The seed of God's Word alone contains the power to create receptive soil and bring about a growing plant and an abundant harvest. Even our fruit-bearing comes only from God's grace. The mighty seed explodes in our lives. He gives us receptive and obedient hearts. We learn to listen and understand, to trust and obey.

May we always be good soil and produce abundant fruit. And may God also make us participants in sowing the seed, so that many may be won for Christ's kingdom.

Prayer

On what has now been sown
Your blessing, Lord, bestow;
The pow'r is yours alone
To make it sprout and grow.
O Lord, in grace the harvest raise,
And yours alone shall be the praise!

A Chariot Witness

Reading: Acts 8:26–40

Text: Acts 8:30a—"Then Philip ran up to the chariot and heard the man reading Isaiah the prophet."

The award-winning film *Chariots of Fire* describes the 1924 Olympic success of the United Kingdom track team. They ran with the intensity of fiery chariots. Eric Liddell, a Church of Scotland believer, anchored that track team and shocked the press by refusing to run on Sunday at the Olympics because of his religious convictions. One year after winning an Olympic gold medal, Liddell journeyed to China as a missionary with the London Missionary Society. He now ran for the Lord as a Christian witness. In addition to teaching science at an Anglo-Chinese college, he served as a rural evangelist, traveling many miles on foot and bicycle. During World War II he spent two years in a Japanese prison camp as an "enemy national" dying there of a brain tumor in 1945. Throughout his career he served as a tremendous inspiration to those around him—a chariot of fire in his witness to Jesus Christ.

In Acts we read about the evangelist Philip, who was asked to seek out a foreign dignitary from Ethiopia traveling home by chariot. "Then Philip ran up to the chariot and heard the man reading Isaiah the prophet." Philip, like Eric Liddell, ran in order to witness to Christ. The Ethiopian eunuch believed and was baptized through Philip's witness. No doubt the Gospel came to Ethiopia as the man's chariot reached his home.

We can also be "chariots of fire" for the Lord. God sent His Son to run the race for us and win the victory on the cross. He endured persecution, suffering, and death to pay for our sins. He chooses us as His own forgiven children. By His power we can run like Philip and Eric Liddell to tell others about Jesus the Savior. What chariot witness does God have in store for you?

Prayer

Give me a faithful heart, Likeness to thee,
That each departing day Henceforth may see
Some work of love begun, Some deed of kindness done,
Some wand'rer sought and won, Something for thee.

The Shadow of God's Hand

Reading: Isaiah 51:12–16

Text: Isaiah 51:16a—"I have put my words in your mouth and covered you with the shadow of my hand."

What could be worse than walking under a mercilessly hot sun with no shade in sight? Skin grows dry and parched. Headache begins. We feel faint. Many times our daily life brings temptations and problems which beat down on our heads like the blazing sun. We try to cover up and protect ourselves but fail to dispel the heat.

Isaiah describes God's salvation with the words, "I have . . . covered you with the shadow of my hand." God with His powerful hand reaches down to us and provides refreshing, cool, life-giving shade to protect us from sin and temptation. Our Bible reading emphasizes both God's might and His mercy. He, the great, merciful God, will take care of His own and will save us, His children, from our enemies.

Alone, we die in sin. But God's Son went to Calvary for us, where He endured the blazing wrath of God on our sins. He won the victory. Now forgiveness is ours through Jesus Christ. God's hand shades us from all guilt and shame.

By speaking the words God puts in our mouth, we can also bring the good news of God's shading hand to others. Repenting of their sins, they too can rest in the shade of God's protecting hand. The next time you seek the shade of a large tree, remember the gracious hand of God available at all times for you in a hot, desert land.

Prayer

I heard the voice of Jesus say,
"Come unto me and rest,"
Lay down, O weary one, lay down
Your head upon my breast."
I came to Jesus as I was,
So weary, worn, and sad;
I found in him a resting place,
And he has made me glad.

The Vault Without Fault

Reading: Hebrews 7:23–28

Text: Hebrews 10:14—"By one sacrifice he has made perfect forever those who are being made holy."

A dramatic moment occurred during the 1984 Olympic Games in Los Angeles. All-around competition in women's gymnastics reached a climax in the vault event. America's first opportunity for a gymnastics gold medal rested on the shoulders of 94-pound Mary Lou Retton, a 16-year-old West Virginian. She needed a perfect score of 10 to capture the individual title. With confidence and dynamic energy, Mary Lou exploded on the vault into not one but two perfect 10s. Her clutch performance has been labeled as "the vault without fault."

Young gymnasts throughout the country aspire to achieve like Mary Lou Retton, but few succeed. We would like to accomplish in our lives at home, in school, and on the job a "vault without fault," but we also fall far short. How many dreams are shattered, goals unreached, and opportunities lost!

The writer to the Hebrews, though, points us to a high priest who brings hope to us all. Other priests, themselves weak and sinful, offered daily sacrifices in the temple for their own sins and the sins of the people. But Jesus Christ, the great High Priest, came down from heaven to earth and lived among us without fault. He was tempted as we are, yet was without sin. In a climactic moment on Calvary, with the future of the whole human race at stake, He needed to make a perfect sacrifice for us. And He did just that!

Now, through His sacrifice, we are perfect in God's eyes— forgiven and cleansed. Now, like Mary Lou Retton, we seek to reach our God-given potential. Therefore, as the Hebrews writer suggests, "Let us consider how we may spur one another on toward love and good deeds" (v. 24).

Prayer
Fight the good fight with all your might;
Christ is your strength, and Christ your right.
Lay hold on life, and it shall be
Your joy and crown eternally.

Spiritual Dryness

Reading: John 7:37–39

Text: Psalm 63:1—"O God, you are my God, earnestly I seek you; my soul thirsts for you, my body longs for you, in a dry and weary land where there is no water."

An old song describes the desert traveler as longing for "cool, clear water." In the old West, desert travel was perilous—hot, dry, dusty conditions, miles and miles of wilderness, prickly cactus, volcanic rock, precious canteens of water for horses and travelers, scarce water holes, sometimes empty, sometimes filled with brackish water, the body dehydrated, weary, tested beyond human endurance. The utter gratitude for reaching journey's end and drinking an unlimited supply of cool, clear water!

In today's psalm verse the writer uses this desert imagery to describe spiritual dryness. David knew the meaning of desert travel from his experiences in fleeing from Saul. He had endured physical thirst and desperation. Here he applies these physical realities to his spiritual thirst for God. Alone, rejected, hopeless, discouraged, he wants a close relationship with the God of Abraham, Isaac, and Jacob, "the spring of living water" (Jer. 2:13).

Do you know the reality of spiritual dryness? Have you felt isolated from God? Troubled on the job, in your family, perhaps even in your church, you wander around desperately seeking a drink of cool, clear water. But you are alone, with a punctured canteen. You cry out to God, but He does not seem to hear. You are spiritually exhausted. You can barely face the next day with its people, problems, and demands. You try to live on what you have within, but your mouth is dry and parched. From time to time you think you see a lake of water ahead, only to discover a mirage. Spiritual dryness has overwhelmed you. Where is God's cool, clear, thirst-quenching refreshment?

Come to Jesus, the Living Water!

Prayer

Lord Jesus, I am spiritually dry. Let me drink Your life-giving water. Amen.

A Drink of Living Water

Reading: Psalm 63

Text: John 7:37b—"If anyone is thirsty, let him come to me and drink."

Yesterday we left David "in a dry and weary land where there is no water" (Ps. 63:1c). But he finds his spiritual thirst quenched by God alone, his Rock and Salvation. The Son of David, Jesus Christ, says to the disciples and to us many years later: "If anyone is thirsty, let him come to me and drink. Whoever believes in me, as the Scripture has said, streams of living water will flow from within him" (John 7:37b–38).

Having spent 40 days and nights in the wilderness, where He was tempted, Jesus relied on the Father and refreshed multitudes with living water. Having cried out in agony from the cross, "I thirst," Jesus won the victory over the evil wilderness forces of sin, death, and the devil.

He now offers us the cool water of His Word and sacraments to quench our spiritual thirst day by day. Spiritual dryness will occur because of our sin and the circumstances around us. But the great thirst-quencher stands ready to help us and through us to pour forth a stream of living water to a dry, thirsty world. With the desert traveler we still cry out for "water, cool, clear water." But God has supplied us with an endless drink of living water through Jesus Christ. How wonderful that we also have water from our spiritual canteen to share with others!

Prayer

I heard the voice of Jesus say,
"Behold I freely give
The living water, thirsty one;
Stoop down and drink and live."
I came to Jesus, and I drank
Of that life-giving stream;
My thirst was quenched, my soul revived,
And now I live in him.

Common Clay Pots

Reading: 2 Corinthians 4:5–10

Text: 2 Corinthians 4:7—"But we have this treasure in jars of clay to show that this all-surpassing power is from God and not from us."

Movie premiere. Limousines arrive. Stars in glittering evening wear sweep through the crowds to the waiting door as cameras flash. Who knows what lies behind the smiling faces—loneliness, fear, arrogance, immorality, emptiness? How often we try to maintain a glittering exterior while hiding what lies inside!

Paul takes an opposite approach in describing his apostolic ministry. He refers to himself as a jar of clay, a common clay pot—ordinary, weak, sinful, no glitter. Why? He wants his treasure, "the light of the knowledge of the glory of God in the face of Christ" (v. 6b), to shine brightly for all to see. That light can shine through the cracks in a common clay pot. No one will mistake the clay jar for the treasure. Everyone will see that "this all-surpassing power is from God and not from us."

We have the same treasure, Jesus Christ, crucified and risen, God's Light in our lives. Admitting that we are common clay pots, sinful but forgiven, calls attention away from ourselves to the treasure of Christ. Others will know that "this all-surpassing power is from God and not from us." Which do you prefer—a glittering exterior like a movie star with nothing inside or the marvelous treasure of Christ in a common clay pot?

Prayer

Wisdom's highest, noblest treasure,
Jesus, is revealed in you.
Let me find in you my pleasure,
Make my will and actions true,
Humility there and simplicity reigning,
In paths of true wisdom my steps ever training.
If I learn from Jesus this knowledge divine,
The blessing of heavenly wisdom is mine.

A Driving Force

Reading: 1 Corinthians 13

Text: 2 Corinthians 5:14—"For Christ's love compels us, because we are convinced that one died for all . . . ."

What causes people to climb formidable mountains, explore unknown frontiers, and push on toward new scientific discoveries? What motivates us to condition our bodies, fight for a higher rung on the career ladder, and struggle to accumulate wealth? Driving forces within us. All too often these driving forces are desire for recognition, greed, and lust for success. At root selfishness and pride.

But Paul describes a far more powerful and helpful motivation. This driving force led the apostles to travel the world, testify boldly, face natural obstacles, persecution, and death itself. They continued loving their enemies, helping ungrateful churches, and clearly proclaiming Jesus Christ as the only way to salvation. What driving force motivated the apostles to lay aside self-interest and greed? Paul simply says, "Christ's love compels us, because we are convinced that one died for all." Paul knew that Jesus went to the cross to pay for the world's sin. Not interested in personal gain and only wanting to obey the Father, Jesus loved us to the death. Overwhelmed by His love, Paul lived boldly and joyfully because Christ's love compelled him.

Thank God for the driving force of Christ's love! We confess our selfish drives and rest in the forgiving love of the Savior. We look to the cross and see the Christ, compelled by love to hang there for us. We soak in His love through Word and sacraments, daily offering His forgiveness. Then we rise to face the challenges of the day—people to love, goals to reach for Him, opportunities for Christian witness. And without striving or struggling, we realize that Christ's love moves us to willing and joyful action. What a driving force!

Prayer

Lord, thanks for Your saving love, which compels us to serve You! Amen.

Internalizing His Death

Reading: 2 Corinthians 5:15–21

Text: 2 Corinthians 5:15—"And he died for all, that those who live should no longer live for themselves but for him who died for them and was raised again."

Smoking causes lung cancer according to research reports. No doubt true. An external fact. Yet people continue smoking. America provides unprecedented freedom for all citizens. No doubt true. An external fact. Yet people either choose to live in bondage or take freedom for granted. When Dad dies of lung cancer or I cough dangerously, I may internalize the cancer research and quit smoking. When I live for a time in a foreign country and experience its lack of liberty, I may internalize America's precious freedom.

"He died for all," Paul writes. True. An external fact. Jesus Christ died on the cross for the sin of the entire world. God declared the whole world righteous for Jesus' sake. I live because God has brought me to faith through the waters of Baptism. Dead to sin, I live in the death and resurrection of Christ. True. An objective fact. But I often live each day as though dead in sin. I fear. I build my own kingdoms. I hate. I reject. I withdraw.

Paul describes internalizing Christ's death, "And he died for all, that those who live should no longer live for themselves but for him who died for them and was raised again." "For all"— external, objective. "For them"—internal, subjective. For us. For me. Because He died for me, a poor sinner, I know God's love and forgiveness. Undeserving, I have eternal life now. I no longer want to live for myself but for Him who died for me and rose again. What a life—rich, challenging, surprising, open, other-directed, praise-filled—when by God's grace I internalize Jesus' death!

Prayer

All that I am and have, Thy gifts so free,
In joy, in grief, through life, Dear Lord, for thee!
And when thy face I see, My ransomed soul shall be
Through all eternity Something for thee.

Godly Sorrow—Worldly Sorrow

Reading: 2 Corinthians 7:5–13

Text: 2 Corinthians 7:10—"Godly sorrow brings repentance that leads to salvation and leaves no regret, but worldly sorrow brings death."

Sin brings sorrow every time. The immediate result may appear exciting, enjoyable, even exhilarating. But in the long run there is guilt and anxiety. Worldly sorrow over sin seeks superficial ways to deal with guilt. We try to blame others. We insist that everyone else does the same thing. We try to make up for sin by doing something good. Worldly sorrow leads to death.

Paul talks about godly sorrow. He writes to the Corinthians, "Godly sorrow brings repentance that leads to salvation and leaves no regret." The Corinthians had sinned in many ways. Paul confronts them with their sin in his First Letter. Initially, they seemed reluctant to listen to his admonition. They displayed only a worldly sorrow.

But in these verses Paul rejoices. A visit by Titus has revealed that God has worked true repentance in their hearts. No longer covering up, they admit their sin and turn to Jesus for forgiveness. Relying on His mercy, their sorrow has produced earnestness, eagerness to be cleared, indignation over wrongdoing, longing to see the wrongs righted, and genuine concern. "Godly sorrow . . . leads to salvation."

God addresses each of us through Paul. Are we dealing with our sin by worldly sorrow, striving desperately to cover up and avoid the truth? Or do we open our lives to the Word of God, admitting our guilt and applying to ourselves the full forgiveness of Christ, won on the cross? "Godly sorrow brings repentance that leads to salvation."

Prayer

Lord, open my heart to sorrow over my sin so that I may receive Your free forgiveness. Amen.

Olympic Torch: Goals

Reading: Philippians 3:12–14

Text: Philippians 3:14a—"I press on toward the goal . . . ."

Since the 1936 Olympic games the Olympic torch has been transported from Greece to the Olympic site. In 1984 a torch relay moved across the United States from New York to Los Angeles. Providing many dramatic and inspiring moments, the relay involved Americans from every walk of life in a common goal. Proceeds from the torch relay helped local sports programs across the country.

Individually and collectively the Olympic Torch Relay provided opportunities to set and accomplish goals. Covering 9,000 miles, the relay started May 8 and ended at the opening ceremonies in Los Angeles on July 28. This major effort required careful planning and the cooperation of groups nationwide. Each runner had the goal of running a kilometer with trained runners covering much more territory in less populated areas of the country.

In running the race of the Christian life, goals provide awesome power. Paul writes to the Philippian Christians, "I press on toward the goal to win the prize for which God has called me heavenward in Christ Jesus." He knew that Jesus had run the race before him to die on the cross for the world's sin. Forgiven by Christ's sacrifice, Paul now strains ahead to live for Christ by serving others every day. He lives with purpose—sharing Christ's salvation with others.

We join with other Christians to press on toward the goal for which God has called us in Christ Jesus. By grace He will lead us to heaven. In the meanwhile, we live with purpose each day, joining hands to carry the torch of Christ's love to every person on the path of life.

Prayer

Run the straight race through God's good grace;
Lift up your eyes, and seek his face.
Life with its way before us lies;
Christ is the path, and Christ the prize.

Olympic Torch: Determination

Reading: James 1:2–4

Text: James 1:3—". . . you know that the testing of your faith develops perseverance."

The Olympic torch relay in 1984 not only provided challenging goals but also developed determination in organizers and runners alike. On Atlanta's Peachtree Street, with crowds four and five deep, a disabled child takes the torch, almost falls off balance, and then moves slowly toward his goal, concentrating on holding the torch aloft. Stumbling several times as the crowd gasps, he reaches his goal to their thunderous cheers. Such determination hardly left a dry eye in the crowd.

We who carry the torch of Christ's love also find our faith tested. James writes, "Consider it pure joy, my brothers, whenever you face trials of many kinds, because you know that the testing of your faith develops perseverance." At the race's start serving Christ seems glorious and exciting, but as the road lengthens and our energy wanes, we struggle and feel like quitting. Then God helps us develop determination. He reminds us of the agony and bloody sweat of His only Son on the final march to Calvary. He supplies us with the encouragement of brothers and sisters in the faith. And we learn to focus on Him and move on toward the finish line.

That determination, developed within us by His grace, serves to strengthen the crowds who watch and equips us to meet greater challenges that lie ahead. We live triumphantly on God's staying power, for His Word endures forever in us, and through us to others. Thank God for the determination of His Son.

Prayer

Jesus, Lord, my heart renew,
Let me bear my crosses,
Learning humbleness from you,
Peace despite my losses.
May I give you love for love!
Hear me, O my Savior,
That I may in heav'n above
Sing your praise forever.

Olympic Torch: Support

Reading: Philippians 2:1–4

Text: Philippians 2:4—"Each of you should look not only to your own interests, but also to the interests of others."

The Olympic torch relay helped to promote teamwork among the American people. Runners supported each other and likewise received support from the crowds. In Kansas City a beautiful retarded girl struggled her way up an incline while her entire class waved balloons and shouted, "Run, Amy, run!" Delayed by a severe thunderstorm in Kentucky, the relay arrived in a small community at 2 o'clock in the morning, expecting everyone to be in bed. Instead, they were greeted by several hundred townspeople holding candles to light the way. Giving and receiving support.

Paul writes to the Philippian Christians, "Each of you should look not only to your own interests, but also to the interests of others." How easily we become self-absorbed, settle into our selfish routine, and look out for number one. We want to star on the team and make the headlines.

Paul points to Jesus, who took on the form of a servant and became obedient to death on the cross. Before we can give support, we need support—His total self-giving sacrifice on the cross for us. And we need the strength of fellow Christians to grow in faith. Then by God's power we can live for Him and for others. He helps us see the needs around us and respond with specific, practical aid. We learn to encourage, commend, sustain, and uplift others as they also support us. The Christian fellowship in action far surpasses any Olympic torch relay and bears eloquent testimony to the saving work of Jesus Christ, the Servant whom God exalted as Lord.

Prayer

We share our mutual woes,
Our mutual burdens bear,
And often for each other flows
The sympathizing tear.

Hold High the Torch

Reading: Hebrews 12:1–3

Text: Hebrews 12:2a—"Let us fix our eyes on Jesus, the author and perfecter of our faith."

The Olympic torch symbolizes the spirit of the Olympic movement—international friendship, national pride, and the pursuit of athletic excellence. Setting goals, developing determination, and sharing support through the torch relay contributed to the Olympic spirit. The runners held high the torch across America, and when Rafer Johnson ignited the permanent Olympic torch in the Los Angeles Coliseum, the games began with high spirits.

As Christians we are called to hold high the torch of our Lord Jesus Christ. Hebrews describes us as running the race surrounded in the stands by all the great heroes of the faith who have gone before us. We are to throw off the weight of our sin and run the race with determination. But the focus of our running always rests on Jesus: "Let us fix our eyes on Jesus, the author and perfecter of our faith." Jesus went joyfully to the cross for us and was raised to the right hand of the Father.

Far from seeking glory or fame, we lift high the cross of our Lord Jesus Christ for all to see. Saved by His death, we set our life's goals to serve Him. Relying on His promises, we develop determination to run the race. Surrounded by the fellowship of believers, we give support to all who alongside of us bear witness to Christ's love. In the darkness of a sinful world, *hold high the torch!*

Prayer

In the cross of Christ I glory,
Tow'ring o'er the wrecks of time.
All the light of sacred story
Gathers round its head sublime.
When the sun of bliss is beaming
Light and love upon my way,
From the cross the radiance streaming
Adds more luster to the day.

Favorite Things: Brown Paper Packages

Reading: Colossians 1:24–29

Text: Colossians 2:3—"Christ, in whom are hidden all the treasures of wisdom and knowledge."

In the Broadway musical *The Sound of Music* Maria comforts the von Trapp children during an evening thunderstorm by singing them a song about her favorite things. She includes in her list "brown paper packages." We delight to receive a package in the mail, even though wrapped in a plain brown paper cover. We eagerly open the plain package to see what treasure lies inside. Whatever the contents, we appreciate receiving the gift with its mystery inside.

In a very real sense God's greatest gift, Jesus Christ, came to us in the equivalent of a brown paper package. The eternal Son of God slipped into this world as a baby wrapped in swaddling clothes in Bethlehem's manger. Although He was and is the most priceless Treasure possible—the Son of God who has won forgiveness for the world—He did not display His glory (except for occasional glimpses) in the cities and towns of the Holy Land or on the ugly road to Calvary. Rather that Treasure remained hidden in the "brown paper package" of His humility and servanthood. Only in His resurrection and ascension did Jesus Christ shine forth as King of kings and Lord of lords.

The next time you receive one of your favorite things in the mail, think of Christ, your greatest Treasure, for now and for eternity!

Prayer

Dear Lord, thank You for coming into this world for me as a "brown paper package." Let me never be offended by the lowly outward form You took when You were here on earth. Amen.

Favorite Things: Ice Cream Cones

Reading: Proverbs 3:5–10

Text: Psalm 132:15a—"I will bless her with abundant provisions."

One of my favorite things is an ice cream cone. Our family used to live on Main Street. On warm summer evenings we would walk several blocks together to our favorite ice cream stand. There we would order double dips of the best ice cream in the world. Those delicious cones would last all the way home.

An ice cream cone for me symbolizes God's special favor. Yes, He provides bread, meat, and potatoes for the supper table. Daily bread indeed. And I suppose many people enjoy gourmet meals in fashionable restaurants by His grace. But an ice cream cone represents a simple extra blessing of God, a taste treat available to most people, a testimony to God's overflowing care.

God speaks of Zion in the psalm verse: "I will bless her with abundant provisions." Abundant—over and above what is needed for survival. Abundant—delicious and delightful. Abundant—like the overflowing gift of eternal life through Jesus Christ, crucified and risen, who said, "I have come that they may have life, and have it to the full" (John 10:10b).

Favorite things—ice cream cones for a growing family on a hot summer evening and abundant life through faith in Jesus Christ, the Savior!

Prayer

Dear Lord, thank You for Your life freely given for us and for the extra delight of ice cream cones on a summer evening. Amen.

Favorite Things: Thoughtful Notes

Reading: Colossians 4:10–18

Text: 2 Corinthians 3:2—"You yourselves are our letter, written on our hearts, known and read by everybody."

How often I have been encouraged by a thoughtful note written by someone who cares—an unexpected thank you, an encouraging word in time of trouble, an invitation to a family gathering, a newsy letter and word of wisdom. I would place thoughtful notes high on my list of favorite things.

Paul wrote many letters to Christian congregations in Europe and Asia Minor. No doubt they brought much encouragement and counsel to embattled believers. But in his letter to the Corinthians, Paul makes a startling statement, "You yourselves are our letter, written on our hearts, known and read by everybody." He considers them letters of recommendation, attesting to the validity of his apostolic ministry. In their daily lives of purity and service they witness to Christ and encourage both Paul and others.

In short, thoughtful notes become an extension of the sender. We show thoughtfulness by the way we live for Christ each day. Jesus Christ by His death and resurrection is God's love letter to us. We receive that love letter in faith and pass it on to others by the life we live and, yes, by the thoughtful notes we send to others. What a privilege for Paul to say of us, "You yourselves are our letter, written on our hearts, known and read by everybody." Thoughtful notes—one of my favorite things!

Prayer

Dear Lord, thank You for Your love letter to us. Help us to be letters of Your love and to send thoughtful notes to others. Amen.

The Seasons

Reading: Psalm 74:12–17

Text: Genesis 8:22—"As long as the earth endures, seedtime and harvest, cold and heat, summer and winter, day and night will never cease."

Vivaldi's *The Four Seasons* provides ongoing delight to lovers of baroque era music. His musical imagery using violin and orchestra portrays spring, summer, autumn, and winter in succession. Four descriptive sonnets accompany the music.

How much a part of life itself, the seasons. We can count on their regularity, their uniqueness, and their individual character. God describes the seasons to Noah as a promise of His loving presence after the Flood: "As long as the earth endures, seedtime and harvest, cold and heat, summer and winter, day and night will never cease."

Year after year we experience the rebirth of spring, the heat of summer, the colors of autumn, and the cold of winter. While varying in intensity from climate to climate, the seasons nevertheless remind us of God's creative power and His orderly rule in nature.

With the passing of years they remind us also of the reality of death and the ultimate end of this world. We recognize our sinfulness and rebellion against God, even as the Flood marked God's punishment of sin.

For this reason we rejoice that God has sent us a "Man for All Seasons," His Son Jesus Christ. Born at winter's midnight hour, He grew up to walk the roads of Palestine at seedtime and harvest, including a winter visit to Jerusalem (John 10:22). He went to death for our sins and rose from the dead during a glorious springtime and offers us eternal life with Him long after the seasons end.

Prayer

Your bountiful care what tongue can recite?
It breathes in the air, it shines in the light,
It streams from the hills, it descends to the plain
And sweetly distills in the dew and the rain.

Summer and Fall

Reading: Psalm 65:9–13

Text: Proverbs 6:8—"Yet it [the ant] stores its provisions in summer and gathers its food at harvest."

God provides the seasons as a demonstration of His creative power and His love. The warmth of summer brings delight. Crops grow and ripen into maturity. People enjoy being outside. They vacation at the seashore, in the mountains, and by the lake. Golf, swimming, picnics, baseball, and fishing trips abound. Withering heat may also take its toll, and drought may cause serious problems. But the God who causes the sun to shine also sends rains to water the earth. God reigns during summer. The writer of Proverbs summons us to avoid laziness by following the example of the industrious ant which "stores its provisions in summer." We are to make the most of our summer opportunities to serve God.

Fall brings its own unique beauty. The days grow shorter, the mornings and evenings cooler. The first frost comes. The leaves change colors, creating a breathtaking panorama of beauty. Farmers gather in the bountiful harvest in preparation for the harsh winter that lies ahead. The leaves fall from the trees. The cold increases. Winter approaches. Again the writer of Proverbs holds up the ant, which "gathers its food at harvest." God wants us to enjoy the days of autumn but also to make the most of the time so that we are ready for winter.

As we reflect on summer and fall, we recognize on the one hand God's magnificent creation and His boundless provision. On the other hand we come face to face with our own laziness and need for God's help. How thankful we are that God sent His Son to pay for our sins and make us His own. Together with all of God's people we praise Him for summer and fall!

Prayer

You forest leaves so green and tender
That dance for joy in summer air,
You meadow grasses, bright and slender,
You flow'rs so fragrant and so fair,
You live to show God's praise alone.
Join me to make his glory known.

Winter and Spring

Reading: Song of Songs 2:11–13

Text: 2 Timothy 4:21a—"Do your best to get here before winter."

Of all the seasons, winter seems the most threatening. While snow can create a winter wonderland and winter sports enthusiasts love skiing, skating, sledding, and snowmobiling, winter nevertheless suggests cold, darkness, and death. Paul writes to Timothy and asks him to "do your best to get here before winter." He also wants Timothy to bring the cloak he left with Carpus at Troas.

Winter reminds us that we will all die, even as leaves wither and fall and green grass grows brown. We rejoice that Jesus Christ died for us. We rejoice that in winter we have always with us the warmth of God's love and that of His people gathered around Word and sacraments.

Spring follows winter. In describing the beautiful relationship between lovers, the beloved exclaims the words of our Bible reading. Winter is bleak. Spring is glorious. Nature comes alive with buds, blossoms, and leaves. Warmth and gentle winds return. Poets wax eloquent. God showers us with His love.

Because spring gives way to summer, summer to fall, and fall to winter, we cannot base our eternal hope on the beauty of spring. But we can anchor our hope on the resurrection of Jesus Christ from the dead, an event which occurred in springtime. Jesus Christ conquered death for us. His death was all-sufficient for our salvation, His life guaranteeing eternal life for those who believe in Him as Savior.

Thank God for the seasons! As we move through life from the springtime of youth, the summer of maturity, and the autumn of aging to the winter of death, we rejoice in the constant presence of the crucified and risen Christ.

Prayer

This the spring of souls today: Christ has burst his prison
And from three days' sleep in death As a sun has risen;
All the winter of our sins, Long and dark, is flying
From his light, to whom is giv'n Laud and praise undying.

Sin and Salvation in Storybook Land: Peter Rabbit

Reading: Genesis 3:1–19

Text: Genesis 2:17—"You must not eat from the tree of the knowledge of good and evil, for when you eat of it you will surely die."

You will remember that Mrs. Rabbit dressed her children one morning in good clothes and sent them out to play. They could pick blackberries. Only one thing was forbidden—to sneak into Farmer McGregor's garden patch and eat his vegetables. Flopsie, Mopsie, and Cottontail obeyed and happily picked blackberries. Not so Peter Rabbit. He immediately slipped under the fence into Farmer McGregor's garden patch. How good those vegetables tasted!

But soon, to his horror, he found himself right under the accusing eye of Farmer McGregor. "Stop, thief!" the farmer cried out as he chased Peter with a hoe. Peter ran as fast as he could, but he got caught in a gooseberry net. Finally, he barely managed to pull free, but he was forced to leave behind his brand-new coat with shiny brass buttons. Now he raced into Farmer McGregor's shed and jumped into a half-full water can. At last, Peter—exhausted, wet, tired, frightened—managed to wriggle under the fence and escape home. He was sent right to bed without supper, while Flopsie, Mopsie, and Cottontail sat down to a delicious meal of fresh blackberries and milk.

Aren't we often like Peter Rabbit? God has placed us in this beautiful world to enjoy everything as we serve Him. Yet we at times insist on going beyond the fence and indulging ourselves. Initially we enjoy these forbidden pleasures—until we start feeling sick. God, the righteous Judge, starts pursuing us. We know He will find us and that we are guilty. There is nothing we can do to escape, no matter how hard we try.

Recognizing our sin against God, we repent and turn to Him. He sent His Son Jesus Christ to rescue us from our sins. We can stop running and let Him heal and forgive us.

Prayer

Dear Father, help us sinners to stop running away and to receive Your Son as our Savior and Lord. Amen.

Sin and Salvation in Storybook Land: Belling the Cat

Reading: James 1:22–27

Text: Proverbs 14:23—"All hard work brings a profit, but mere talk leads only to poverty."

Once there was a dangerous cat who constantly attacked a group of mice. Eventually the mice decided to summon a council where they could discuss the problem. A young, self-assured mouse came forward with a brilliant idea. He said, "Let's put a bell around the cat's neck. Then whenever he comes near us, we will hear the bell and be able to escape in plenty of time."

The mice nodded their approval. "A wonderful plan, brilliantly conceived. It's bound to work," they cried. "Shall we select a silver bell, a gold bell, or a brass bell? What color ribbon should we use to fasten the bell around the cat's neck?" Enthusiasm grew by leaps and bounds.

At length, a very old, wise mouse spoke. "Wait a moment! I want to ask one question: Who is going to put the bell on the cat's neck?" Complete silence. Several mice nervously cleared their throats. A few shuffled their feet. No one stepped forward to volunteer, least of all the young, self-assured mouse. The elder mouse said, "That shows it's not enough just to talk about something unless you can also do something about it."

Despite what we learned from Peter Rabbit about our rebellion against God, we somehow think we can come up with a brilliant plan to atone for our failures. But can we? We talk a great deal about how our lives will change. We make New Year's resolutions. But how often do we back up our talk with actions? How often we sit at church for hours in meetings and make plans for evangelism, education, and service! Often we believe our task accomplished because we have talked about our responsibilities. As Proverbs says, "Mere talk leads only to poverty."

And so this story shows the futility of our attempts to justify ourselves before God. We need to turn to God's Son Jesus Christ. He alone can save us.

Prayer

Dear Father, forgive us for empty talk. Turn us to Your saving action in Jesus Christ. Amen.

Sin and Salvation in Storybook Land: The Emperor's New Clothes

Reading: Acts 12:19b–23

Text: Proverbs 11:2—"When pride comes, then comes disgrace, but with humility comes wisdom."

There was once an emperor who loved beautiful clothes. One day two men came to his palace claiming to be weavers. They promised him the world's most beautiful suit of clothes. So he hired the men and gave them a generous advance. Day after day they labored, although they had no cloth. After a time the king sent some of his advisers to see how the work was proceeding. They saw nothing, but not willing to risk the emperor's wrath, they returned with glowing praise. Finally the weavers summoned the king to see the finished product and to march in a special parade. Eager to wear the new suit, the king came. Although he could see nothing, the weavers talked about the suit and fitted it to his body with a flourish. "Could I be ignorant?" thought the king. "I can't admit such a thing." And so the king permitted the men to dress him in nothing, while praising them.

When he walked in the parade, none of the thousands of viewers could see anything, but no one dared say a word. Finally a young boy cried out, "Look at the king, he doesn't have any clothes on." But the proud emperor continued to walk in the parade with his head held high, wearing nothing but his birthday suit.

We laugh at the emperor, at his pride and stupidity. But doesn't he mirror our relationship to God? Somehow we think we are such fine people. Pointing the finger at others, we pat ourselves on the back. Proudly we walk before God sporting our "fine" clothes. But God sees us as we really are—poor, miserable, sinful human beings.

But we need not stand naked before God. He offers us a brandnew suit of clothes, made of the finest cloth. He sent His Son to die for our sins and rise again. We can put on the clean robe of Christ's righteousness and stand before God as His beautiful, well-dressed sons and daughters.

Prayer

Gracious Father, forgive us for our pride and foolishness. Clothe us in Christ's righteousness. Amen.

Sin and Salvation in Storybook Land: The Ugly Duckling

Reading: Isaiah 53:1–6

Text: 2 Corinthians 5:17—"Therefore, if anyone is in Christ, he is a new creation; the old has gone, the new has come!"

Once a mother duck hatched her eggs. Little fuzzy ducklings joined their mother, one at a time. One egg took longer to hatch. It looked different from the other eggs. When it hatched, an ugly little duckling emerged. This duckling didn't look or act like the others. She could not swim as well. The other animals ridiculed the ugly duckling for being so different. Finally, the duckling had to set out on her own. She tried to be a farmyard chicken, a dog, and other animals. But she simply failed to belong. All alone and unhappy, the ugly duckling weathered the winter.

In spring the duckling came to a pond where some beautiful white swans were swimming. She started to swim toward them. She expected them to avoid her, but they accepted her and invited her to stay. Then she looked down at the water and saw her own reflection—not the reflection of an ugly duckling, but of a beautiful white swan.

We are all ugly ducklings at first, because of our sinful nature. But God cared about us. He sent His own Son Jesus Christ to be an ugly duckling for us. "He was despised and rejected by men" (Is. 53:3). They nailed Him to a cross, to die. He did not stay in the grave, however, but rose from the dead on the third day as a beautiful white swan.

He makes us beautiful swans too in our baptism. "If anyone is in Christ, he is a new creation." Unfortunately, some of our ugly duckling nature is still with us, but gradually He is transforming us into something new. And someday He will permit us to take our places at His throne forever as beautiful white swans.

Prayer

Gracious Father, thank You for transforming us ugly ducklings into beautiful white swans by the death and resurrection of Jesus Christ. Amen.

You Feed Them

Reading: Matthew 14:13–21

Text: Matthew 14:16—"They do not need to go away. You give them something to eat."

The scene: a lonely wilderness place by the Sea of Galilee. The situation: a hungry crowd of 5,000 men plus women and children. The startling command: You feed them. The disciples ask Jesus to send the crowds away to the villages where they can buy food. Jesus says, "They do not need to go away. You give them something to eat." Taken aback, the disciples reply, "We have here only five loaves of bread and two fish." Impossible!

Does that scene look familiar to you? We live in a world of hungry people—physically hungry and spiritually hungry, hungry at day's end, week's end, and year's end. We recognize their hunger and would like to send them somewhere else for help. Then Jesus startles us with the words of our text. Taken aback, we look at our checkbook balance, our cupboard, and our social calendar. Reporting we say, "We have here only two one dollar bills, a can of sauerkraut, and 15 minutes a week." Impossible! What is that for a hungry world?

But Jesus replies, "Bring them here to me." He proceeds to work a miracle. Having the crowd sit down on the grass, He takes the five loaves and two fish, gives thanks to the Father, and then the disciples distribute it to people. The entire crowd eats, with 12 basketfuls remaining. Impossible? No, not for Jesus working through the disciples.

Jesus says to us, "Bring them here to me." We invite them to come and sit. He takes our gifts and multiplies them for all to receive. Then He asks us to feed them. He has fed us. He gave His body as bread for the world. He feeds us with His body and blood in the Sacrament. And He asks us to distribute our physical and spiritual blessings to the hungry. Impossible? On our own, yes, but with His bountiful grace, no. The Crucified and Risen One supplies us and then commands, "YOU FEED THEM!"

Prayer
O Bread of Life, help us to feed the hungry! Amen.

A Lesson in Faith: Jesus on the Water

Reading: Matthew 14:22–27

Text: Matthew 14:27—"But Jesus immediately said to them: 'Take courage! It is I. Don't be afraid.' "

Feeding 5,000—a heady miracle for the disciples who distributed the food and saw the loaves multiply—surely a faith-strengthener. But immediately thereafter they experience paralyzing fear in a boat. Asked by Jesus to travel alone at night by boat to the other side of the lake, they run into strong winds and high waves. Though seasoned fishermen, the rough conditions and eerie night hour grip them with fear. Add a ghostlike figure walking on the water, and they cry out in terror. Faith tested.

Could a lesson in faith be in order for us? We participate daily in God's Word-and-sacrament miracles among His people. We see others come to saving faith and experience His daily providence in our own lives. But then stormy circumstances arise—difficult family situations, illness and death of loved ones, mountains of bills. We feel surrounded by the eerie darkness of loneliness. When a shadowy figure appears which we understand as a judging and condemning God, fear paralyzes us too. Faith tested.

Help in sight through the darkness. Jesus says to them, "Take courage! It is I. Don't be afraid." Their Friend. Their Savior. Nothing to fear. His voice comforts. The darkness remains. The wind continues to blow. The waves buffet the boat. But they need fear no longer. A lesson in faith.

Jesus walks on the water in the midst of our paralyzing fears and says, "Take courage! It is I. Don't be afraid." He came into this dark world in the little town of Bethlehem. He triumphed over sin and fear in the darkness of Good Friday. Faith tested, the darkness remains. The wind continues. The waves buffet the boat. But our Savior says, "It is I." We need fear no longer. For us too, a lesson in faith.

Prayer

Dear Jesus, thank You for teaching us a lesson in faith on the night waves of Galilee. Reassure us with Your presence. Amen.

A Lesson in Faith: Getting Out of the Boat

Reading: Matthew 14:28–36

Text: Matthew 14:29b—"Then Peter got down out of the boat, walked on the water and came toward Jesus."

The lesson in faith continues. Reassured by the voice of Jesus, Peter boldly asserts, "Lord, if it's you, tell me to come to you on the water." Then he gets out of the boat and walks on the waves toward Jesus. Impetuous? Yes. But nevertheless a genuine faith response to do the impossible.

"Get out of the boat to serve others," Jesus tells us. "Don't just play it safe." Reassured by His voice, we get out of the boat and walk on the water to Him as we serve Him.

But then fear returns. A second test of faith. Peter looks at the waves and feels the wind. Afraid and beginning to sink, he cries out, "Lord, save me!" Problems enough in the boat, but out here on the water, only a watery grave!

We, too, learn the meaning of fear when we step out of the boat. We reach out to others, take risks for the Lord, testify to our faith in Christ. In the process we often take our eyes off Jesus and look at the waves. We begin to sink. Desperately afraid, we cry out, "Lord, save me!"

Immediately Jesus reached out His hand and caught Peter. When they climbed into the boat, the wind died down. A third lesson in faith. Jesus said to Peter, "You of little faith, why did you doubt?" Those in the boat worshiped Him, saying, "Truly you are the Son of God." And they traveled on to land, where they got out of the boat to continue ministering to people.

Recognizing our fear and weakness, Jesus reaches out His hand and catches us, guiding us safely to the boat. Our sin of doubt rebuked, we see Jesus as the true Son of God and our Savior. We follow Him to land and get out of the boat again to minister to people in need.

Prayer

Dear Jesus, sustain me in the stormy waves and strengthen my faith in Your salvation so that I may serve You daily. Amen.

Faith that Works

Reading: Matthew 15:21–28

Text: Matthew 15:28a—"Woman, you have great faith! Your request is granted."

The Canaanite woman has saving faith in Jesus Christ, so her faith works in her life. With Jesus traveling near Tyre and Sidon, the woman demonstrates her God-given faith by crying out, "Lord, Son of David, have mercy on me!" And she is an outsider. We often feel that God is not for us, perhaps for pastors and "strong" Christians, but not for us. But this Canaanite woman looks not to her faith but to her God. Faith in Jesus Christ as Savior works because we have a great God.

The woman comes with faith in God to meet a specific need: "My daughter is suffering terribly from demon possession." Her faith is severely tested. First silence. "Jesus did not answer a word." Then ridicule. The disciples urged Jesus, "Send her away, for she keeps crying out after us." Finally discouragement from Jesus. "I was sent only to the lost sheep of Israel." And further, "It is not right to take the children's bread and toss it to their dogs." But the woman, believing that Jesus can heal her daughter, persists. "Lord, help me!" And again, "Yes, Lord, but even the dogs eat the crumbs that fall from their masters' table." The woman's God-given faith works. Jesus answers, "Woman, you have great faith! Your request is granted." And the daughter is healed from that very hour.

Blessed with God's gift of saving faith, we come to Him with our specific needs—strength in financial crisis, restored health, wisdom in difficult decisions. Our faith is often tested. First silence. No apparent answer from God. Then ridicule. Others mock our faith as they seemingly prosper. Finally discouragement. "Maybe your faith isn't strong enough." By God's grace we persevere. Christ's death and resurrection brings us forgiveness, life, and salvation. We continue to pray with the woman, "Lord, help me!" And He does—in His own way and at His own time, because He has given us freely a *faith that works!*

Prayer
Lord, thank You for a faith that works. Amen.

Learning Still?

Reading: Proverbs 9:1–12

Text: Proverbs 9:9b—"Teach a righteous man and he will add to his learning."

School days. Graduations. Finished at last. You may feel saturated with learning and content just to live a little. However, we never stop learning as long as we live. In our rapidly changing society, everyone struggles to keep abreast of constantly growing knowledge. Who would have expected that computers would become so essential to daily life? If learning stops, we can scarcely adapt to modern life.

Unfortunately, we also may think of our knowledge of God and His Word in terms of graduation. We attended Sunday school and perhaps a Christian elementary school. We received confirmation instruction. Now we think we have arrived!

The writer of Proverbs would disagree. Mockers refuse to learn or accept correction. But Proverbs 9:9 tells us, "Instruct a wise man and he will be wiser still; teach a righteous man and he will add to his learning." The righteous person, declared righteous by Christ's death on the cross, rejoices in salvation and never ceases to want more knowledge about God's love in Christ. Humbly and simply, the wise come to the waters of life again and again for a drink. Not like a cup, which fills with water and can hold no more, but rather like a sponge, which absorbs more and more water, the wise keep learning and sharing with others.

God's Spirit creates in us the desire to absorb more and more of God's good news. The more we live for Christ like a sponge emptying, the more we need to learn like a sponge absorbing. Jesus Christ fills our lives with His forgiving love. Yes, as God's wise and righteous people, we are learning still!

Prayer
Preserve your Word and preaching, The truth that makes us whole,
The mirror of your glory, The pow'r that saves the soul.
Oh, may this living water, This dew of heav'nly grace,
Sustain us while here living Until we see your face.

Prisoners of the Law

Reading: Galatians 3:23–29

Text: Galatians 3:23a—"Before this faith came, we were held prisoners by the law."

Prisons restrict and confine. The days stretch into endless weeks. Usually activities are regimented and restricted. Oh, to live freely again and make choices!

Paul speaks of a different kind of prison when he writes the words of our text. He knew personally the bondage of living by the Law. As a Pharisee he attempted to live a disciplined life in total obedience to God's commands, thereby earning God's favor. After his experience on the Damascus road, he realized that he had been a prisoner of the Law, trying to bear the burden of his sin all alone.

Do you live as a prisoner of the Law? Are you filled with rules and expectations which run your life? Do you constantly feel guilty because you are failing to live up to the standards of others? Do you act out of obligation, guilt, and fear of reprisal? Do you end up unhappy with your performance, burdened to try harder but certain you will fall short? How painful and discouraging to live by the Law! Oh, to live freely again!

Paul discovered the freedom of faith in Jesus Christ. He writes: "You are all sons of God through faith in Christ Jesus, for all of you who were baptized into Christ have clothed yourselves with Christ" (vv. 26–27). Christ lived perfectly under the Law and then died on the cross to break its bondage. He now frees from prison all who trust in Him for salvation. Paul now didn't have to be burdened with the expectations and demands of the Law, because Christ had already carried those burdens.

You, too, can live freely through faith in Jesus Christ. Admitting your inability to keep the Law, you turn to Jesus, who kept it for you. You can now live freely and joyfully.

Prayer

I lay my sins on Jesus, The spotless Lamb of God;
He bears them all and frees us From the accursed load.
I bring my guilt to Jesus To wash my crimson stains
Clean in his blood most precious Till not a spot remains.

Bodies Offered as Living Sacrifices

Reading: 2 Corinthians 11:22–29

Text: Romans 12:1a—"Therefore, I urge you, brothers, in view of God's mercy, to offer your bodies as living sacrifices."

Today people are encouraged to donate organs of their body at the time of death for use in organ transplants. A heart, a kidney, or a liver can bring new life to a seriously ill person.

St. Paul in Romans 12 urges the early Christians to offer their bodies as living sacrifices. He is asking them to commit themselves totally—body, mind, and spirit—to the service of Christ, which he calls a "spiritual act of worship." In many respects a living sacrifice requires much more than a sacrifice of body organs at the time of death. A living sacrifice means daily commitment. Not always or even usually dramatic. Sometimes dull and routine. Time-consuming. Unpopular at times. Often unnoticed. Contrary to human nature. Living sacrifices demand more than we can possibly give on our own power.

That's why Paul makes this a Gospel appeal: ". . . in view of God's mercy." Paul has described God's mercy in the 11 glorious chapters of Romans preceding this text. He is "not ashamed of the gospel" (1:16). He faces the ugly reality of sin and the Law which condemns the whole human race, but rejoices in God's free "gift of . . . eternal life in Christ Jesus our Lord" (6:23b). Jesus presented His body as a living sacrifice in perfect obedience to the Law. He then went to the cross and sacrificed Himself in payment for the world's sin.

In view of this mercy of God, Paul urges us to offer our bodies—ourselves—as living sacrifices. Forgiven and empowered by the Gospel, we freely and joyfully give ourselves to the Lord. We love, care, give, share, witness, and obey in view of God's mercy. Falling short, we repent and receive Christ's forgiveness; then we offer our bodies again as living sacrifices.

Prayer

Dear Lord, based on Your sacrifice of mercy, help us to offer ourselves as living sacrifices each day. Amen.

Metamorphosis

Reading: Galatians 5:19–26

Text: Romans 12:2a—"Do not conform any longer to the pattern of this world, but be transformed by the renewing of your mind."

Paul urges Christians to offer their bodies as living sacrifices. Negatively, he asks them not to conform to the pattern of this world. The Greek word for "conform" suggests a rigid, assembly-line approach to life in which you look and act like everyone else. How boring, drab, and restricted the life of conformity to the world's pattern! Positively, Paul admonishes, "Be transformed by the renewing of your mind." The Greek word for "be transformed" suggests an interesting illustration from the world of nature— metamorphosis.

How does the lowly caterpillar become a beautiful butterfly? The caterpillar looks nothing like the adult butterfly. We are helpless to bring about a change in the lowly caterpillar. Someone quipped, "You can't change a caterpillar into a butterfly by Scotch-taping on wings and sending him to aviation school." But God has provided a marvelous transforming process to accomplish the metamorphosis. The caterpillar or larva passes through an inactive stage in which body changes take place inside a cocoon. When the cocoon is broken open, out flies the colorful butterfly, totally transformed.

In the same way we are by nature lowly caterpillars. We are only capable of conforming to the world. But God sent His Son to live and die for us. From the cocoon of His grave He emerged on the third day as a colorful butterfly, triumphant over sin and death. God transforms us by a spiritual metamorphosis. He works faith in our hearts through His Word and sacraments. Christ lives in us. We are transformed into beautiful butterflies, free to serve Him with our lives. Through our regular exposure to His Word, God renews our minds. We can shun conformity and are transformed to offer our bodies as living sacrifices. Thank God for His metamorphosis!

Prayer
Dear Lord, transform us to serve You. Amen.

By the Sweat of Your Brow

Reading: 2 Thessalonians 3:6–10

Text: Genesis 3:19a—"By the sweat of your brow you will eat your food until you return to the ground."

In September Americans pause to observe Labor Day. How does Scripture view work?

God created human beings to work in the Garden of Eden and care for it. Work must have been a joyful blessing. With the fall into sin, work became more of a burden. God tells Adam, "By the sweat of your brow you will eat your food." Now thorns and thistles would complicate farming. Much sorrow would enter the picture.

Work still represents God's purpose for people. Much blessing and fulfillment accompanies faithful labor. But, like Adam, we toil by the sweat of our brow because of sin in the world. Work problems multiply. Labor-management strife develops. Unemployment affects many. Some work takes a tremendous physical toll. Other work exacts a serious mental and emotional price. Sometimes we deify work and let it rule our lives with no room for God or people's needs. Sometimes we devalue work and become lazy sluggards, expecting others to provide for us. Both distortions reveal our sinful rebellion against a loving God.

But in our labor we remember Jesus Christ. He is the One who worked with His hands as a carpenter and called to Himself rugged fishermen and tax collectors. He did the work of Him who sent Him (John 9:4). In prayer His sweat was like drops of blood (Luke 22:44). He completed His saving work on the cross and rose from the dead.

Jesus knows our needs and our labor problems. He promises to be with us. He restores our work to its joyful significance in God's creation. We continue to toil by the sweat of our brow, but through the sweat we see His face.

Prayer
Father, move us to work joyfully for Jesus' sake. Amen.

The Discipline of Work

Reading: 2 Thessalonians 3:10–13

Text: 2 Thessalonians 3:11a—"We hear that some among you are idle."

There is a lazy streak in all of us. We glorify Tom Sawyer for cleverly getting his friends to do his fence painting. Our nation, founded on the Puritan work ethic, has experienced a breakdown in moral fiber. We watch television for hours at a time and want to be entertained.

Paul writes the Thessalonian believers regarding a similar problem, "We hear that some among you are idle." They expected the immediate second coming of Christ. Therefore many quit their jobs, sat around idly, became busybodies and gossips. Paul strongly condemns idleness: "If a man will not work, he shall not eat" (v. 10).

The problem of idleness stands in sharp contrast to God's purpose of work. Paul urges them "to settle down and earn the bread they eat" (v. 12). Work involves a daily discipline—quiet, steady, positive effort to serve God and others. We carry out God's creation plan and find joy and meaning in the discipline of work. However, in the routine and drudgery of everyday life we often lose sight of God's purpose for work.

Only God can supply the power for work in our lives. Paul writes, "We command and urge in the Lord Jesus Christ to . . . earn the bread they eat" (v. 12). God sent His Son to work for the world. A carpenter's son, Jesus worked tirelessly to proclaim the kingdom of God, to heal the sick, and to teach the disciples. He endured the suffering of the cross for us. His saving work complete, He offers us free salvation based on faith and not the works of the Law. Free from earning salvation, we can work while it is day to serve Him before the night comes when no man can work (John 9:4). Yes, the discipline of daily work provides the foundation for a life of Gospel service.

Prayer

Dear Father, bless our daily work to Your glory, because of the finished work on the cross of Your Son Jesus Christ. Amen.

Witnessing Excuses: Moses and You—No. 1

Reading: Exodus 3:1–12

Text: Exodus 3:11—"But Moses said to God, 'Who am I, that I should go to Pharaoh and bring the Israelites out of Egypt?' "

What a challenge God gives us when He tells us that we will be His witnesses to the ends of the earth! We have witnessing opportunities among family and friends, neighbors, co-workers, and fellow church members.

What a challenge God gave Moses to free Israel from bondage in Egypt. Alone as a shepherd in the Sinai desert for 40 years, Moses, a fugitive from Egypt, is now asked to return to Pharaoh and free his people.

Moses begins to make excuses because he fears the awesome challenge. When God asks Moses to go to Pharaoh, Moses replies with the words of our text. In effect Moses tells God that he is a nobody. What sounds like humility on the surface turns out to be cowardice. Moses, once a prince of Egypt, reared in Pharaoh's household, now feels inadequate for the task.

We often ask with Moses, "Who am I that I should witness about my faith in Jesus Christ to others?" We may have a college education and hold a responsible job, but we feel like a nobody when it comes to witnessing.

God answers Moses, "I will be with you" (v. 12a). He was preparing him in the wilderness. He would send the Messiah to save Moses from his sin. He promises to be with Moses constantly. Hence Moses' first excuse is countered. Because of God, Moses is a somebody, able to go to Pharaoh.

God answers us, "I will be with you." He made us as special people with gifts and abilities. He sent His Son to be our Savior. He made us His children in our baptism. And He promises to be with us each day. We are somebodies, able to witness to others about our faith in Jesus Christ.

Prayer

Dear Father, thank You for making us special in Your sight through Jesus Christ. Empower us to witness to Your love every day. Amen.

Witnessing Excuses:
Moses and You—No. 2

Reading: Exodus 3:13–17

Text: Exodus 3:13—"Moses said to God, 'Suppose I go to the Israelites and say to them, "The God of your fathers has sent me to you," and they ask me, "What is his name?" Then what shall I tell them?' "

Moses presents a second excuse which stands in the way of the liberation challenge. He questions God's identity. He wants to know God's name. Moses really wants that certainty for himself, so that he can go to Israel and then to Egypt's leader.

When God presents us with the witnessing challenge, we also raise the question about His identity. We may frame the question in terms of other people, "What if they ask me about who my God is? What if they ask me theological questions I can't answer?" But we want that certainty about God's identity for ourselves.

God answers Moses' second excuse by telling him: "I AM WHO I AM. This is what you are to say to the Israelites: 'I AM has sent me to you' " (v. 14). He is Yahweh, the eternal, all powerful God who gives life to the world. He will continue to act in the history of His people, bringing them salvation through His Son, the Messiah.

God answers our second excuse with the same clarification: "I am who I am." We see Him as the covenant God of the Old Testament. We see Him in Jesus Christ, the Word-Made-Flesh, who said: "I am the Bread of Life . . . the Resurrection and the Life . . . the Way, the Truth, and the Life." Crucified and risen, Jesus also said, "I am with you always." Assured of God's identity, we have fresh power to witness to His love within our church and out in the world where we live daily.

Prayer

Dear Father, thank You for revealing Yourself to us in Your Son Jesus Christ. Continue to deepen our understanding of Your identity so that we may witness more boldly about Your love. Amen.

Witnessing Excuses: Moses and You—No. 3

Reading: Exodus 3:18–4:9

Text: Exodus 4:1—"Moses answered, 'What if they do not believe me or listen to me and say, "The Lord did not appear to you"?' "

Moses has questioned his own identity and God's identity. Both excuses failed to relieve Moses of his awesome challenge to free Israel from slavery. God promised to be with Moses and identified HImself as Yahweh, the "I AM" God.

Now Moses presents a third excuse: "What if they do not believe me?" What if God's powerful words are called into question? What if people are skeptical about my message?

Don't we raise a similar excuse? We want to witness to our faith, but we fear that others will doubt our message. They may question the Bible or doubt God's power in today's world. How can we possibly accept the witnessing challenge?

God answers this excuse not with words but with actions. He asks Moses to throw his staff on the ground. Moses complies, and the staff becomes a snake. Recoiling, Moses is asked to pick up the snake by the tail, and it becomes a staff again. Moses is then asked to put his hand inside his cloak. Withdrawing it, he sees that it is leprous, like snow. Repeating the procedure, Moses' hand is restored. God also tells him about a third sign— taking water from the Nile and turning it to blood. These signs of God will confirm His powerful words as authentic.

God likewise shores up His powerful words for us with actions. God delivered His people from Egypt with signs and wonders, led them through the wilderness to the Promised Land, and at the right time sent His Son as the Word-Made-Flesh to live, die, and rise again for the world. He acts today in the fellowship of His people through Word and sacraments. He changes lives, heals family divisions, restores people to health, and works in wonderful ways among His people. God's actions confirm His powerful words.

Prayer

Dear Father, thank You for Your marvelous actions in Jesus Christ, which reinforce Your powerful words. Help me to speak Your words boldly. Amen.

Witnessing Excuses: Moses and You—No. 4

Reading: Exodus 4:10–17

Text: Exodus 4:10—"Moses said to the Lord, 'O Lord, I have never been eloquent, neither in the past nor since you have spoken to your servant. I am slow of speech and tongue.'"

Excuses abound when a challenge seems overwhelming. Moses tried to avoid the challenge of liberating Israel. We try to avoid witnessing. But God persists. We are part of His plan.

Moses tries one more excuse, and God becomes angry with him. He claims that he is a poor speaker, lacking eloquence, slow of speech and tongue.

Before we condemn Moses for a feeble excuse, do we not plead the same deficiency? We often claim that we don't have the right words or feel awkward. Strangely, we may be able to discuss current events, sports, and the weather at great length. But we freeze when trying to witness about Christ.

God reminds Moses that He is the one who gives us a mouth to speak. He also promises that He will help Moses speak and even teach him what to say. After Moses tries to bow out, God arranges for Aaron to be his spokesman. All excuses exhausted, Moses heads for Egypt to face his greatest challenge. God brings the victory.

The same God comes to us with His promise of help. He will help us speak and teach us what to say. He provides others to go with us and support us. He sent His Son to the cross for us. He has opened our eyes to see the cross and the empty tomb, the baptismal font and the bread and wine. We have seen, heard, tasted, and touched the living Christ. We have something to share with others. All excuses exhausted, we head for our witnessing challenge. God will bring the victory.

Prayer

Dear Father, thank You for giving me the words to speak and the courage to speak them. Help me to accept the witnessing challenge without excuses, so that many may come to know Jesus Christ as their Savior and Lord. Amen.

Abraham: Test of Obedience

Reading: Genesis 22:1–19

Text: Genesis 22:2—"Take your son, your only son, Isaac, whom you love . . . . Sacrifice him there . . . ."

Whom do you hold dearest in life—a husband or wife, a child, a friend? Imagine being asked by God to give this person up at a moment's notice as evidence of your loyalty to Him.

That's precisely what God asked Abraham to do when He spoke to him the words of our text. Yes, Isaac was Abraham's only son from his marriage to Sarah. For years they had been childless. What a special joy when Isaac was born in their old age! But beyond that, Isaac represented the fulfillment of God's promise to Abraham that he would have many descendants and be a blessing to the world through the promised Messiah.

Now God tests Abraham to the limit, asking him to take Isaac up on Mount Moriah and offer him on an altar as a human sacrifice. How does God test you? He knows the most vulnerable part of our lives—health, family security, financial stability. Problems in these areas become tests of obedience for us.

How does Abraham respond to God's test? He obeys without question. With heart pounding, he saddles his donkey, cuts enough wood for the offering, takes his son to the offering location, binds his son, places him on the altar, and raises the knife. What obedience! An obedience based on Abraham's God-given faith. He had told Isaac, "God himself will provide the lamb." God did spare Isaac and supplied a ram for the burnt offering. He then reaffirmed His promise to Abraham.

God likewise provides for our needs in the time of testing. He sent His Son Jesus to be the Sacrificial Lamb in our place. He died for our sins so that we might live forever. God gives us faith in His promises so that we might be able to obey Him in the midst of trials.

Prayer

The God of Abr'am praise, Whose all-sufficient grace
Shall guide me all my pilgrim days In all my ways.
He deigns to call me friend; He calls himself my God.
And he shall save me to the end Through Jesus' blood.

Joseph: God Uses Evil for Good

Reading: Genesis 50:15–21

Text: Genesis 50:20—"You intended to harm me, but God intended it for good to accomplish what is now being done, the saving of many lives."

Evil stops us. Others treat us unfairly. We try hard but receive little recognition. Power-hungry people use us and then discard us. How easy to grow cynical and depressed!

Joseph could have felt that way. Certainly evil attacked him at every point. He was left in a pit by his brothers and sold as a slave to traders. A slave in Egypt, he was thrown into prison when he refused the advances of Potiphar's wife. But we don't find Joseph complaining against God or growing bitter toward others. He served faithfully in Potiphar's household. In prison he gained trust and respect. When the time came, he was ready to help the country through a famine and bring his family to Egypt.

How often we permit problems and troubles to consume, discourage, and destroy us! Unlike Joseph, we complain and grow bitter. We forget to trust God and fail to obey Him.

Near the end of his life, Joseph's brothers beg forgiveness for the evil they have inflicted on him. In tears, Joseph tells them, "You intended to harm me, but God intended it for good to accomplish what is now being done, the saving of many lives." Joseph recognized God's loving hand in his life. God used evil for good.

Turn from Joseph to Jesus. See Him as One surrounded by evil—tempted in the wilderness by Satan, opposed angrily and unfairly by the scribes and Pharisees, convicted and crucified unjustly by Pontius Pilate. Yet He faithfully trusted the Father, lived obediently, and died to defeat the combined forces of evil. God used evil for good.

He has a plan for your life too. He promises His constant presence. And He wants to use you to carry out His plan for the salvation of the world. God uses evil for good.

Prayer

Dear God, help us to see how You use evil for good in our lives, for Jesus' sake. Amen.

Aging: Prospects for Long Life

Reading: Psalm 92:12–15

Text: Psalm 91:16—"With long life will I satisfy him and show him my salvation."

America is growing older. As the postwar baby boomers age, the population is steadily turning gray as the year 2000 approaches. Because of public health and medical advances, people live longer. Our society is changing as a result. Work, leisure, housing, finance, advertising, health, education, and religion— all are experiencing the impact of the aging of America.

According to God's Word, what are the prospects for long life? The Scriptures seems to link long life with a vital relationship to God. The psalmist says of the God-fearing person: "With long life will I satisfy him and show him my salvation." Of the righteous the psalmist says: "They will still bear fruit in old age, they will stay fresh and green" (Ps. 92:14). According to Proverbs 10:27, "The fear of the Lord adds length to life." God seems to promise long life to those who trust in Him. That long life includes both quantity and quality. "Gray hair is a crown of splendor; it is attained by a righteous life" (Prov. 16:31). Only God makes joyful long life possible.

How do you face the aging process? Do you anticipate problems in your old age? Or do you picture long years of high-quality life? Only God knows your future. He alone can grant the prosperity of long life and joyful years. He sent His Son to die for you so that you might live for Him now and with Him eternally in heaven. He invites you to call upon His name and rest in His shadow. He promises you long life and salvation.

Prayer
Take my life, O Lord, renew,
Consecrate my heart to you;
Take my moments and my days;
Let them sing your ceaseless praise.

Aging: Problems of Growing Old

Reading: Ecclesiastes 12

Text: Ecclesiastes 12:1—"Remember your Creator in the days of your youth, before the days of trouble come and the years approach when you will say, 'I find no pleasure in them.' "

America is aging. Many glowing words can be spoken about retirement, travel, leisure time, and enjoying the fruits of our labor. The fact remains, however, that old age brings many problems as the body deteriorates. Who has not felt the pain of a loved one suffering physical or mental torment as the result of the aging process?

The writer of Ecclesiastes describes the inevitable process of aging in a grim, poetic fashion, demonstrating that everything is vanity. He labels old age as "the days of trouble." He writes, "When the keepers of the house tremble, and the strong men stoop [formerly muscular arms now weak and trembling, strong legs now stooped and gnarled], when the grinders cease because they are few [loss of teeth], and those looking through the windows grow dim [eyesight failing]; when the doors to the street are closed and the sound of grinding fades [loss of hearing]; when men rise up at the sound of birds, but all their songs grow faint [inability to sleep and poor hearing]; when men are afraid of heights and of dangers in the streets . . . Then man goes to his eternal home and mourners go about the streets." Pessimistic, but also realistic. We can make use of medicine, diet, and exercise, and wear eyeglasses and hearing aids, but we cannot stop the onslaught of aging.

Our problems remind us of our need for God. He wants us to trust Him for each day's problems. He has saved us by the suffering and death of Jesus on the cross. We can remember our Creator, not only in the days of our youth but also as we grow older. And we know that the deterioration and decay of our bodies will be followed by the resurrection to eternal life, where "there will be no more death or mourning or crying or pain, for the old order of things has passed away" (Rev. 21:4).

Prayer
In mercy, Jesus, bring us
To that dear land of rest!

Aging: Promises of God's Presence

Reading: Psalm 128

Text: Isaiah 46:4a—"Even to your old age and gray hairs I am he, I am he who will sustain you."

In America increased longevity is a fact. Problems abound for the aging population. But God promises His presence. Through the prophet Isaiah, God speaks the words of our text to the faithful remnant of the house of Judah. God's people were forced into exile in Babylon. Seventy years would elapse before they could return to Jerusalem. Many would grow old and die in a foreign land, separated from the temple of God. How discouraged they must have felt! Enormous problems. Yet God promises His presence. He says, "I am he." Words similar to those He spoke to Moses at the burning bush, identifying Himself as Yahweh. "I am he who will sustain you." He will give them the staying power to make it through difficult times. He promises to carry them when they falter and can no longer walk on their own. He will rescue them with His salvation.

Whatever your problems, God is present with you also. You may be concerned about money, with a meager fixed income and the uncertainty about future medical expenses or the possible need for a nursing home. You may be experiencing failing health and wondering how long you can care for yourself. You may have lost your spouse and struggle with loneliness. You may sense that you are becoming more forgetful and fear increasing senility. Whatever your concerns, listen to God's own promises. "Even to your old age and gray hairs I am he, I am he who will sustain you. I have made you and I will carry you; I will sustain you and I will rescue you." The "I am" God came to earth in the person of Jesus Christ. He carried our burdens, problems, and sins on His own shoulders as He went to the cross. He promised, "Surely I am with you always" (Matt. 28:20b). He sustains you and rescues you in the hour of trial and will carry you home to heaven.

Prayer

Dear Lord, thank You for Your promise to be with me always. Amen.

Aging: Purpose of Long Life

Reading: Genesis 47:28–31; 49:28–33

Text: Psalm 71:18—"Even when I am old and gray, do not forsake me, O God, till I declare your power to the next generation, your might to all who are to come."

All too often society looks at the aging as a special group in need of help. What programs need to be provided for the aging so that they will be able to survive this difficult period?

Nothing could be further from the truth. Everyone of us bears responsibility for growing old with real purpose in life. The psalmist suggests a profound purpose for living: to declare God's power to the next generation. That's what aged Jacob did when he gathered his 12 sons together for a final blessing before he died. He reminded them of God's promise to Abraham by asking to be buried with his fathers in Canaan.

How exciting to picture the elderly reaching out in service to one another and telling the following generations about the power of God! Simeon and Anna, waiting for the Messiah, rejoice at Jesus' birth. John, the beloved disciple, in his later years provides the comforting vision of God's kingdom in the Book of Revelation. Veteran pastors help younger colleagues face the demands of pastoral ministry. Elder statesmen continue to provide leadership for our country. White-haired men and women take their grandchildren by the hand and show them love and guidance. Older women teach young women the almost-lost art of quilting. Retired businessmen offer advice to young people starting small businesses.

Through all of these examples runs a common thread. The aging live with a purpose—declaring the love of God to younger people by word and deed. When we become self-absorbed and self-pitying, He shows us our sin and points us to the self-giving sacrifice of His Son Jesus Christ. Forgiven, we look beyond ourselves to others who need forgiveness and love. We declare God's power until He takes us to continue praising Him before the heavenly throne.

Prayer

Dear Father, fill us with Your purpose all the days of our life. Amen.

Life in a Mini-World

Reading: 1 Corinthians 1:18–31

Text: 1 Corinthians 1:28—"He [God] chose the lowly things of this world and the despised things."

To many Americans bigger is better—skyscrapers, domed stadiums, multinational corporations. But in reality we live in a mini-world. Much of our recent progress traces to the microscope, the transistor, the atom, and the computer chip. Small automobiles, radios, and calculators count for real value in today's world.

As Paul suggests in Corinthians, God has not worked through the wisdom and power of the world but through lowly and despised things. Jesus Christ was born in a lowly manger in Bethlehem, a small town in a subjugated nation. He lived only 33 years. While He walked the dusty roads of Palestine, the Roman legions were marching proudly and successfully through the world. But that one man, Jesus Christ, the Son of God, pursued a mission that would turn the world upside down. He came to give His life on a despised cross. His death brought forgiveness of sins as a gift to the world. By historical accounts at the time, His death was a mini-happening. The big news events occurred in Rome. But Christ's death cost God the precious blood of His Son. And it brought about a new breed of people called Christians, dedicated to glorify God and serve others. Though initially not wealthy or influential, they changed the course of history.

You may view your Christian life as a mini-event, but the example of your life and the testimony of your lips will influence the world. Drawing on the Savior's sacrifice for you and feeding regularly on His Word, you can live boldly for Him in a huge world. God's Son can take your mini-life and use it to help write the story of His salvation large across the world.

Prayer
Dear Father, help me to value my life, though seemingly small, as Your instrument for reaching others. In Jesus' name. Amen.

Living on the Growing Edge

Reading: Luke 2:41–52

Text: Luke 2:52—"And Jesus grew in wisdom and stature, and in favor with God and men."

Although we know little about Jesus' childhood, we do have the story of His visit to the temple at the age of 12. Luke tells us at the end of that story: "And Jesus grew in wisdom and stature, and in favor with God and men."

On the trip to Jerusalem He no doubt grew in many ways. He heard more of the Word of God, which He had been studying. He learned to relate to adults on the pilgrimage and then teachers in the temple. He was challenged to question the teachers and to speak the Word as well. He was being prepared for His public ministry of salvation for the world. If Jesus grew in His relationships to His Father, Himself, others, and His world, should we not also be growing every day?

Bruce Larson in his book *Living on the Growing Edge* describes a favorite teacher who year after year produces classes of children who are motivated to achieve and develop their potential. Her secret: She tries to meet them on their "growing edge," where they are ready and able to learn—not too challenging and therefore discouraging and not too repetitive and therefore boring.

Are you living on your growing edge? What is God teaching you right now? Are you growing "in wisdom . . . and in favor with God and men"? Do you find yourself in a boring rut? Or are you frustrated with too great a challenge?

God knows your needs and has a plan for your growth. His Son lived on the growing edge in daily ministry and on His way to the cross, where He won the victory over Satan. God has made you His own dear child through faith in Christ. You have eternal security. Therefore He frees you to live on the growing edge of service and witness.

Prayer

Dear Father, help me to live on the growing edge in my relationships to You, myself, others, and the world, so that I might serve You more joyfully and faithfully. Amen.

A Key to Miracles: Accepting His Timing

Reading: John 2:1–11

Text: John 2:4–5—" 'Dear woman, why do you involve me?'
Jesus replied. 'My time has not yet come.' His mother
said to the servants, 'Do whatever he tells you.' "

Jesus changes water to wine at a wedding in Cana of Galilee.
Notice how Mary accepts His timing. First, she recognizes and
admits a need. The wine supply is short. Jewish wedding cele-
brations lasted for a week, and hospitality dictated an abundance
of wine. Mary admits the need for more wine and feels inadequate
to handle the problem. Though we claim self-sufficiency in our
public and private lives, we come to the point where we must
recognize and admit our need for help.

Then Mary brings her need to Jesus. She trusts Him to help
her. She simply says, "They have no more wine." We need to
bring all of our needs and problems to Jesus, the One who died
for our sins and asks us to come to Him. Personal, church, and
vocational needs all can be handled by the Forgiver and Healer.

But Jesus seemingly rebukes Mary by saying, "My time has
not yet come." He wants her to learn to accept His timing. He is
saying, "Let Me handle your problems My way and at My time."
His action in this instance relates to His whole mission on earth,
ultimately to His greatest hour, being glorified on the cross. Led
by the Spirit, Mary humbly instructs the servants to do whatever
He tells them. She accepts His timing in faith.

We hear the same words from Jesus, "My time has not yet
come." He wants us to participate in His plan of salvation and
uphold His cross as we humbly trust Him to meet our needs. By
faith we accept His timing.

And Jesus changed water into wine in a magnificent way,
giving glory to God. We, too, witness God at work in a miraculous
way in our lives as He brings many to faith and uses us to point
others to His redeeming love.

Prayer
Lord, help us to accept Your timing in our lives. Amen.

A Key to Miracles: Accepting His Authority

Reading: Matthew 8:5–13

Text: Matthew 8:8–9—"The centurion replied . . . 'But just say the word, and my servant will be healed. For I myself am a man under authority . . . .' "

A Roman centurion comes to Jesus at Capernaum on behalf of his servant who suffers paralysis at home. Jesus offers to go with him and heal his servant. The centurion has demonstrated a genuine compassion. He cares but realizes that he needs outside help, from Jesus.

Now comes the remarkable part of the story. The centurion tells Jesus that he is not worthy to have Jesus come under his roof and adds, "But just say the word, and my servant will be healed." He explains that he is under authority and has soldiers under him to whom he can issue orders. In effect the centurion is saying, "I believe that You, Jesus, have authority to speak the word and heal my servant. I accept Your authority." He then obeys by accepting Jesus' word and returning home to a healed servant.

How often we challenge Jesus' authority like the scribes and Pharisees. We value our own authority over others but question our obedience to Him. Consequently, we also doubt His Word. Then we wonder why we seem to be ineffective Christians.

The key to miracles—accepting His authority. Jesus Christ accepted the Father's authority and lived as a servant. He exercised that authority by reaching out to others. He preached with authority, cast out demons, stilled the storm, and defeated Satan on the cross by His humble obedience.

Jesus likewise healed us, His servants, by paying for our sins, and now He empowers us to trust and obey Him. We accept His authority in Word and sacrament. We help those under our care. We live effective Christian lives as instruments of God's miraculous power. We accept both His timing and His authority as we tell the world about Jesus Christ, our Savior and Lord!

Prayer

Lord, help us to accept Your authority in our lives. Amen.

Jeremiah's Call: The Word of the Lord

Reading: Jeremiah 1:1–3

Text: Jeremiah 1:4—"The word of the Lord came to me, saying . . ."

What is God calling you to do with your life? How can you best serve Him? How do you know whether you are responding to your own desires or to His purposes for your life? These questions challenge every Christian. In the next several devotions we will examine Jeremiah's call into prophetic ministry. While he as an Old Testament prophet received God's call directly from Him, and New Testament ministers of the Word receive their call through the church, we will seek guidelines in Jeremiah for every Christian's calling.

Living in a definite historical setting, "the thirteenth year of the reign of Josiah, son of Amon king of Judah" (v. 2), "Jeremiah son of Hilkiah, one of the priests at Anathoth" (v. 1), received a definite call from God. Not Jeremiah's personal whims, not a carefully worked out vocational plan with the help of guidance counselors, not a radical vision of his own making, but the clear, simple, direct Word of the Lord. That Word, as we shall see in subsequent devotions, provided both the direction and the power to answer God's call. Ultimately, the Word of the Lord was made flesh and dwelt among us, full of grace and truth, namely, Jesus the crucified and risen Savior.

In our specific historical situation, with our own personal background, we turn not to our own whims, or to a carefully contrived plan for reaching the top of the corporate ladder, or to frenetic visions for overcoming mid-life crisis. We simply seek the Word of the Lord speaking to our heart. In that Word, received corporately among God's people and individually in our solitude, we find both direction for daily service and power flowing from the cross of our Lord Jesus Christ, the Word-Made-Flesh. Yes, Jeremiah's call and ours begin with the Word of the Lord.

Prayer

Dear Father, direct and empower me for service through the Word of Your Son, Jesus Christ. Amen.

Jeremiah's Call: Set Apart as Prophet

Reading: Jeremiah 1:4–5, 9–16

Text: Jeremiah 1:5—"Before I formed you in the womb I knew you, before you were born I set you apart; I appointed you as a prophet to the nations."

We listen to the Word of the Lord, addressed to us for our lives. What do we hear? God's Word to Jeremiah issues a jarring call—set apart as a prophet to the nations. "Before I formed you in the womb I knew you, before you were born I set you apart; I appointed you as a prophet to the nations."

Jeremiah lived in a troubled time, much turmoil for Judah, with mighty nations seeking to control and destroy her, much wickedness within Judah, including idolatry, injustice, and reliance on political manipulation rather than on God. Jeremiah a prophet of God in such a time? A prophet to Judah? Overwhelming. A prophet to the nations? Impossible. Yet the Word of the Lord clearly tells him of his call to be a prophet. And God reveals that he has been set apart for this role even before he was born. He has been appointed and prepared all his life for this prophetic ministry. What a call indeed!

And your call? Not exactly like Jeremiah's. Different historical situation. Different person. Different calling. Yet before God formed you in the womb, He knew you. He knew you with His tender love as Creator and with His forgiving love as Redeemer. Christ's death and resurrection avails for you. And before you were born, He set you apart. That's what "holy" means, set apart for God's purposes. Baptized in the triune God, you have been set apart. He has called you in a sense as prophet, as one who "speaks forth" His Word in daily life, and yes, as proclaimer to the nations with a "making disciples of all nations" scope. What a call, indeed!

Prayer

Father, thank You for setting us apart as Your forgiven children. Help us to answer Your call as proclaimer of Jesus' saving love to the nations. Amen.

Jeremiah's Call: Doubts Expressed

Reading: Jeremiah 20:14–18

Text: Jeremiah 1:6—" 'Ah, Sovereign Lord,' I said, 'I do not know how to speak; I am only a child.' "

The Word of the Lord speaks. We hear. "Set . . . apart . . . as a prophet to the nations." A tremendous challenge for Jeremiah. A difficult application for us as modern-day proclaimers of Christ's love. We hear. But now what?

Jeremiah expresses serious doubts about his own ability to answer God's call. He responds, "Ah, Sovereign Lord, I do not know how to speak; I am only a child." He trembles. What good is a prophet who can't speak? Echoes of Moses by the burning bush! How can an immature teenager (which Jeremiah may have been) stand before kings and princes? Good questions. Serious doubts. And Jeremiah would indeed be tested beyond human endurance—physically, emotionally, and spiritually. He would suffer rejection after rejection. But assurance and maturity would come from God's words and His steady presence. But for the moment Jeremiah's doubts remain.

Do you have serious doubts about your ability to speak God's Word and stand boldly as a Christian in difficult situations? Do you feel like a child in your spiritual maturity even though you may have gray hair and a solid standing in society? Like Jeremiah, we can also expect stiff tests of our faith as we answer God's call to service—possible rejections, day-by-day temptations, and flagging zeal. "Ah, Sovereign Lord, I do not know how to speak; I am only a child."

Serious doubts. But God will supply the words to speak, and His forgiving presence in Jesus Christ, the Crucified, to mature us. The call stands.

Prayer

Dear Father, quell our doubts with Your love in Jesus Christ. Amen.

Jeremiah's Call: God's Assurance

Reading: Jeremiah 1:6–8, 17–19

Text: Jeremiah 1:8—" 'Do not be afraid of them, for I am with you and will rescue you,' declares the Lord."

Real doubts about his ability to serve as a prophet to the nations. Jeremiah hears the call and knows that God speaks. Afraid and uncertain, he needs reassurance. The Lord declares, "Do not be afraid of them, for I am with you and will rescue you." Words of promise and comfort. Jeremiah takes the assignment and begins to speak God's Word of judgment and mercy. How he will need those words of assurance as he repeatedly faces kings and priests with a message of repentance! They plot against his life. They arrest and imprison him. They beat him and leave him to die in an open cistern. He wants to die. He complains against God. But he keeps speaking the Word of the Lord. And always there are those words of assurance for him: "Do not be afraid of them, for I am with you and will rescue you."

We need those words also. We hear God's call and know that He speaks to us. We also see the world in which we live—immorality, cheating, scoffing at religion, power plays, social climbing. Real doubts grip our hearts when we try to proclaim the Word of the Lord to our age. But the Lord declares, "Do not be afraid of them, for I am with you and will rescue you." We see the Lord come into a world that rejects Him. We hear the taunts and feel the whip gouge His back. We observe His faithfulness on the cross and hear His loving Word of forgiveness. We experience His forgiveness in our lives and dwell on His continuing Word of comfort. We falter. We speak hesitatingly. We wince at rejection. But we keep speaking His message, for those words of assurance continue, "Do not be afraid of them, for I am with you and will rescue you."

Prayer

Thank You for Your words of assurance to Jeremiah and us. Amen.

Jeremiah's Call:
God's Words in My Mouth

Reading: Jeremiah 20:7–13

Text: Jeremiah 1:9—"Then the Lord reached out his hand and touched my mouth and said to me, 'Now, I have put my words in your mouth.' "

The Word of the Lord came to Jeremiah, announcing his call. He learned that he was set apart as a prophet to the nations. Doubts rose within him that he could not speak and was only a child. God's assurance came with the words, "Do not be afraid of them." Now the Lord provides Jeremiah with the words he will speak as a prophet. "Then the Lord reached out his hand and touched my mouth and said to me, 'Now I have put my words in your mouth.' "

That Word consumes Jeremiah. He later writes, ". . . his word is in my heart like a fire, a fire shut up in my bones. I am weary of holding it in; indeed, I cannot" (Jer. 20:9). He simply obeys God and speaks powerfully against Judah's sins. Sometimes he illustrates the Word with symbols of God's message. But always he communicates God's message. The result—God's Word of judgment is vindicated in the destruction of Jerusalem, and His Word of promise materializes in the new covenant ushered in by Jesus Christ, the Crucified One.

What a powerful description of God's call! He specially entrusted Jeremiah with His very own words of judgment and mercy. He also gives His Word to called and ordained servants as they publicly preach the Word and administer the sacraments. They are to speak God's Word, not their own message. He also touches the mouth of each Christian and puts in His words. We are touched by the Word in Baptism and made new creatures in Christ. We feed on that Word as proclaimed by pastors. And we share that Word with others in our daily calling. Yes, Jeremiah's call has much to teach us about God's call in our lives. And His Word holds the answers.

Prayer

Father, thank You for touching my mouth with Your words of life. Open my mouth to speak to others. Amen.

Living Water and Broken Cisterns

Reading: Jeremiah 2:13–19

Text: Jeremiah 2:13b—"They have forsaken me, the spring of living water, and have dug their own cisterns, broken cisterns that cannot hold water."

Jeremiah speaks to a sinful Judah with powerful imagery. Precious water meant life to ancient peoples in the dry Near East. Attacking military forces laid siege to walled cities and tried to cut them off from their water supply. Now Jeremiah suggests Judah's twofold foolishness. First, they have forsaken Him, their "spring of living water." Second, they have dug their own cisterns, which turn out to be broken and unable to hold water. Their own efforts have failed miserably.

Don't we often try to construct our own cisterns to hold the water of this world? We want wealth, pleasure, success, happiness, recognition. But these cisterns don't hold water. All the while we have forsaken the never-ending spring of living water provided by a loving God. Confession time.

Jesus refers to Himself as Living Water which will forever quench our thirst. Our selfish attempts to trap water for ourselves fail in broken cisterns. But He offers us Himself. He lived, died, and rose again for us. In the waters of Baptism we receive Him as our Spring of living water. The Spirit flows forth from us as we regularly use His Word and sacraments. Broken cisterns abandoned, we come in faith to God's spring of living water, where we invite others to drink as well.

Prayer

I heard the voice of Jesus say,
"Behold I freely give
The living water, thirsty one;
Stoop down and drink and live."
I came to Jesus, and I drank
Of that life-giving stream;
My thirst was quenched, my soul revived,
And now I live in him.

Bush in the Wastelands?

Reading: Jeremiah 17:1–6

Text: Jeremiah 17:5a–6a—"Cursed is the one who trusts in man . . . . He will be like a bush in the wastelands."

Our town features a botanical conservatory. One walks from a seasonal display room through a tropical forest into a desert with barren terrain and cactus. The contrast startles. Jeremiah stoutly addresses a wicked Judah with the real possibility of eternal life in a wasteland.

He writes against their idolatry: "Cursed is the one who trusts in man, who depends on flesh for his strength and whose heart turns away from the Lord. He will be like a bush in the wastelands; he will not see prosperity when it comes. He will dwell in the parched places of the desert, in a salt land where no one lives" (vv. 5–6). How stark and hopeless these words are for those who trust in themselves.

Would Jeremiah describe you as a bush in the wastelands? You may be seeking prosperity, fashioning success with your own hands, and gaining praise from people in the world. But if your heart turns away from the Lord and you depend on flesh for your strength, you will be like an isolated bush in the wastelands, with no hope for the future.

Shocked to attention, we realize our pride and our foolishness. We look to the One tempted in a wilderness to depend on flesh for strength by changing stones into bread and to turn away from the Father by bowing down and worshiping Satan. But we know how Jesus overcame these temptations. On our behalf He was willing to hang, so to speak, on a lonely tree in the wastelands, where He fully paid for our sins. Because He thirsted and died, we need not dwell alone as a bush in the wastelands but can sing His praises forever in heaven.

Prayer
When I survey the wondrous cross
On which the prince of glory died,
My richest gain I count but loss
And pour contempt on all my pride.

Tree Planted by the Water?

Reading: Psalm 1

Text: Jeremiah 17:7a–8a—"But blessed is the man who trusts in the Lord . . . . He will be like a tree planted by the water . . . ."

Leaving the desert in the botanical conservatory, one enters the tropical forest complete with waterfall and lush greenery. What a refreshing contrast to the arid wasteland! Jeremiah offers a similar contrast to Judah in need of repentance.

While disobedience and rebellion against God lead a person to be cursed like a bush in the wastelands, Jeremiah describes the opposite hope: "But blessed is the man who trusts in the Lord, whose confidence is in him. He will be like a tree planted by the water that sends out its roots by the stream. It does not fear when heat comes; its leaves are always green. It has no worries in a year of drought and never fails to bear fruit" (vv. 7–8). How glorious and inviting this description of one who trusts in the Lord!

Would Jeremiah identify you as by God's grace a tree planted by the water? The Savior died for you on that barren tree in the wastelands. A stream of living water flows forth from Him—a stream of healing, forgiveness, and refreshment. God has planted you as a flourishing tree by the waters of Baptism. Repentant of sin, your roots reach out to that living stream. Despite the heat and drought of temptation around you, your leaves remain green, and through God's never-failing supply of living water in Word and sacraments, you bear fruit daily among family and friends, co-workers, and fellow Christians. What a joy to trust in the Lord "like a tree planted by the water"—His water of life!

Prayer

He like a tree shall thrive,
With waters near the root;
Fresh as the leaf his name shall live;
His works are heav'nly fruit.

September 30

The Potter and the Clay

Reading: Jeremiah 18:1–10

Text: Isaiah 64:8—"Yet, O Lord, you are our Father. We are
the clay, you are the potter; we are all the work of your
hand."

We seek control of our own destiny. We want to shape our
future and often the lives of those around us. We forget the Creator and arrogate that role to ourselves.

In Jeremiah's time Judah likewise was headed away from
God and toward gods of human making. So God sends Jeremiah
to the potter's house to observe the potter shaping the clay on
his wheel. He takes a marred piece of clay and totally reshapes
it into a new pot. Unless Judah repents, Jeremiah cries, she will
be destroyed like this clay pot and another nation fashioned in
her place. Strong words of divine judgment on sin!

Isaiah offers a beautiful prayer on the other side of God's
judgment. A repentant Judah in exile will pray, "Yet, O Lord,
you are our Father. We are the clay, you are the potter; we are
all the work of your hand." Willing to let God shape her, God's
people will return home to rebuild.

God, who formed man from the dust of the ground, would
also send His own Son in human form. Begotten of the Father
from eternity, Jesus lived a perfect life of obedience and even
yielded to death on the cross. Because of Jesus' death, we are
now perfect in God's eyes. He also desires to make us a new
creation in Christ and to mold us according to His will. He wants
to use us in His service. He continues shaping and reshaping
us, removing the blemishes and rough spots. By His grace, He
continues to make us what in His eyes we already are.

Prayer
"Yet, O Lord, you are our Father. We are the clay, you
are the potter; we are all the work of your hand. Amen."

Ordinary Days

Reading: Psalm 90:12–17

Text: Psalm 90:14—"Satisfy us in the morning with your unfailing love, that we may sing for joy and be glad all our days."

Special days stand out in our memory—birthdays, graduations, wedding anniversaries, and job promotions. Terrible days likewise sear our minds—the death of a close friend, a serious auto accident, or loss of a job. But what of ordinary days? Same old routine, normal ups and downs, the hours dragging a bit, not much excitement. Most days qualify as ordinary days. How we handle them probably determines how well we live.

Psalm 90 offers us a perspective for dealing with ordinary days. We are reminded of God's eternal presence in our lives. The One who always has existed dwells in our midst. As New Testament Christians we recall how "the Word became flesh and made his dwelling among us" (John 1:14). Jesus Christ, crucified and risen, dwells with us in the midst of God's people. The psalm goes on to expose the reality of our sinfulness and the shortness of our days on earth. We have reason to number our days.

From this perspective on God and the human life span comes our text's approach for dealing with ordinary days. God's unfailing love awaits us every morning, including days that seem like all the others. His love in Jesus Christ cleanses us from our sins and refreshes us for another day of service. We daily remember His unfailing love in the waters of Baptism. As a result, we "sing for joy . . . all our days," the good ones and the bad ones, the special ones and the terrible ones, and, oh yes, the ordinary ones. In fact, because of God's unfailing love a good case can be made for labeling them extraordinary.

Prayer

Let each day begin with prayer, Praise, and adoration.
On the Lord cast every care; He is your salvation.
Morning, evening, and at night Jesus will be near you.
Save you from the tempter's might, With His presence cheer you.

Man's Best Friend

Reading: John 15:12–15

Text: John 15:15b—"Instead, I have called you friends."

You probably know the familiar quotation, "A man's best friend is his dog." A strong case can be made for the truth of this statement. Currently our lovable white and tan "B.J." of mixed breed brings much more than 17 pounds of love into our household. Sometimes naughty and other times a nuisance, "B. J." nevertheless delights each member of the family in a special way. He greets us at the door, romps for his ball, cuddles up close, begs for scraps, and offers to help whether help is desired or not. Somehow he accepts us when no one else will.

You see, we need accepting friends and spontaneous relationships because we don't always deserve acceptance, and people place formal barriers in the way of openness. Consequently, we often wear masks and give grudgingly to others, lest we get hurt in return. But with our dog we can "let our hair down" and not have to worry about the response.

In reality dogs don't replace people in our need for lasting friendship. Our best friend is Jesus Christ. In the upper room He said to His disciples, "I no longer call you servants . . . . Instead, I have called you friends, for everything that I learned from my Father I have made known to you."

Despite our enmity with God because of our sinful rebellion, Jesus laid down His life for us. He covers us with His righteousness and, as a result, God accepts us as His own. Friends of God through Jesus Christ, we can also be best friends to others by accepting them as they are and loving them with God's love. We learn from dogs like "B. J." how to receive Christ's undeserved friendship for us and how to become "best friends" to others.

Prayer

What a friend we have in Jesus,
All our sins and griefs to bear!
What a privilege to carry
Ev'rything to God in prayer!
Oh, what peace we often forfeit;
Oh, what needless pain we bear—
All because we do not carry
Ev'rything to God in prayer!

Coming to the Well

Reading: John 4:4–26

Text: John 4:15a—"The woman said to him, 'Sir, give me this water so that I won't get thirsty . . . .' "

A woman comes to Jacob's famous well near Sychar around noon to draw water. A Samaritan woman, despised by the Jews, she has deeper needs than getting drinking water. She is living in sin. After five husbands, her current lover is not her husband. Does she feel guilty, lonely, and rejected down deep? But she prepares to meet her immediate need for water.

We come to the well often. We are always trying to quench our thirst for physical things—food, shelter, money. At best we temporarily quench our thirst. Like the woman, we have deeper needs. We too have problems with sin, because we have rebelled against God. Do we feel guilty, lonely, and rejected down deep? Yet we continue meeting our immediate need for thirst-quenching.

The woman meets a Stranger at the well, who unexpectedly asks her for a drink and then offers her Living Water that will forever quench her thirst. Not understanding at first, she grows skeptical. Then He exposes her sin and causes her to respect Him as a prophet. She learns that He is the Messiah. He has probed her deeper needs, and now at the well she discovers Him as the Living Water that refreshes her soul. No longer guilty but forgiven, no longer lonely but belonging, no longer rejected but accepted, she rejoices at her new life.

When we come to the well with thirst-quenching in mind, we meet Jesus, who reaches out to us and offers Living Water. Uncomprehending and even skeptical, we probe further. He exposes our secret sin and lays bear our deepest needs. Repentant, we see Him as the Messiah, the One who died for our sins and rose again on the third day. Guilt forgiven, loneliness and rejection replaced by belonging and acceptance, we rejoice in our new life. We continue coming to the well each day and week to meet Jesus.

Prayer

Lord Jesus, thank You for bringing me to the well of Your salvation and giving me the Living Water which forever quenches my thirst. Amen.

Returning from the Well

Reading: John 4:27–30, 39–42

Text: John 4:28–29—"Then, leaving her water jar, the woman went back to the town and said to the people, 'Come, see a man who told me everything I ever did. Could this be the Christ?' "

She came to the well seeking physical water, with deep spiritual needs buried. She returns from the well with those deep needs met by her encounter with Jesus Christ, the Water of Life. Transformed, she has good news to tell her countrymen, the very people who previously looked down upon her for her sinful life. Very simply she tells them, "Come, see a man who told me everything I ever did. Could this be the Christ?" The living water is flowing through her now, for many came out of the town and made their way toward Jesus. We are told, "Many of the Samaritans from that town believed in him because of the woman's testimony" (v. 39a). Later, after talking with Jesus, they are confirmed in their belief that "this man really is the Savior of the world" (v. 42c).

How do we return from the well? There our deepest spiritual needs have been met. We have seen Jesus and drunk deeply of the living water. The water flowed in our baptism and continues quenching our thirst through the Word, wafer, and wine. Like the woman, we return from the well with good news to share. Very simply we need to tell people, "Come, see a man who is the Christ." Living water flows through our testimony. Others will come and see. Others will hear the Word preached and will read, study, and learn for themselves that Jesus Christ is their crucified and risen Savior. The more we come to the well for water, the more powerfully and lovingly we can return from the well with a never-ending stream of living water for the world.

Prayer
Lord Jesus, as I return from the well, let Your Living Water flow through my words to a thirsty world. Amen.

The World Series: Thoughts for the Faith Life

Reading: Hebrews 11:1–8, 20–40; 12:1–3

Text: Hebrews 11:1—"Now faith is being sure of what we hope for and certain of what we do not see."

Hebrews 11 and 12 illustrate the faith life by presenting examples of great heroes of faith. Baseball's World Series with heroes galore sparks some thoughts on our faith in Jesus Christ.

There's something almost religious about a World Series. The true fan radiates undying loyalty toward the favorite team, year in and year out, no matter what the record. Along with loyalty comes a sense of trust. In the fire of intense World Series competition, the fan believes in the popular slugger, fastball pitcher, or manager, even after they fall short a time or two. For every dyed-in-the-wool baseball fan there is a future hope. If the team doesn't make the Series, even if they finish in the cellar, the fan always looks ahead to next year.

Loyalty, trust, and hope for the future are joined by a type of exciting ritual service—a half hour of pregame activities, the formal introduction of players, the singing of the National Anthem, the throwing out of the first ball, the home team taking the field, the first batter digging in at the plate, the seventh-inning stretch, the sweet taste of victory, and then retelling the story of victory to everyone within earshot.

The same ingredients characterize the life of faith. Loyalty to God, unswerving even when the going gets tough and we are outnumbered by the skeptics. Trust in God's promises. We believe firmly that God loves us and has freed us by sending His own Son to suffer and die for our sins. A future hope, that God will complete our joy and give us eternal life in heaven.

Prayer

Dear heavenly Father, graciously fill us with loyalty, trust, hope, and joyful worship so that we may live as Your forgiven children. Amen.

Friends in the Name of the Lord

Reading: 1 Samuel 20:18–42

Text: 1 Samuel 20:42a—"Jonathan said to David, 'Go in peace, for we have sworn friendship with each other in the name of the Lord.' "

What makes a true friend? How many friends do you have? We have many acquaintances but few friends. Common interests, convenience, mutual gain will bind people together for a time. But when trouble arrives, friends can quickly become enemies.

Jonathan and David stand out as a great model of true friendship. King Saul burned with an insane jealousy of David, the slayer of Goliath, the one anointed by Samuel to succeed Saul. David trusted God and obeyed His commands. Jonathan was caught in the middle. As Saul's son, he stood in line to become king and owed his father obedience. As David's friend, he wanted to help him.

The moment of testing arrives. Saul seeks to kill David. David waits in hiding to get word of Saul's intent. Jonathan stands up for David and becomes a target for Saul's spear. He realizes David must flee. According to a prearranged signal, he warns David and then runs to him for a final embrace. In the words of our text he reaffirms their friendship. They were loyal friends because they trusted in the same Lord and called on Him as witness. Jonathan remained loyal until his untimely death on the battlefield. David grieved for his friend and later welcomed Jonathan's son at his own table.

Friends in the Lord. Only God can bind two people together in a lasting friendship. Because of our rebellion, we shun God's friendship. Similarly, we betray friends when selfishness takes over. But God sent His Son as Friend of sinners to die on the cross. Through Christ, God has changed us from enemies into His friends. We, then, can make friends with others.

Prayer Thoughts

Discuss the qualities of a good friend. Describe someone you consider a friend. Thank God for friends and ask Him to make you a friend for Jesus' sake.

Sow the Seed Worldwide!

Reading: Luke 10:1–18

Text: Luke 10:2—"The harvest is plentiful, but the workers are few. Ask the Lord of the harvest, therefore, to send out workers into his harvest field."

My wife and I planted tulip bulbs yesterday before the rain. The bulbs were of high quality. We followed the instructions carefully. Next spring we hope to enjoy some colorful tulips and share their beauty with others.

In Luke 10 Jesus describes a plentiful harvest before sending out the Seventy into the villages of Galilee. Sowing and harvesting both involve sharing God's love with others. When we sow the seed of God's Word, sometimes we are privileged to harvest a soul for Christ, and sometimes someone else reaps the harvest. In either case, Christ asks us to *sow the seed worldwide!*

The harvest is plentiful. Seventy suggests the whole number of nations and therefore a worldwide mission. We start sharing the good news of salvation through faith in Jesus Christ at home but expand our vision to include people from many ethnic groups all over the world. God is preparing a bountiful harvest.

The laborers are few. Starting with 12 disciples, and now 70, Jesus points to the seemingly impossible task. How precious He regards each worker who sows the seed and reaps the harvest! We ask the Lord of the harvest to send forth laborers, and then make ourselves available for that task. He died to pay for our sins. He gives us new life and then sends us out on His mission.

How very much like planting tulips! We sow the seed. The powerful Word of God is of high quality. We follow the instructions carefully by praying and going. We place our planting in God's hands. Next spring we will rejoice to see everything in full bloom.

Prayer
So when the precious seed is sown,
Your quick'ning grace bestow
That all whose souls the truth receive
Its saving pow'r may know.

Going Nowhere?

Reading: Exodus 14:1–29

Text: Exodus 14:11b—"What have you done to us by bringing us out of Egypt?"

Have you ever felt that you were going nowhere? You started out with enthusiasm but soon encountered discouragement, danger, and dull routine. For every step forward, you seemed to take four steps backward. The Lewis and Clark expedition experienced "going nowhere" when they tried to row their huge flatboat *Discovery* up the Missouri River against the current. A few yards of hard-won progress up the river quickly disappeared as the boat hit a sandbar or plunged into rapids. The tired men had to start all over again.

In our text Israel felt they were going nowhere. Excited to leave Egypt, they now found themselves boxed in by the Red Sea and the desert, with Pharaoh's army converging. They railed against Moses, "What have you done to us by bringing us out of Egypt?" Seemingly trapped, the people quickly forgot about God. On their own, they were going nowhere. How familiar the problem!

But God was clearly leading His people somewhere, to the Promised Land. He took the initiative. He instructed Moses to stretch out his hand over the sea, and the Israelites walked through on dry land while Pharaoh's army perished. God's grace makes the difference. When bogged down and discouraged, we look to God for strength and direction. He sent His Son Jesus as "the way" (John 14:6a). He leads us. Ultimately He brings us to eternal life in heaven. Going somewhere indeed!

Prayer
I walk with Jesus all the way,
His guidance never fails me;
Within his wounds I find a stay
When Satan's pow'r assails me;
And by his footsteps led,
My path I safely tread.
No evil leads my soul astray:
I walk with Jesus all the way.

Going Astray?

Reading: Proverbs 1:8–19

Text: Proverbs 14:12—"There is a way that seems right to a man, but in the end it leads to death."

"I'm going somewhere in life. I know my mind. I have confidence in myself." Sometimes we come to a crossroads. One path looks broad and straight, with much promise. The other looks narrow and winding, with an unknown destination. Relying on our own judgment, we may quickly choose the broad path which leads to destruction. As the proverb says, "There is a way that seems right to a man, but in the end it leads to death."

We examine our current path. Are we living mostly for ourselves? Do we value material possessions more than we should? Do we seek recognition, success, and power? Did we start on the right path only to stray away on a yellow brick road which leads to danger? Are we depending on our own wisdom?

God directs us to the only way that leads to life. His own Son walked the narrow path of the cross. Tempted to go astray, He never wavered. Because of His atoning death, God opens to us the narrow way of salvation. He offers protection along the way through His Word and sacraments. He brings us back when we go astray and will bring us at last to heaven.

Prayer

I walk in danger all the way.
The thought shall never leave me
That Satan, who has marked his prey,
Is plotting to deceive me.
This foe with hidden snares
May seize me unawares
If I should fail to watch and pray.
I walk in danger all the way.

Going Straight

Reading: Psalm 1

Text: Proverbs 3:6—"In all your ways acknowledge him, and he will make your paths straight."

The prison doors clank shut for the last time, and the paroled convict marches out into the blinding sunlight carrying his few belongings. The words of the warden still ring in his ears, "We know you have served as a model prisoner in here. Now you have a chance. Are you going straight? It's up to you."

Going straight. Words ridiculed by some, intent on fighting the system. Words treasured by others, determined to make good, to conquer the alcohol or drug problem, to turn over a new leaf. What of us? We have admitted at times going nowhere, bogged down by routine, trapped in our own lifestyle. We have also confessed at times going astray on the alluring road to destruction.

The proverb simply states, "In all your ways acknowledge him, and he will make your paths straight." We can't go straight on our own. The devil, the world, and our sinful flesh conspire to defeat us. But God can make our paths straight. He acknowledges us as His children because His Son traveled that straight path to the cross, where He defeated the unholy trinity mentioned above. In our baptism and Christian education God places our feet on the straight path and gives us the desire and the strength to acknowledge Him in all our ways. Prison doors of sin and death clank behind us, and we walk out into the sunlight of a new life—*going straight,* by God's grace—with heaven as the destination.

Prayer

My walk is heav'nward all the way;
Await, my soul, the morrow,
When God's good healing shall allay
All suff'ring, sin, and sorrow.
Then, worldly pomp, begone!
To heav'n I now press on.
For all the world I would not stay;
My walk is heav'nward all the way.

A Lesson in Grace: Equal Pay for Unequal Work

Reading: Matthew 20:1–16

Text: Matthew 20:14—"Take your pay and go. I want to give the man who was hired last the same as I gave you."

Jesus tells a parable. A landowner goes out early in the morning to hire men to work in his vineyard. He agrees to pay each worker one denarius for the day. He then goes out again at 9:00 a.m., 12 noon, 3:00 p.m., and finally at 5:00 p.m., each time hiring additional laborers. When day is done, the workers collect equal wages. The full-day workers complain but are told they are receiving exactly what has been agreed upon.

We learn a lesson in grace with three parts. First, working in God's vineyard (kingdom) is a privilege. Workers gathered in the marketplace with their tools, desperately needing work because one denarius was required to put food on the table for the family. Today God gives us the privilege of entering His kingdom and serving Him there. The alternative is spiritual hunger and deprivation.

Second, workers are chosen by grace alone. In the parable the owner didn't choose workers based on their merit but simply because he desired to give them work. We are *not* chosen for God's kingdom because we are such good workers. No! Sinners all, lazy, rebellious, self-righteous, we don't deserve the Kingdom. Our work record cannot stand before God for a moment. No, we are chosen by God's grace for Christ's sake through faith.

Third, workers are compensated by grace alone. In the parable all the workers were given the same pay no matter how long they worked. Each, therefore, had enough to put bread on the table that day. Yet the all-day workers complained. We often complain too as we compare ourselves with others. But God gives eternal life in heaven to all who believe in Jesus Christ as Savior, whether they are lifetime believers or deathbed converts. All by grace.

Prayer

Dear Father, help me to work for the Kingdom joyfully and willingly, by Your grace. Amen.

291

Enlarge Your Tent

Reading: Isaiah 54:1–8

Text: Isaiah 54:2—"Enlarge the place of your tent, stretch
   your tent curtains wide, do not hold back."

Israel struggled to survive. Her territory was shrinking.
First, a divided kingdom. Then enemy attacks from outside.
Gone the glory days of David and Solomon. In this pessimistic
setting Isaiah cries out the word of the Lord, "Enlarge the place
of your tent, stretch your curtains wide, do not hold back." The
Messianic kingdom is coming. Many will be added to the people
of God. Even though current conditions look bleak, do not be
afraid. Reach out. God cares.

Today's church often seems outnumbered by her enemies.
Christians fight each other. Christian morality appears to lose
ground in every generation. We may spend time remembering
sadly the glory days of our church in our town. But God says
also to us through Isaiah, "Enlarge the place of your tent, stretch
your tent curtains wide, do not hold back." Jesus Christ has
come. He has paid the price for the world's sin. The Holy Spirit
works powerfully in the church through Word and sacraments.
Don't be afraid. Reach out. Believe God's promise of a mighty
church with believers daily being added.

Open the doors. Give generously. Tell others of Jesus' love.
Prepare your tent for more people. Think worldwide in your vision. God cares. God brings in the harvest of souls. He strengthens us for the great task. *Enlarge your tent!*

Prayer

Jesus shall reign where'er the sun
Does its successive journeys run;
His kingdom stretch from shore to shore
Till moons shall wax and wane no more.
People and realms of ev'ry tongue
Dwell on his love with sweetest song;
And infant voices shall proclaim
Their early blessings on his name.

The Rain and Snow of God's Word

Reading: Isaiah 55:8–13

Text: Isaiah 55:10a, 11a—"As the rain and the snow come down from heaven . . . so is my word that goes out from my mouth."

Words, words, words. So many words bombard us that we take them lightly. As a result, we may also trifle with God's Word—spoken by the pastor on Sunday morning, read out loud and sung in worship, taught in Bible classes, or read silently at home. "The same old words," we say. "I already know that."

But the Word of God creates and saves, as Isaiah says so poetically, "As the rain and the snow come down from heaven, and do not return to it without watering the earth and making it bud and flourish, so that it yields seed for the sower and bread for the eater, so is my word that goes out from my mouth: It will not return to me empty, but will accomplish what I desire and achieve the purpose for which I sent it."

God spoke, and the world was created. "In these last days [God] has spoken to us by his Son" (Heb. 1:2a). "The Word became flesh and made his dwelling among us . . . full of grace and truth" (John 1:14). The apostles spoke God's Word regarding Jesus as the Savior, and many believed and were baptized. As surely as rain and snow water the earth and bring about abundant crops, so surely God's unfailing Word brings new life to His people.

No wonder Paul admonishes us to "let the word of Christ dwell in [us] richly" (Col. 3:16). God accomplishes His purposes for us individually and for His church through His unfailing Word.

Prayer

Preserve your Word and preaching,
The truth that makes us whole,
The mirror of your glory,
The pow'r that saves the soul.
Oh, may this living water,
This dew of heavenly grace,
Sustain us while here living
Until we see your face.

One Thing Desired

Reading: Psalm 27:4–6

Text: Psalm 27:4—"One thing I ask of the Lord . . . that I may dwell in the house of the Lord all the days of my life . . . ."

Many fairy tales revolve around the central character receiving an opportunity to choose one thing. One wish is granted by a genie. Or the king offers one request, up to half of his kingdom. Scripture contains some interesting verses where "one thing" receives attention.

David writes, "One thing I ask of the Lord, this is what I seek: that I may dwell in the house of the Lord all the days of my life, to gaze upon the beauty of the Lord and to seek him in his temple." Aware of many enemies and major problems confronting him, he nevertheless rejoices at the opportunity to worship the Lord. There in God's presence he finds shelter and safety; he experiences victory over his enemies; he sings and makes music to the Lord. The one thing he asks of the Lord is to worship Him perpetually in His house. A rather interesting choice for a warrior and political leader.

Would you choose, as your one thing desired, to dwell in the house of the Lord all the days of your life? Problems loom large. Challenges occupy our attention. But nothing brings greater joy than focusing on the God of our salvation, the One who gave His life as a sacrifice for the world. Dwelling in His house means living for Him each day aware of His saving presence and rejoicing with praise to Him. How thrilling to gather with God's people around Word and sacrament each Sunday in the house of the Lord! It is the *one thing desired!*

Prayer

Open now thy gates of beauty,
Zion, let me enter there,
Where my soul in joyful duty
Waits for God, who answers prayer.
Oh, how blessed is this place,
Filled with solace, light, and grace!

One Thing Needed

Reading: Luke 10:38–42

Text: Luke 10:42—"But only one thing is needed. Mary has chosen what is better, and it will not be taken away from her."

What one thing do you most need? A difficult question. You might answer—a steady job, a marriage partner, a close friend, money for your children's college education. Your answer probably would differ depending on the circumstances. A man lost in the desert might most need a drink of water. The hospital patient awaiting major surgery probably needs the assurance of life. What one thing do you most need?

Martha worried about many things as she tried to host her friend Jesus. Mary sat and listened to what Jesus said. Jesus, referring to Mary's choice, commented: "But only one thing is needed." Hearing God's Word is the one thing needed. Mary no doubt learned about Jesus as the Messiah bringing in the kingdom of God. The Word offers salvation and strength for living.

No matter what our worries and problems, Jesus offers the one thing needed—His Word, which offers us forgiveness and life through His death on the cross for our sins. Taking the time to listen, we learn to live joyfully for Him. His Word helps us to place our other needs in perspective and to receive comfort and direction for daily living. *One thing is needed!*

Prayer

One thing's needful; Lord, this treasure
Teach me highly to regard;
All else, though it first give pleasure,
Is a yoke that presses hard.
Beneath it the heart is still fretting and striving,
No true, lasting happiness ever deriving.
The gain of this one thing all loss can requite,
Can teach me in all things to find true delight.

One Thing Lacking

Reading: Mark 10:17–24

Text: Mark 10:21—" 'One thing you lack,' he [Jesus] said. 'Go, sell everything you have and give to the poor, and you will have treasure in heaven.' "

What do you give to the person who has everything? Quite a problem these days in our affluent society. The rich young man in our text seemed to have everything. He was wealthy. He had a solid religious background, even claiming that he had kept all the Commandments since he was a boy. He therefore assumed that he would inherit eternal life.

Imagine his shock when Jesus said to him, "One thing you lack." He must have wondered what in the world could be lacking. Jesus proceeds, "Go, sell everything you have and give to the poor, and you will have treasure in heaven." He lacked treasure in heaven because he was placing his trust in earthly possessions. Sadly he went away because he had great wealth. He preferred lacking heavenly treasure to lacking earthly treasure.

Do you have one thing lacking? Do you trust earthly wealth instead of Jesus Christ as your only Savior from sin? One thing lacking means eternal punishment in hell. Possessing that one thing means lacking nothing else. As Paul writes, "He who did not spare his own Son, but gave him up for us all—how will he not also, along with him, graciously give us all things?" (Rom. 8:32). Yes, believers in Christ lack nothing!

Prayer

Therefore you alone, my Savior,
Shall be all in all to me;
Search my heart and my behavior,
Root out all hypocrisy.
Through all my life's pilgrimage, guard and uphold me,
In loving forgiveness, O Jesus, enfold me.
This one thing is needful, all others are vain;
I count all but loss that I Christ may obtain!

One Thing Known

Reading: John 9:1–12

Text: John 9:25b—"One thing I do know. I was blind but now I see!"

Often we feel ignorant about theological matters. We hesitate to speak up in Bible class because others might regard our question or comment as foolish. We falter in our witness to the neighbor or friend because we fear that they will raise religious questions beyond our ability to answer. We wish we knew more about God and His Word.

The man blind from birth, healed miraculously by Jesus, could have worried about his theological knowledge. Neighbors asked him about the healing in skeptical tones. The Pharisees with their superior knowledge grilled him and tried to discredit Jesus as a sinner who defiled the Sabbath. But the humble man doesn't hesitate to testify of Christ. "Whether he is a sinner or not, I don't know. One thing I do know, I was blind but now I see!"

Whether or not we have memorized the entire Scripture and have mastered Christian doctrine, we can say, "One thing I know, I was blind but now I see!" Jesus Christ through His atoning death and resurrection has brought us out of darkness into His marvelous light. God's Spirit has restored our spiritual sight so that we know Him as our Savior and Lord. Unafraid we can witness. *One thing known!*

Prayer

He lives, all glory to his name!
He lives, my Savior, still the same;
What joy this blest assurance gives:
I know that my Redeemer lives!

One Thing Remembered

Reading: 2 Peter 3:8–13

Text: 2 Peter 3:8—"But do not forget this one thing, dear friends: With the Lord a day is like a thousand years, and a thousand years are like a day."

Time runs our lives. Either our hectic schedules drive us to race frantically from one day to the next or because of troubles and boredom time drags on endlessly. In either case we easily lose perspective. We live for the moment and forget God's eternal plan.

St. Peter writes to Christians who wondered why Christ had not yet returned for judgment: "But do not forget this one thing, dear friends: With the Lord a day is like a thousand years, and a thousand years are like a day." On the one hand, the Lord loves us so much that He shows great patience. He wants everyone to come to repentance. The length of days also spells fresh opportunities to witness to our faith in Jesus as Savior and to serve God with our lives. What a blessing to fill our days with praise, service, and witness!

On the other hand, the day of the Lord will come like a thief. Every day may be the last day. Urgency prevails. We want to maximize each hour to live thankfully for Him in service to others. Jesus redeemed the time. His short public ministry was filled with obedience to the Father and service to people in need. On the cross the hours must have seemed like years. Yet He endured patiently to save us for eternity. *One thing remembered*—all time is God's time.

Prayer

A thousand ages in your sight Are like an evening gone,
Short as the watch that ends the night Before the rising sun.
Time, like an ever-rolling stream, Soon bears us all away;
We fly forgotten, as a dream Dies at the op'ning day.
Our God, our help in ages past, Our hope for years to come,
Still be our guard while troubles last, And our eternal home.

Fainthearted?

Reading: Numbers 14:1–12

Text: Numbers 14:3a—"Why is the Lord bringing us to this land only to let us fall by the sword?"

What an opportunity for Israel! God sends 12 men to explore the land of Canaan, a land flowing with milk and honey. They come back with a report of a good land, but a land inhabited by powerful peoples and fortified cities. Joshua and Caleb favor trusting God to capture the land. But the other 10 explorers disagree. Israel responds in a grumbling, fainthearted manner: "Why is the Lord bringing us to this land only to let us fall by the sword?" They add, "Wouldn't it be better for us to go back to Egypt?" You know the result of their faintheartedness—40 more years of wandering in the wilderness!

What opportunities we have to live for God today—people ripe for our Christian witness, churches to be planted, missionaries to be sent, Christian schools to expand. We hear about the great possibilities but also about the problems, dangers, obstacles, and high costs. Are we fainthearted as we complain and say no? Do we prefer standing still or going backward to the good old days? This rebellion against God brings serious consequences.

God's Son saw the plan of His Father for saving the world. He also knew the dangers, the opposition, and the high cost of faithfulness. But with a strong heart He depended on the Father and went boldly to the cross, where He won the victory against incredible odds. Through Him and strengthened by His Word and sacraments, we need be fainthearted no more. We can move forward in service and participate in Christ's saving action for the world.

Prayer
Faint not nor fear, his arms are near;
He changes not who holds you dear;
Only believe, and you will see
That Christ is all eternally.

Halfhearted?

Reading: Jeremiah 3:6–11

Text: Jeremiah 3:10—"In spite of all this, her unfaithful sister Judah did not return to me with all her heart, but only in pretense."

One of the greatest ills of American society is apathy. Many citizens do not bother to vote on election day. Civic organizations struggle to find volunteers. People express strong opinions about needed changes, but then do little about making those changes happen. We give only halfhearted support.

Jeremiah writes against Judah for being halfhearted. Her sister nation Israel has openly rebelled against God with adultery and immorality. But Judah stands equally guilty, pretending to love God but not returning to Him with all her heart. In fact, Jeremiah says, "Faithless Israel is more righteous than unfaithful Judah." Halfhearted service to God deserves eternal punishment.

Even as we confess our halfhearted response to God, He promises to be our faithful Husband. He gives us shepherds after His own heart to care for us. They point us to the Chief Shepherd, Jesus Christ, who wholeheartedly obeyed the Father and died for our sins. Jesus draws us to Himself. Forgiven and restored, our love for God increases. The Spirit fills us with enthusiasm to live for God and others. By grace God fills our hearts with praise to Him. With God's heart in us, we are halfhearted no more.

Prayer

On my heart imprint your image,
Blessed Jesus, king of grace,
That life's riches, cares, and pleasures
Never may your work erase;
Let the clear inscription be:
Jesus, crucified for me,
Is my life, my hope's foundation,
And my glory and salvation!

300

Whom Do You Serve—God or Money?

Reading: Matthew 6:24–34

Text: Matthew 6:24—"You cannot serve both God and Money."

Headlines often feature economic news about unemployment, inflation, or the stock market. We rejoice or weep, feel relieved or worried, based on the news as it affects our pocketbook. Who says the Bible doesn't speak to the issues of today? Jesus in His Sermon on the Mount makes the point in clear-cut terms: "You cannot serve both God and Money."

Mammon is the Aramaic word for material possessions. Unfortunately, many people trust in mammon or money like a god. Depending on the situation, trusting money leads either to self-seeking greed (wanting more) or to worry (being anxious about food, drink, and clothes).

While money has a legitimate use as a gift entrusted to us by God, we must not put our trust in it. Money can easily gain a stranglehold on us. We end up serving money instead of God. The root sin is unbelief.

Serving God means regarding Him as the Pearl of Great Price, worth everything we have. Instead of self-seeking, Kingdom-seeking. Instead of worry, trust in God's promises. Serving God means using our money for Him—joyfully, sacrificially, expectantly.

With the choice clear between serving money and serving God, we confess our self-seeking greed and faithless worry. Who can help us? The God who asks us to serve came to us in the form of a servant. Jesus Christ refused Satan's offer of worldly kingdoms and chose to serve the Father. He went to the cross. "Though he was rich . . . he became poor, so that [we] through his poverty might become rich" (2 Cor. 8:9). Made God's children in Baptism, we now serve Him each day as He freely supplies faith to replace our worry, and Kingdom-seeking to replace our self-seeking.

Prayer

Dear Father, transform our greedy, anxious hearts (pursuing money) into serving, trusting hearts (seeking only You), through Your Son, Jesus Christ our Lord. Amen.

Greed: A Dead End

Reading: Luke 12:13–21

Text: Luke 12:15—"Watch out! Be on your guard against all kinds of greed."

Greed, an ugly word. One of the deadly vices recognized already by philosophers in the ancient world. Condemned by the New Testament. The Greek word simply means "wanting more." How deceptively simple, yet how deadly! Just one more piece of candy. Just one more amusement park ride before heading home.

Jesus tells the story of the rich man with a good crop who tears down his barns and builds bigger ones to store his grain and goods. Relishing his plenty, the man plans to take life easy— eat, drink, and be merry. Then comes the door slamming in his face, the evidence that greed leads only to a dead end. God says to him, "You fool! This very night your life will be demanded from you."

Two lessons from the barn builder: (1) Don't seek material wealth instead of God's riches. (2) Selfish acquiring leads to death, generous giving to life. Think about the surrounding culture. Greed prevails under the guise of the good life. Professional sports figures escalate salaries. Television game shows encourage and produce greedy contestants with an insatiable urge for more. And our day-by-day lives quickly fill with the quest for more—savings, investments, cars, houses, and appliances. Selfish acquiring replaces generous giving to God and others. A serious sin to confess.

Comes Christ with life. "For you know the grace of our Lord Jesus Christ, that though he was rich, yet for your sakes he became poor, so that you through his poverty might become rich" (2 Cor. 8:9). The riches of full and free forgiveness. Greed crucified with Christ. Greed-forgiven saints rising to new life. No need for new barns. Rich in God's grace. "Wanting more" no longer, because we already have glorious riches in Christ. "Giving more" now from His inexhaustible supply.

Prayer

Lord, replace my greed with contentment in Your forgiveness. Amen.

An Investment for Eternity

Reading: Luke 12:32–40

Text: Luke 12:32—"Do not be afraid, little flock, for your Father has been pleased to give you the kingdom."

What kinds of investments do you have—insurance, savings, property, stocks, bonds? How secure are they? How well do they prepare you for the future? In preparing the disciples for their future, Jesus describes God's eternal investment in us.

God made a major investment in His kingdom on earth. He placed human beings on earth as managers of His kingdom. Initially God received a very poor return on His investment. Adam and Eve fell into sin. The world rebelled against Him. But God continued investing His love and mercy in His kingdom on earth. In the fullness of time He invested the ultimate, His own dear Son Jesus Christ, who paid the price of giving up His life on the cross. That costly investment produced rich dividends.

God has now made all believers in Christ's death and resurrection co-managers in the work of His kingdom. And to us beleaguered managers, wrestling with worries, burdens, and temptations, Jesus says, "Do not be afraid, little flock, for your Father has been pleased to give you the kingdom."

Jesus moves us to examine our investment portfolio. He urges us to get rid of the investments that fail—purses that wear out, treasures that can be stolen, and clothes eaten by moths. Conversely, He directs us to safeguard those eternal investments given to us by a loving Father—purses that will not wear out, heavenly treasures that will not be exhausted or stolen, and clothes which no moth can destroy. He means the free gift of eternal life based on the forgiveness of sins through His death on the cross. God's eternal investments move us to share our possessions with the poor. We joyfully engage in Kingdom work, serving others, witnessing to our faith, rearing a Christian family, and giving our financial resources to the Lord's work.

Prayer
Father, help me to live unafraid because of Your eternal investment. Amen.

What's Your Measuring Stick?

Reading: John 3:22–36

Text: John 3:30—"He must become greater; I must become less."

When my son was growing up, he was constantly measuring to see how tall he was. A number of marks on the wall told the story. How do you measure your place in life? John the Baptizer uses an unusual measure in our text when he says of Jesus, "He must become greater; I must become less," instead of "I must become greater."

Jesus had arrived on the scene and was calling disciples, some of them former disciples of John. Furthermore, He was starting to gain popularity with the multitudes. Certainly some of John's disciples were concerned. "Everyone is going to him," they said (v. 26). By their measuring sticks, John was failing in his competition with Jesus.

Is your measuring stick, "I must become greater"? Are you seeking recognition, success, advancement, higher income, greater social standing? Do you view your relationship to Christ and the church as an opportunity for personal gain? Do you become jealous when others outshine you or Christ receives the credit? An "I must become greater" measuring stick simply measures our sin and selfishness.

But John was using a totally different measuring stick. He rejoiced that Jesus was active in ministry to save the world—the Lamb of God taking away our sins (John 1:29). He saw his own mission as pointing to Jesus and our need for Him. John now wanted to become less, so that Jesus could become greater. He was content to be friend of the Bridegroom. That was his great joy (John 3:29).

The best measuring stick for us is "He must increase." Jesus loves us, died to save us, and lives to strengthen us in His service. He is our life and hope. The greater He becomes, the greater is our joy.

Prayer

Lord, help me to become less, so that in the eyes of many You will become greater as Savior and Lord. Amen.

The Need for Spiritual Healing

Reading: Matthew 9:1–8

Text: Matthew 9:2—"Take heart, son; your sins are forgiven."

Jesus teaches in Galilee. Crowds gather in a small house to hear Him. Four men bearing a paralytic on a stretcher devise a method to lower the man to Jesus from the flat rooftop. What is the man's greatest need? Obviously he is paralyzed and cannot walk. Jesus sees that the man needs forgiveness. Dead in sin, he needs a miracle of spiritual healing. He cannot lift a finger to help himself. The need for spiritual healing always comes first.

Are you willing to let Jesus diagnose your needs? He comes with a keen eye and a sure knowledge of your condition. He explores every nook and cranny of your life. You may identify a host of physical needs—illness, injuries, financial problems, family difficulties—all very real and painful to you. But Jesus probes beneath the obvious problems to your need for forgiveness and spiritual healing.

Jesus says to the man, "Take heart, son; your sins are forgiven." What sweet music to his ears—sins forgiven! He experiences peace inside. Still physically paralyzed, the man feels unburdened, clean, and whole. Jesus has authority to forgive sins because He is God. He will earn forgiveness for the world by dying on the cross in full payment of sin. Spiritual healing accomplished!

Jesus says to us, "Take heart; your sins are forgiven you." He announces it every Sunday morning in the liturgy, bestows it through the preached Word and the Holy Supper. What sweet music to our ears! Physical problems may remain, but we have peace with God through our Lord Jesus Christ. We feel unburdened, clean, and whole. Thank God for daily forgiveness. Spiritual healing accomplished!

Prayer

Today your mercy calls us To wash away our sin.
However great our trespass, Whatever we have been,
However long from mercy Our hearts have turned away,
Your precious blood can wash us And make us clean today.

The Need for Physical Healing

Reading: Matthew 9:1–8

Text: Matthew 9:6—"Get up, take your mat and go home."

Grumbling in the crowd. Teachers of the Law accuse Jesus of blasphemy for daring to forgive sins. They don't think about the man's need for spiritual healing. They don't rejoice about his forgiveness and new life. They just complain about Jesus exceeding His authority.

Jesus, knowing their thoughts, prepares to address the man's other need, the need for physical healing. "Which is easier: to say, 'Your sins are forgiven,' or to say, 'Get up and walk'? . . . Then he said to the paralytic, 'Get up, take your mat and go home.' " He demonstrates His authority to perform the greater miracle (forgiveness) by performing the lesser miracle (healing the man's paralysis).

The physical miracle is recorded simply and powerfully, "The man got up and went home" (v. 7). No fanfare. No headlines. No vivid, detailed account of the miracle. "The man got up and went home." Yet in those few words we see a man given a new lease on life—no longer helpless, unable to walk, depending on others to carry him, now able to walk and perhaps run and care for himself. A physical need supplied. A precious gift. But not as great or as profound as the spiritual healing of forgiveness.

Today Jesus still goes about the task of both physical and spiritual healing. When He heals physically through doctors or in unexplained ways, He reminds us of His authority to forgive sins and change lives. We can come to Him with our hurts, our diseases, our problems, our concerns, physical and spiritual. He will meet our needs. Always the offer of full and free forgiveness, that inner spiritual healing. Sometimes also the physical healing, meeting our needs on both levels. Jesus still has the same power He demonstrated when He healed the paralytic.

Prayer
Lord, grant Your total healing, that I may praise You. Amen.

Giving vs. Hoarding

Reading: Proverbs 11:24–28

Text: Proverbs 11:24—"One man gives freely, yet gains even more; another withholds unduly, but comes to poverty."

All we have comes from God, and He expects us to share with others what has been entrusted to us. We are indeed to give generously and sacrificially to the Lord and to those in need. And God blesses, not because we have earned it but simply because He loves us.

Or we can choose a life-style of hoarding: "Another withholds unduly, but comes to poverty." We started hoarding when as children in the sandbox we kept our own blocks from our playmates. That same hoarding spirit leads us to withhold gifts from the Lord. Hoarding needs to be labeled for what it is—sin. Though we withhold to gain riches, the proverb is correct in saying that hoarding leads to eternal poverty.

How can we learn to give generously? St. Paul gives the answer, "For you know the grace of our Lord Jesus Christ, that though he was rich, yet for your sakes he became poor, so that you through his poverty might become rich" (2 Cor. 8:9). God freely gave us His Son Jesus to become poor so that we might be rich—rich in forgiveness, grace, and mercy. Because of His death, we are motivated to give.

Giving is living. Hoarding is death. God gives us His Son so that we might adopt a life-style of giving. Keep that in mind as you respond to the many opportunities for giving that are all around us.

Prayer

Grant us hearts, dear Lord, to give you
Gladly freely of your own.
With the sunshine of your goodness
Melt our thankless hearts of stone
Till our cold and selfish natures,
Warmed by you, at length believe
That more happy and more blessed
'Tis to give than to receive.

Wanted: Stewards of God's Gifts

Reading: 1 Peter 4:7–11

Text: 1 Peter 4:10a—"Each one should use whatever gift he has received to serve others."

The scene: first-century Asia Minor. Christians persecuted for their faith. A world to be won for Christ. Desperate need for light in the darkness. "Wanted: stewards of God's gifts. Long hours. Hard work. Purpose: serving others and praising God through Jesus Christ. Reward: probably more suffering." An unlikely want ad? God's people responded with love and service, using their unique gifts within the fellowship to reach an alien world with the saving news of Jesus Christ.

The scene: twentieth-century America. Christians ignored for their faith. Growing secularism and pluralism. A world to be won for Christ. Desperate need for light in the darkness. "Wanted: stewards of God's gifts. Not just an hour on Sunday. Not just a church job. Long hours. Hard work. Purpose: serving others and praising God through Jesus Christ. Reward: probably less credibility with the world." How will you respond? Identifying and using your unique gifts of God's grace to reach an alien world with the saving news of Christ? Or deciding to play the role of spectator on the sidelines, safe and removed from the battle?

Peter describes the key to faithful stewardship of God's gifts: "Do it with the strength God provides" (v. 8). Any gift points to the giver. God freely gave His Son for us all. He lived in a hostile world, used His gifts in love and service, died to pay for our sins, and rose triumphantly from the grave. "The gift of God is eternal life through Jesus Christ our Lord" (Rom. 6:23b). He provides us with His strength to live for others to His praise and glory. "Wanted: Stewards of God's gifts!"

Prayer

Lord, make me a good steward of Your varied grace in my daily life, so that others may trust in You as their Savior. Amen.

Unemployed?

Reading: Psalm 73:21–26

Text: Psalm 73:21–22a—"When my heart was grieved and my spirit embittered, I was senseless and ignorant."

How difficult to be unemployed! You want to work, to earn a living, to pay your bills, to support your family. But you have lost your job through unforeseen circumstances. You are trying so hard to find something, anything, but no one seems willing to hire you. The days stretch out endlessly. The bills mount. Every "no" in an employment line reduces your hope a little more. You feel helpless and worthless. You doubt your ability to perform adequately. You turn inward and spend hours moping. Others try to comfort you, others who have a good job, but their words seem hollow. They pity you and don't understand. You begin to envy those who have a job and to question why God is letting this happen to you.

The psalmist must have felt similarly when he observed his own poverty in the face of the wicked people's success. He cries out, "When my heart was grieved and my spirit embittered, I was senseless and ignorant." He recognizes his own self-pity and bitter attitudes. The psalmist's answer comes from his faith in a caring God who would later send His Son to the cross: "Whom have I in heaven but you? And earth has nothing I desire besides you. My flesh and my heart may fail, but God is the strength of my heart and my portion forever" (vv. 25–26). Words of encouragement for the unemployed. God will guide you through the difficult period and sustain you. He will help you serve others and will in His good time open the doors of opportunity to you.

Prayer

Fear not, I am with you, oh, be not dismayed,
For I am your God and will still give you aid;
I'll strengthen you, help you, and cause you to stand,
Upheld by my righteous, omnipotent hand.

An Autumn Meditation on Sin

Reading: Romans 7:14–25

Text: Romans 7:19—"For what I do is not the good I want to do; no, the evil I do not want to do—this I keep on doing."

I just finished three hours of hard work in our backyard. Autumn leaves had deluged our lawn. I raked and bagged more leaves than I care to count. I mowed the lawn to get any remaining leaves. Now I sit exhausted looking out the window. Already a few leaves dot the backyard. And the front yard, which I cut yesterday, sports a carpet of more leaves. When will the cycle ever end?

I can't help but think of Paul's struggle with sin described in Romans 6: "For what I do is not the good I want to do; no, the evil I do not want to do—this I keep on doing." He adds, "What a wretched man I am! Who will rescue me from this body of death?" (v. 24). When will the cycle ever end?

We share Paul's struggle. Our spiritual nature wants to do right and avoid what is wrong, but our sinful flesh leads us astray. We feel helpless. We rake leaves and bag them, but they just keep coming back like a nightmare. With Paul, helpless on our own, we cry out, "Who will rescue me from this body of death?" When will the cycle ever end?

Paul answers his own question, "Thanks be to God—through Jesus Christ our Lord!" (v. 25a). God's Son has set me free from the cycle of sin and death. The Law could not free me. But Christ paid the full price for the sin of the world. He is our Righteousness. Therefore we are controlled not by our sinful nature but by the Spirit of God. We live by the Lord's power, and so we can defeat sin in our lives every day.

I look out the window and know that while the battle with the leaves will last yet for a week or so, I will win the victory because these dead leaves are almost gone. And I thank God that He likewise has put sin to death and will give me the victory in my daily struggle.

Prayer
Dear Father, help me win daily victories over sin through the victorious power of Your Son Jesus Christ. Amen.

Really Free

Reading: Romans 3:1–20

Text: John 8:36—"So if the Son sets you free, you will be free indeed."

On Reformation Day we celebrate the gift of God to the church through His servant Martin Luther. Luther reminded us of our freedom from the Law in the Gospel of Jesus Christ.

Jesus told the self-satisfied religious leaders of His time, "Everyone who sins is a slave to sin" (v. 34). You see, they thought, "I've got it made." They believed that their birth automatically made them free. In the 16th century many religious people felt much the same way: "I've got it made." Birth and religious vocation give a false sense of freedom. Is it possible for lifelong church members with good records to make the same mistake— "I've got it made"?

Another tragically mistaken group says, "I've got to make it." People in Jesus' day followed the Pharisees and tried to keep their religious laws to the finest detail. Paul once lived by those standards: "I've got to make it." In the 16th century many struggled to gain freedom from guilt through prayers, fastings, pilgrimages, and indulgences. Is it possible that today many depend on church attendance, financial contributions, church work, and acts of service to make it before God? A hopeless task!

Then we eagerly realize: The Son makes me free. Jesus Christ took on the slavery of the Law and died to atone for the world's sin. God declares the world righteous for Jesus' sake. "So if the Son sets you free, you will be free indeed." When Luther discovered that freedom through faith in Christ, the gates of paradise opened to him. We rejoice in our movement from slavery to freedom and live in that freedom.

Prayer

Dear Jesus, thank You for making me really free. Keep me always in that freedom. Amen.

Alive with the Heartbeat of the Reformation

Reading: Romans 3:21–31

Text: Romans 3:23–24—"All . . . are justified freely by his grace through the redemption that came by Christ Jesus."

How vital our beating heart! Often taken for granted, the heart assures circulation of fresh blood. When problems arise, we realize how very important the heart is to the body.

The heartbeat of the Reformation is the Scriptural teaching of justification by grace for Christ's sake through faith. This vital teaching provides fresh life for the church at all times. When this teaching predominates, a healthy church worships, obeys, serves, and grows. When this teaching is neglected, the very existence of the church is threatened.

The early church had heart problems. Paul's opponents held up the Law as the means to salvation. This teaching led either to self-righteousness or despair. Paul writes about this in Romans 3. The 16th century also had heart problems. The church recommended doing penance, buying indulgences, and venerating relics as ways to earn salvation. Once again people became either self-righteous or despairing. Then Martin Luther spoke out boldly. Today's church faces heart problems too whenever we make the Law a means of justification before God. If we think our giving, serving, witnessing, and church-involvement will justify us, we grow either self-righteous or despairing. The church develops sluggish blood, grows tired and breathless.

But Paul renews the church with the ringing affirmation of our text. We stand before the Judge. Are we guilty or innocent? The evidence of our sins against the Law cries out for a guilty verdict. But God looks to the sacrifice of His sinless Son on Calvary and declares us righteous, not guilty. He gives us faith in Christ's death and resurrection, and as a result we are justified by grace. Our spiritual heart beats strong, and we serve Him. The church's heart beats strong, and the Gospel sounds forth to the world.

Prayer

Lord, keep us alive with the heartbeat of the Reformation. Amen.

Building with the Heart

Reading: Nehemiah 4:1–23

Text: Nehemiah 4:6—"So we rebuilt the wall till all of it reached half of its height, for the people worked with all their heart."

What a task! Rebuilding the walls of Jerusalem. The city lies in shambles. After years of captivity in Babylon, a small group returns to the scene of former glory. Where to begin? Led by Nehemiah, the people begin to rebuild the city walls. Opposition mounts. Nearby peoples threaten to attack every day. The Jews have to build with a sword in one hand and a trowel in the other. What obstacles!

But the walls are getting built because the people work with all their heart. Previously Judah's heart strayed from God to idolatry and personal gain. But now, chastened by captivity and repentant, the returning exiles desire with all their heart to restore the sacred city as a monument of praise to God. They are willing to struggle and sacrifice to accomplish the task.

What building does God have in mind for you? A church? A Christian school? Your own Christian family? Whether or not brick and mortar are involved, God calls us to build. What a task! Money seems lacking and relationships often lie in shambles, with much brokenness, misunderstanding, hurt, and jealousy. Opposition mounts as other people say it can't be done. What obstacles!

But we can build when we work together with all our heart. When our hearts stray from God, we get wrapped up in selfish desires and seek material gain. But God shatters our self-serving dreams and points us to His heart, a heart willingly broken on the cross in payment for our sins. Chastened, repentant, restored, forgiven, we begin to build. God gives us a heart for the work. The building proceeds to the glory of God. God's kingdom comes. His church is built into a temple of living stones. What a joy to participate with all our heart!

Prayer

Dear Father, fill our hearts with courage for the task of building Your kingdom. Amen.

God's Building Project

Reading: Nehemiah 6:1–16

Text: Nehemiah 6:15, 16b—"So the wall was completed . . . in fifty-two days . . . . They realized that this work had been done with the help of our God."

Building project complete! Walls rebuilt in 52 days. A major accomplishment. Despite the constant opposition, Nehemiah completes the city walls. Yes, the people build with all their heart. Yes, Nehemiah is a capable leader. But something far more significant leads to this amazing result.

God is the builder! He wants those walls completed. He wants the faithful remnant to praise Him again in Jerusalem. God's people know who deserves credit. They assemble to hear Ezra read the Law from daybreak to noon (Neh. 8:2–3). They then thank and praise God in celebration with Nehemiah's reminder: "The joy of the Lord is your strength" (v. 10c). And even the enemies of the Jews must recognize the rebuilt city walls as God's building project. We are told they lose their self-confidence, "because they realized that this work had been done with the help of our God."

When we participate in the physical building of a church or Christian school, we certainly rejoice when the project is complete. When we see a Christian fellowship growing in size, depth, and closeness, we feel a sense of accomplishment. Yes, people work together with all their heart. Yes, faithful pastors and lay members provide good leadership. But something far more significant is involved.

God is the builder! He wants His church to grow and serve Him. He built His church on the foundation of the apostles and prophets, with Jesus Christ as the Chief Cornerstone. Christ gave His life for the church. We assemble to hear His life-changing Word and to celebrate God's grace in sacramental worship. Even enemies of the Gospel have to recognize that "this work has been done with the help of our God."

Prayer

Dear Father, thank You for the privilege of participating in Your building project. Amen.

Time of Trouble: The Fowler's Snare

Reading: Psalm 91:1–4; Matt. 6:26

Text: Psalm 91:3—"Surely he will save you from the fowler's snare."

The psalms provide a treasure chest of practical help for the Christian life. Psalm 91 especially addresses the believer in time of trouble. The psalmist writes, "Surely he will save you from the fowler's snare." Unsuspecting birds faced serious trouble when a wooden cage was dropped on top of them. Hopelessly trapped, they could not escape.

We are often trapped by our own troubles just like the unsuspecting bird. Other people set traps for us, and sometimes we set traps for ourselves. We may choose the wrong kind of friends and so be led into sin. The fowler's snare drops on us. Trapped.

We develop a hectic pace of life. Work takes long hours if we expect to advance in rank and salary. Social engagements crowd our calendar—part of the good life, we think. We encourage the children to participate in sports, music lessons, and school events. We struggle to make our home and yard a showplace. The fowler's snare drops on us. Trapped.

We spend money to buy necessities and then luxuries which we call necessities. We borrow money to pay for house, cars, boats, and campers. Then we get additional jobs to earn extra money to pay off our loans. But we can't keep up. The fowler's snare drops on us. Trapped.

The psalmist talks about God's rescue. "He will cover you with his feathers, and under his wings you will find refuge" (v. 4a). The mother bird stretches out her wings to protect you from the snare of the fowler. God has rescued you by sending His Son to break forever the snares of sin and death by His death on the cross. When Satan thought Jesus was trapped, the Son won the victory and burst the bonds of death on the third day. Freed from our self-made traps, we are gathered under the warm protective wings of the Almighty.

Prayer
Lord, keep us from getting trapped! Amen.

Time of Trouble: Terror and Pestilence

Reading: Psalm 91:5–16

Text: Psalm 91:5–6—"You will not fear the terror of night . . . nor the pestilence that stalks in the darkness."

The psalmist continues describing times of trouble with the imagery of the terror of night and the pestilence that stalks in the darkness.

We still fear darkness. When a violent storm cuts the electric power supply, we grope for candles. A small child calls out in the night for reassurance.

Dread diseases of mysterious origin strike fear in our hearts. A few years ago Legionnaire's disease caused much concern nationwide. AIDS, with its terminal nature and contagious character, has created panic worldwide. Sometimes we feel that nothing is safe to eat, drink, wear, drive, or breathe! Sickness, whether acute or chronic, creates a time of trouble which drains our energies and brings discouragement.

We also face spiritual and supernatural troubles. Satan attacks at every opportunity, including at night when we are alone with our thoughts. He wants to rob us of peace by magnifying our guilt. We cannot handle physical or spiritual trouble on our own.

But the psalmist suggests the remedy: "He will call upon me, and I will answer him; I will be with him in trouble, I will deliver him and honor him" (v. 15). God promises to shelter us from danger. He sent His Son to penetrate the darkness as the Light of the world. Triumphant on the cross in the darkness of Good Friday, Jesus lives with us and in us. No physical or spiritual trouble can separate us from His love. He also prepares a heavenly home for us who believe in Him as Savior. Whether endangered by the fowler's snare or attacked by pestilence in the darkness, we have God as our very present Help in time of trouble.

Prayer

Father, thank You for rescuing us in time of trouble through Your Son, Jesus Christ. Amen.

Penetrating the Fog

Reading: John 1:7–9

Text: Psalm 119:105—"Your word is a lamp to my feet and a light for my path."

I just returned from driving my daughter to high school through a thick fog. Heavy, dense fog. Visibility zero. My headlights barely penetrated. Cars crept along. Drivers strained to see a few feet ahead. What can penetrate the fog?

Life often seems shrouded in a dense, thick fog. So much confusion in our world. Knotty problems. Moral breakdown. Strident voices. Many conflicting opinions, but no solid answers. Uncertainty regarding the future of the world, our country, our town, and our lives. What can penetrate the fog?

The psalmist suggests, "Your word is a lamp to my feet and a light for my path." Though afflicted with much suffering and tempted to go astray by the wicked, the psalmist continues to trust in the promises and guidance of God's unchanging Word.

The apostle John further identifies that light with the Word made flesh, Jesus Christ: "In him was life, and that life was the light of men. The light shines in the darkness, but the darkness has not understood it" (John 1:4–5). "The true light that gives light to every man was coming into the world" (John 1:9). Yes, the light of God's Word penetrates the fog of sin and death by revealing Jesus Christ as Savior.

The fog remains. We admit the inadequacy of our feeble efforts to penetrate the sin, confusion, and uncertainty of our world. But we turn to God's Word. In it God shines forth to penetrate the fog with His Son, the crucified and risen Savior. We can see again. We can drive confidently through the fog and even light the way for others.

Prayer
Visit then this soul of mine,
Pierce the gloom of sin and grief;
Fill me, radiancy divine,
Scatter all my unbelief;
More and more thyself display,
Shining to the perfect day.

Come for the Cleansing!

Reading: Isaiah 1:15–20

Text: Isaiah 1:18—" 'Come now, let us reason together,' says the Lord. 'Though your sins are like scarlet, they shall be as white as snow.' "

Scripture contains some beautiful "Comes"—God's gracious invitations. Through Isaiah He exposes the rebellion and guilt, the insincere offerings and prayers, of His Old Testament people. He pictures them lifting hands in prayer—hands full of blood. Then Isaiah offers the invitation of God, "Come now, let us reason together. Though your sins are like scarlet, they shall be as white as snow." Those blood-stained hands will be washed clean by God's forgiving action.

These words strike to our hearts. We also rebel against God in many ways, walking from Him to the lure of our selfish goals— money, prestige, power, success. We come to worship piously, only to raise sin-stained hands in prayer. He pleads with us, "Come now, let us reason together. Though your sins be as scarlet, they shall be as white as snow."

We know how God's forgiving action works. We see the blood-stained hands of the Son of God. His nail-pierced hands bore our sins as He died on the cross. We have been washed clean in the blood of the Lamb. Through Baptism we experience a daily cleansing of our sins as we live the life of repentance. How precious those promises to our ears: *Come for cleansing!*

Prayer

Today your mercy calls us
To wash away our sin.
However great our trespass,
Whatever we have been,
However long from mercy
Our hearts have turned away,
Your precious blood can wash us
And make us clean today.

Come for Refreshment!

Reading: Isaiah 55:1–7

Text: Isaiah 55:1—"Come, all who are thirsty, come to the waters; and you who have no money, come, buy and eat! Come, buy wine and milk without money and without cost."

Isaiah describes the plight of a rebellious Israel with wilderness imagery. Because of her sin she wandered in a trackless wasteland with no water to drink. Her captivity in Babylon far from Jerusalem would be a spiritual wilderness. Now God issues the beautiful invitation of our text to a hopeless, despairing people. God's overflowing love is freely poured out for sinners. Refreshing water to drink. Food and drink for sustenance. Spiritual refreshment that lasts forever. All without cost!

In the wilderness of our existence, God also issues an invitation to us. "Come, all who are thirsty, come to the waters . . . ." Having squandered our money on food that doesn't satisfy (v. 2), having rebelled against God, we now come to Jesus Christ for refreshment. He has paid the full price for our sins and offers us spiritual food and drink without cost. The living water of His Word refreshes our parched throats. The solid food of His love and forgiveness nourishes us for daily living. Now we can sound the summons for others to come and drink at the waters and to eat the food freely offered. *Come for refreshment!*

Prayer

I heard the voice of Jesus say,
"Behold, I freely give
The living water, thirsty one;
Stoop down and drink and live."
I came to Jesus, and I drank
Of that life-giving stream;
My thirst was quenched, my soul revived,
And now I live in him.

Come for Rest!

Reading: Matthew 11:25–30

Text: Matthew 11:28—"Come to me, all you who are weary and burdened, and I will give you rest."

Jesus places a yoke of discipleship on each of His followers. His own road to Calvary involved many burdens and trials, but He bore them willingly. He candidly told His followers that they also would experience crosses in their lives. John the Baptist's imprisonment and death for exposing King Herod's sin witnessed to the cost of discipleship.

But Jesus never asks for anything He does not freely bestow. He offers a most comforting invitation to struggling disciples: "Come to me, all you who are weary and burdened, and I will give you rest." "Come to me." All sins and failures are covered by His sacrificial death. "All you who are weary and burdened." He has already shouldered our burdens. He understands them, and He cares about us. He puts His arms around us and comforts us. "And I will give you rest." We don't deserve rest. But He gives us rest nevertheless. Peace in His forgiveness. Shelter from the storms of life. Quiet meditation on His promises. Rest for today and the promise of that eternal rest which belongs to the people of God.

The discipleship goes on with the yoke of obedience shouldered. But He makes our yoke easy and our burden light (v. 30), because of His death and resurrection. He gives rest to our souls. *Come for rest!*

Prayer

I heard the voice of Jesus say,
"Come unto me and rest;
Lay down, O weary one, lay down
Your head upon my breast."
I came to Jesus as I was,
So weary, worn, and sad;
I found in him a resting place,
And he has made me glad.

Come to the Banquet

Reading: Matthew 22:1–14

Text: Matthew 22:4c—"Everything is ready. Come to the wedding banquet."

The beautiful word "Come" fills Scripture. Come for cleansing. Come for refreshment. Come for rest. In Matthew 22 our attention is directed ahead to the heavenly invitation: *Come for the banquet.*

In the parable a king prepares a banquet for his son. His servants invite many to come, but they refuse. He tells his servants to invite the guests again with the news that the oxen and fattened cattle have been butchered, and "everything is ready. Come to the wedding banquet." They pay no attention but work in the fields and tend to business. Swift judgment came upon these ungrateful guests who had mistreated his servants. Now he sends servants into the streets and gathers all they can find to the banquet. The king then provides wedding garments for these new guests.

Our King invites us to the heavenly banquet. All things are ready. His Son Jesus Christ, the crucified and risen Lord, attends as guest of honor. We do not deserve to attend because of our sin. But the King searches in the streets and alleys: "Everything is ready. Come to the wedding banquet." He then furnishes us with the wedding garment of Christ's righteousness, so that we are worthy to enter the banquet hall. Accepting the invitation by God's grace, we also extend the invitation to others as long as we live: *Come to the banquet!*

Prayer
"And whosoever cometh, I will not cast him out."
O patient love of Jesus, Which drives away our doubt,
Which, though we be unworthy Of love so great and free,
Invites us very sinners To come, dear Lord, to thee!

Baking Blessings

Reading: 1 Kings 17:7–16

Text: Luke 6:38—"Give, and it will be given to you. A good measure, pressed down, shaken together and running over, will be poured into your lap. For with the measure you use, it will be measured to you."

Kitchen delight. Baking in process. Sift the flour. Measure and pack down the brown sugar. Stir in the eggs and vanilla. Mix the ingredients. Spoon out the teaspoonfuls on the cookie sheet. Bake. Smell the aroma and eat the finished product. A blessing of God!

As Jesus says, "Give, and it will be given to you. A good measure, pressed down, shaken together and running over, will be poured into your lap." An abundance of grain poured into the fold of the garment for use in preparing the daily meal. The widow of Zarephath discovered that the cruse of oil and flour in the jar never emptied as she continued to bake bread for Elijah and her family. God's bountiful blessing!

Baking blessings. As we prepare good things for others and lovingly use the ingredients He supplies, God's blessings flow in abundance. God spared not His Son but gave Him up for us all. "Freely [we] have received, freely give" (Matt. 10:8). The lesson learned in the kitchen applies to life in the factory, the school, the neighborhood, and the church. "For with the measure you use, it will be measured to you." All by grace. All from God's love. Shared with others freely and abundantly, freshly baked cookies are indeed *baking blessings!*

Prayer
All the plenty summer pours;
Autumn's rich, abundant stores,
Flocks that whiten all the plain,
Yellow sheaves of ripened grain:
Lord, for these our souls shall raise
Grateful vows and solemn praise.

Cleaning the Refrigerator

Reading: Psalm 51

Text: Isaiah 64:6a—"All of us have become like one who is unclean, and all our righteous acts are like filthy rags."

Baking may provide blessings, but cleaning the refrigerator, that's another matter. The refrigerator looks shiny on the outside. What modern kitchen can survive without a refrigerator to preserve food and keep drinks cold? We fill it with produce, meat, and dairy products. We store leftovers for use at a later time. What a service to the family!

But then comes the time for cleaning. Nothing else will fit inside. The process begins. Everything removed. Plastic containers emptied. Spoiled food everywhere. Black and green mold. Heavy glass jars discarded. Soap applied inside. Elbow grease on the sponge. At last sparkling clean and plenty of room! The cycle begins again.

How much our life resembles a refrigerator! Shiny on the outside. Potentially useful to others. Constantly taking in words and experiences from the world, stored for future use. But then we have to examine the inside. "All of us have become like one who is unclean, and all our righteous acts are like filthy rags." Within our rebellious hearts the world's input quickly sours and molds. We are so cluttered that our ability to help others is hindered. Only God can clean us properly. The sins confessed and removed are covered by the blood of Christ. The waters of Baptism continue to cleanse us daily. Sparkling clean in Christ and useful again for service, we begin again the cycle of God's love as we live for Him. What a lesson from *cleaning the refrigerator!*

Prayer

Lord, on you I cast my burden.
Sink it to the depths below.
Let me know your gracious pardon,
Wash me, make me white as snow.
Let your Spirit leave me never;
Make me only yours forever.

Spiritual Dullness

Reading: Micah 4:6–13

Text: Micah 4:12a—"But they do not know the thoughts of the Lord; they do not understand his plan."

"That knife couldn't cut hot butter." Frustration at trying to cut something with a dull blade. "You don't catch on to anything I'm saying." Frustration of a teacher with a dull student. Dull means ineffective and slow.

Micah describes the spiritual dullness of nations gathered against Israel: "But they do not know the thoughts of the Lord; they do not understand his plan." These people may have been powerful and clever, much to be feared, but spiritually they could neither cut hot butter nor catch on to the simplest teaching. Therefore, as Micah prophesies, they will be broken to pieces (v. 13).

Do we have a problem with spiritual dullness? "Called . . . out of darkness into his wonderful light" (1 Peter 2:9), we nevertheless at times fail to understand and live effective lives in relation to God's plan for us. Why? Our sinful flesh rebels against God. Micah promised a new day for Judah after the Babylonian captivity and a Ruler to come out of Bethlehem, One who would "shepherd his flock" (5:2, 4). That Ruler, Jesus, has come to be our Light in darkness, to replace our spiritual dullness with bright understanding and keen-edged living. We turn to His Word for illumination. As a result we know His thoughts, understand His plan, and live joyfully each day. Thank God for His Son, who carried out the Father's plan on Calvary and lives in our hearts forever.

Prayer
Renew me, O eternal Light,
And let my heart and soul be bright,
Illumined with the light of grace
That issues from your holy face.

Spiritual Discernment

Reading: 1 Kings 3:5–15

Text: 1 Kings 3:9a—"So give your servant a discerning heart to govern your people and to distinguish between right and wrong."

The story of Solomon's dream deserves attention. As he began his reign over Israel, God appeared to him during the night and said, "Ask for whatever you want me to give you" (v. 5b). Solomon could have asked for wealth or long life. Instead he prayed, "So give your servant a discerning heart to govern your people and to distinguish between right and wrong."

Solomon showed spiritual discernment by his request and asked for a discerning heart as he governed. He recognized the difficulty of his task and the need for dependence on God's wisdom. God granted his request and promised wealth and long life as well. Unfortunately we also know that in later years Solomon grew distracted by his many foreign wives and his wealth, thus dulling his spiritual discernment.

What better request could we make than for a discerning heart—the spiritual discernment to know the difference between right and wrong, to admit our sins and ask forgiveness, to look to God's Son Jesus Christ, "one greater than Solomon" (Matt. 12:42), as our Savior from sin, and to live joyfully according to God's commandments. Though we don't rule a nation, we also have heavy responsibilities in our home, church, and employment. Only God's gift of a discerning heart will enable us to serve Him wisely and lovingly.

Prayer

Give me the strength to do With ready heart and willing
Whatever you command, My calling here fulfilling.
Help me do what I should With all my might, and bless
The outcome for my good, For you must give success.

Fingers in the Cookie Jar

Reading: Psalm 32:1–5

Text: Proverbs 28:13—"He who conceals his sins does not prosper, but whoever confesses and renounces them finds mercy."

Mother tells Junior, "You can play now until supper. Whatever you do, stay out of the cookie jar. Those chocolate cookies will spoil your supper." Junior plays with one thought dominating his mind—those chocolate cookies. Nothing could ever taste better. Just one cookie can do no harm while Mother works in another room. He sneaks into the kitchen, gets up on a stool, takes off the lid, and grabs a delicious cookie. Time enough to get away. Just one more. With fingers in the cookie jar, Junior hears footsteps and then a voice, "Junior, what did I tell you— no cookies! No dessert for you tonight."

I still love cookies and pass the cookie jar frequently. No penalty awaiting me from a parent, but I still rationalize to myself that one or two won't add any pounds. Then I think of the proverb, "He who conceals his sins does not prosper, but whoever confesses and renounces them finds mercy." We still live with our fingers in the cookie jar. We know what God says in His Word about cheating, stealing, lying, adultery, and gossip. We have much freedom to live and enjoy His creation. Yet our minds focus on the forbidden object or action. We decide that one time won't hurt, and no one will know.

But inevitably we get caught, at least by God, who found Adam and Eve hiding in the garden. With fingers in the cookie jar and chocolate on our face we try to conceal our sin, but to no avail. The better course—openly confessing our sin and asking forgiveness. God sent His Son for us. He defeated those cookie jar temptations and died for our sins. He offers full forgiveness. His mercy—dessert of the best kind. Ahead by grace through faith in Jesus—the heavenly feast. Who needs fingers in the forbidden cookie jar anyway?

Prayer

Dear Lord, help me to come clean with my misdeeds. Point me to Your forgiveness won on Calvary. Help me to desire Your will only. Amen.

Songs of Joy or Wails of Brokenness?

Reading: Isaiah 65:11–16

Text: Isaiah 65:14—"My servants will sing out of the joy of their hearts, but you will . . . wail in brokenness of spirit."

Through the prophet Isaiah, God articulates a clear choice for the people of Israel. On the one hand, those who disobey can expect wails in brokenness of spirit. They provoke God, forget His holy mountain, offer sacrifices to idols, and walk in evil ways. God vows to pay them back in full for their sins and the sins of their fathers.

How easily we can forget God in the midst of our selfish pursuits, follow the example of those who pursue modern idols, and say that we are above reproach! Persistent disobedience can lead to anguish of heart and wails of brokenness when we experience God's wrath against our sins.

But, on the other hand, God offers us salvation freely by His grace. He sent His Son to pay for our sins by dying on the cross. Chosen by Him in Baptism, we sing out of the joy of our hearts. We treasure our inheritance, thank Him for many blessings, hear the answers to our prayers before we even ask, and anticipate new heavens and a new earth which He will create for us. No wonder we fill the air with songs of joy.

"The Sovereign Lord says: 'My servants will eat, but you will go hungry; my servants will drink, but you will go thirsty; my servants will rejoice, but you will be put to shame.' " *Songs of joy or wails of brokenness?* Thank God for the gift of His Son!

Prayer
Oh, grant the consummation
Of this our song above
In endless adoration
And everlasting love;
Then shall we praise and bless you
Where perfect praises ring
And evermore confess you,
Our Savior and our King!

A New Thing!

Reading: Isaiah 43:18–21

Text: Isaiah 43:19—"See, I am doing a new thing!"

Israel lived in the past. Israel developed elaborate laws and practiced formalized religion. Her corporate life resembled a desert wasteland. Disobedient and rebellious, she faced destruction.

Today's church sometimes lives on tradition in the desert of disobedience and rebellion. We often bring God the leftovers and weary Him with our offenses.

Isaiah electrifies the discouraged nation by bringing the Word of the Lord: "See, I am doing a new thing!" He refers to God's new covenant of grace initiated by the coming of the Messiah, Jesus Christ. God will make a new way in the desert, where streams of water will flow to quench the thirst of His chosen people. Jesus by His death on the cross would blot out the transgressions of the world.

That new thing continues to bring new life today. Our society falls over itself for the latest fad and the newest discoveries. These fads quickly fade. But in a modern desert of selfishness, materialism, and rebellion against God, He continues to pour forth the streams of life to quench our thirst. Baptized, we drink the clear, cold water of God's Word and sacraments. Refreshed, we participate in God's new thing which is drawing people to Himself from every nation, tribe, and clan. We witness God at work in our own lives and share His goodness with those around us. "See, I am doing a new thing."

Prayer
Let the earth now praise the Lord,
Who has truly kept his word
And at last to us did send
Christ, the sinner's help and friend.

Trivial Pursuit

Reading: Ecclesiastes 7:5–12

Text: Ecclesiastes 1:2—" 'Meaningless! Meaningless!' says the Teacher. 'Utterly meaningless! Everything is meaningless.' "

The box game Trivial Pursuit captured the hearts of millions of Americans a few years ago. The game appeared at many parties and family gatherings. It has difficult questions in a wide variety of categories such as arts and literature, history, and sports and leisure—questions that challenge the most knowledgeable participants. And the questions stress trivia, often obscure and otherwise unimportant facts but tantalizing morsels for game enthusiasts.

Trivial pursuit, unfortunately, describes the life-style of many people. We choose unimportant goals, waste time on activities without much value, and fill our heads with useless knowledge. Our world bombards us with glittering goods, exotic travel, promising investments, and get-rich-quick schemes. We often pursue the trivial, forgetting eternal values.

The Teacher in Ecclesiastes points out the trivial nature of most things: "Meaningless! Meaningless! Utterly meaningless! Everything is meaningless." While admittedly pessimistic, the Teacher helps us to question values and choices. By contrast, says the same writer, "Wisdom, like an inheritance, is a good thing and benefits those who see the sun" (Eccl. 7:11). In our New Testament understanding, wisdom refers to a right relationship with God. He sent His Son, the Word made flesh (John 1:14) to live and die for our sins. Christ is the Power and Wisdom of God. Because of His faithful pursuit of the cross, we can live with clear goals of service and witness as members of God's family. In the light of eternity, no trivial pursuits for us!

Prayer
Forth in your name, O Lord, I go,
My daily labor to pursue,
You, only you, resolved to know
In all I think or speak or do.

Monopoly

Reading: Ecclesiastes 5:8–20

Text: Ecclesiastes 5:10—"Whoever loves money never has money enough; whoever loves wealth is never satisfied with his income. This too is meaningless."

How I used to love the board game Monopoly! I would eagerly purchase all the property I could afford and start placing houses and hotels on it. My excitement grew as I won more and more money and continued amassing property. Of course, sometimes I lost everything I had while someone else grew wealthy. Monopoly has experienced enduring sales over the past 50 years. Obviously a strong appeal to game lovers.

Monopoly mirrors life. The Teacher in Ecclesiastes refers to our insatiable desire for material possessions: "Whoever loves money never has money enough; whoever loves wealth is never satisfied with his income." We want more money, clothes, televisions, automobiles, and the list goes on. We think we can handle additional income circumspectly, but our sinful nature pushes us to spend and keep it for ourselves. We seek monopoly in the sense that we want to amass wealth, even if it comes at the expense of others. The Teacher cuts us short: "This too is meaningless." We need to face reality, to admit the fleeting nature of possessions and to repent of our greed.

Enter God. He shares abundantly with the righteous and the unrighteous alike (Matt. 5:45b). He gives everything away. He gave us His Son, who gave His life for us on Calvary. Jesus learned contentment in doing the Father's will. Now in possession of the free gift of eternal life, we can spend a lifetime not gaining a monopoly, but giving everything away to others—our life, our Savior, and our material possessions. Such a life-style will not be judged "meaningless."

Prayer

All that I am and have, Thy gifts so free,
In joy, in grief, through life, Dear Lord, for thee!
And when thy face I see, My ransomed soul shall be
Through all eternity Something for thee.

Clue

Reading: Ecclesiastes 12:9–14

Text: Ecclesiastes 12:13—"Now all has been heard; here is the conclusion of the matter: Fear God and keep his commandments, for this is the whole duty of man."

A third popular board game, Clue, engages the players in a who-done-it mystery. A murder has been committed, and the purpose of the game is to identify the murderer, the weapon, and the location of the murder. Clues are provided to lead toward a solution, but usually one clue sheds the most light on the mystery.

How does one make sense out of the game of life? With all the confusing values, philosophies, and life-styles, how does one choose the right path? What clues can lead to a solution? The Teacher in Ecclesiastes has systematically eliminated one option after another—knowledge, wealth, and pleasure.

But the significant clue comes near the end of the book: "Now all has been heard; here is the conclusion of the matter: Fear God and keep his commandments, for this is the whole duty of man." The clue comes from God, not from human beings. God wants us to fear Him and keep His commandments: "Love the Lord your God and your neighbor as yourself" (Matt. 22:37, 39). Not selfish living, but selfless living.

The clue points toward the solution. We can't fear God or keep His commandments on our own. That's why God sent His Son to live the life and pay the price. A murder in a sense. They nailed Him to a tree. But in the end He did it Himself. He willingly died for us on Calvary. Now you know the solution for your life. He works faith in your heart. He instills in you a fear of God and obedience to His commandments. Purpose for living. Sure hope in dying. The saving clue—Christ crucified.

Prayer
Not the labors of my hands
Can fulfill thy law's demands;
Could my zeal no respite know,
Could my tears forever flow,
All for sin could not atone;
Thou must save, and thou alone.

Our Family: Together in Thanksgiving

Reading: Psalm 128

Text: Psalm 128:1, 3—"Blessed are all who fear the Lord, who walk in his ways . . . . Your wife will be like a fruitful vine within your house; your sons will be like olive shoots around your table."

With the Thanksgiving holiday approaching, we think of celebrating together with our families or at least remember the many family blessings of the past. The ideal Thanksgiving dinner pictures a bountifully laden table with the family gathered around it.

In reality the Thanksgiving meal often features bickering and complaining. "Mom, she's taking all the white meat." "Why are there so many onions in the dressing?" "Can I be excused to watch football on television?" "No one thanks me for the meal—all that work and no appreciation!" "Will everyone be quiet? I can't stand all the nagging and the noise. Why can't we relax on a holiday?"

The psalmist, however, describes how family togetherness can be a reality. "Blessed are all who fear the Lord, who walk in his ways." God sent His Son Jesus for us. At the cross He bridged all divisions between God and human beings, including families. God chooses us as His own people in our baptism and brings us to faith in Christ. As we grow in faith, He fills us with reverence and obedience. By His power we reach out to our family members at Thanksgiving and throughout the year.

What blessings flow from God to us by His grace! "You will eat the fruit of your labor; blessings and prosperity will be yours. Your wife will be like a fruitful vine within your house; your sons will be like olive shoots around your table" (vv. 2–3). By faith we rejoice in God's Thanksgiving blessings. *Our family: together in thanksgiving.*

Prayer

With voices united our praises we offer
And gladly our songs of thanksgiving we raise.
With you, Lord, beside us, your strong arm will guide us.
To you, our great Redeemer, forever be praise!

Have You Learned to Be Content?

Reading: Philippians 4:10–20

Text: Philippians 4:11b—"I have learned to be content whatever the circumstances."

A picture of contentment. The family gathers around the bountiful Thanksgiving table with turkey and all the trimmings. Norman Rockwell captures the moment. A precious but fleeting moment. The larger question, however: Have you learned to be content?

Leaving the serene Thanksgiving tableau, many live in perpetual discontent, ruled by circumstances. Paul writes to the Philippians that "whether well fed or hungry, whether living in plenty or in want" (v. 12c), he has learned to be content. For the discontented, circumstances always spell trouble. Never enough. Always wanting more, more, more. We want more wages, profits, possessions. Perhaps we even want more of the turkey's white meat than the person sitting next to us.

Some seek a false contentment. They strive to be self-sufficient and self-satisfied. The Stoics used the Greek word for contentment to describe a life-style of wanting little and not caring. Both desire and feelings were eliminated by an act of the will. Such an attempt at self-imposed contentment robs us of joy and peace.

Paul describes true contentment as Christ-sufficient and Christ-satisfied. "I can do everything through him who gives me strength" (v. 13). Jesus Christ was content to do the Father's bidding. He came to earth in difficult circumstances, with the forces of hell pitted against Him. Yet He could enjoy the lilies of the field, sleep peacefully in a storm-tossed boat, stand silent before His tormentors, and ultimately cry, "It is finished" (John 19:30). "He died for all" (2 Cor. 5:15a). He forgives sins of both discontent and false contentment.

As you celebrate Thanksgiving and savor the pumpkin pie, learn the meaning of true contentment—doing everything through Christ, who strengthens us.

Prayer
Lord, let me rest content in Your salvation. Amen.

Thanksgiving Confession and Praise

Reading: Psalm 103:1–5

Text: Luke 17:18—"Was no one found to return and give praise to God except this foreigner?"

Aware of God's overflowing blessings recorded in Psalm 103 and conscious of being more often like the nine cleansed lepers than the one who returned to give thanks, we confess to God:

O Lord, we come before You as often thankless people—
    rich in turkey and dressing, but poor in thanks,
    rich in houses, cars, and TV sets, but poor in thanks,
For our thanklessness, forgive us Lord.
We often forget to thank You, Lord—
    for comfortable homes and abundant food,
    for pardon and forgiveness,
    for Your suffering and death on the cross,
    for Your resurrection and ascension,
    for our baptism and new life,
    for togetherness with Your family.
For our forgetfulness, forgive us, Lord.
Sometimes, Lord, we are thankful for blessings,
but not thankful enough to share them with others—
    our new-found life with the lost,
    our food with the hungry,
    our clothes with the ill-clad,
    our love with the unlovable.
For our selfishness, forgive us, Lord.
Forgive us, Lord, for our thanklessness,
    our forgetfulness, and our selfishness.

God forgives us our sin for the sake of His Son, Jesus Christ, and fills our hearts with true thanksgiving as we live for Him and for others. Now we can rejoice and praise Him with all our heart, as our Bible reading and our closing hymn verse do.

Prayer
Sing to the Lord of harvest, Sing songs of love and praise;
With joyful hearts and voices Your alleluias raise.
By him the rolling seasons In fruitful order move;
Sing to the Lord of harvest A joyous song of love.

A Thief in the Night

Reading: 1 Thessalonians 4:13–5:5

Text: 1 Thessalonians 5:2—"For you know very well that the day of the Lord will come like a thief in the night."

We all dread the possibility of a thief in the night. With the family sleeping, a thief quietly breaks in and enters through a window or door. Armed with knife or gun, he stealthily sneaks around looking for money and valuables. Just thinking about it strikes terror in our hearts, giving grotesque meaning to shadows in our room or strange noises in the night.

Paul uses this imagery to describe the sudden coming of the day of the Lord at the end of the world. People will be talking about "peace and safety" when destruction comes suddenly. We think of the days of Noah, when the Flood came without warning.

At the end of the church year Christians contemplate the end of the world. For everyone living in darkness that day spells terror, destruction, punishment. Judgment Day means a day of reckoning, with no escape, no warning.

But Paul has good news for us, "You, brothers, are not in darkness so that this day should surprise you like a thief. You are all sons of the light and sons of the day" (vv. 4–5a). "God did not appoint us to suffer wrath but to receive salvation through our Lord Jesus Christ" (v. 9). In the very darkness of Good Friday, Jesus shone forth on the cross as the Savior of the world. Easter morning light brought proof of His victory.

We live in the light of Easter. We have been "called . . . out of darkness into his wonderful light" (1 Peter 2:9b). Forgiven, we wait expectantly for the day of the Lord, when Jesus will appear again to take us to heaven. We don't know the day or the hour when He will return. But as children of the light we will not be surprised but will welcome our salvation with open arms.

Prayer

Lord, prepare us with Your saving light for Your sudden return. Amen.

Living in the Daylight

Reading: 1 Thessalonians 5:6–11

Text: 1 Thessalonians 5:8a—"But since we belong to the day, let us be self-controlled."

Many discussions about the end of the world focus on the exact time sequence and various other details. Paul, however, emphasizes the implications of Christ's Second Coming for daily living—living in the daylight. "Since we belong to the day, let us be self-controlled." He first admonishes that we be awake and sober, not asleep and drunk. Does the world tranquilize us with its many pleasures so that we fall asleep? How easy to get wrapped up in television, bowling, social clubs, shopping, and travel! These activities, fine in themselves, can divert us from God's plan for our lives. In addition, Satan tempts us to succumb to the sinful deeds of the night—revelry, drunkenness, and sexual immorality.

Second, Paul encourages us to put on the armor of God. The breastplate of faith enables us to trust God with each day's problems. The breastplate of love flows from faith. Love penetrates the darkness as nothing else can. The helmet of hope equips us to live soberly each day. No matter how dark the day, the hope of Christ's return keeps the light burning.

Third, Paul asks us to "encourage one another and build each other up." The world discourages us and tears us down. People scoff at our faith and ridicule our Christian standards. But we have the precious Gospel message to share with one another. "He [Christ] died for us so that, whether we are awake or asleep, we may live together with him" (v. 10).

Yes, living in the light naturally follows from the fact that God has made us children of the light. By God's grace we stay awake, wear the armor of God, and encourage one another with salvation through our Lord Jesus Christ.

Prayer

I am the light; I light the way,
A godly life displaying;
I help you walk as in the day;
I keep your feet from straying.
I am the way, and well I show
How you should journey here below.

Ready for the Bridegroom?

Reading: Matthew 25:1–13

Text: Matthew 25:10b—"The virgins who were ready went in with him to the wedding banquet. And the door was shut."

The time—7:15 a.m. The place—the MGM Hotel in Las Vegas. Many asleep, unsuspecting. Suddenly the unexpected, a devastating fire sweeps through the hotel. Over 100 lives lost, 500 injured. Tragedy. Not ready for the crisis.

The text describes a more joyful event—a wedding feast. But readiness remains the issue. The ten maidens await the wedding procession with lamps. Five are wise, with lamps trimmed and well-supplied with oil. Five are foolish, with lamps not supplied with oil. Unexpectedly at midnight the Bridegroom comes. Our text tells what happened.

Are you looking forward to the Bridegroom's coming? When you consider Jesus Christ coming again at the end of the world, do you thrill with anticipation or stir uneasily? Are you ready to die and go to heaven? Do these events remind you more of a destructive hotel fire or a joyful wedding feast? Confession time. Are you prepared for the Bridegroom's coming? Preparation means trusting Jesus Christ alone for salvation. God prepared the way for Him to take on human flesh, to live a perfect life, and to die for the world's sin. God prepares us to meet Jesus through Baptism, the Word of God, and the Lord's Supper.

Lacking motivation and discipline, we often neglect God's grace for us. Like the foolish virgins we may find that the lamps of our faith are going out. But God is faithful and just to rekindle our faith, to forgive us our sins of poor preparation, and to cleanse us from all unrighteousness. Thus we await His coming.

Prayer

The bridegroom comes, awake!
Your lamps with gladness take!
Alleluia! With bridal care
And faith's bold prayer,
To meet the bridegroom, come, prepare!

Thanksgiving Before the Throne

Reading: Revelation 7:9–17

Text: Revelation 7:12—"Amen! Praise and glory and wisdom and thanks and honor and power and strength be to our God forever and ever. Amen!"

Thanksgiving Day and the end of the Christian church year occur around the same time, near the end of November. They present contrasting scenes. The first conjures up thoughts of the family gathered around a bountiful table, voraciously consuming turkey and dressing. Thanksgiving, yes, but short-lived and often directed more toward material blessings.

The second suggests Judgment Day and then the gathering of the saints around the throne of the Lamb. There the multitudes of the redeemed join with the angels in an endless song of praise. It continues forever and focuses on God—Father, Son, and Holy Spirit—who loves us and chose us as His people. This celebration combines Christmas Eve and Easter worship, infinitely magnified.

How can our thanksgiving each day become less like a short-lived Thanksgiving Day and more like the endless thanksgiving before the throne described in Revelation? We first confess that our old nature, still clinging to us, is indeed thankless. On our own, we cannot participate in endless thanksgiving.

Admitting our failure, we look to the Lamb. Jesus Christ came for us. His perfect life and self-giving death on the cross offered a spotless sacrifice to the Father. God now stands before us with His love and forgiveness, not just on Thanksgiving Day but 365 days a year. We also join the praising crowd in the fellowship of God's people gathered around Word and sacrament. There we join with angels and archangels and all the company of heaven in praising God. Every Sunday a *thanksgiving before the throne.*

Prayer

All praise and thanks to God The Father now be given,
The Son, and him who reigns With them in highest heaven,
The one eternal God, Whom earth and heav'n adore;
For thus it was, is now, And shall be evermore.

Deliverance on the Interstate

Reading: Psalm 107:4–9

Text: Psalm 50:15—"Call upon me in the day of trouble; I will deliver you, and you will honor me."

The Saturday afternoon began peacefully enough. After an enjoyable visit home, our family was headed back to the city where I served as pastor. The car headed west on the interstate into the afternoon sun. My wife and two small children fell asleep. With the monotonous drive and glare of the sun, I found myself getting drowsy. Suddenly I saw the grass rushing up at us. Applying the brakes, I watched the front bumper smash through a barbed wire fence and the front wheels finally come to rest in the mud a few feet from a creek. The final landing was gentle. No one was hurt.

We took stock of our situation. The interstate was way up a hillside. Another car, seeing the problem, had stopped up on the road. The people in that car invited us to drive with them to a nearby town to contact the police. They also provided us with hot food and shelter. We were so thankful to be safe, although shaken. A few hours later we returned to the scene. Two wreckers with pulleys had pulled our car up the hillside back to the road. Except for the grillwork, our vehicle had sustained no damage. We were able to get in and continue our journey.

"Call upon me in the day of trouble; I will deliver you, and you will honor me." I had only a fleeting moment to call on God in the midst of the accident. But certainly He delivered us in a marvelous way. We concluded that He had a purpose for the remainder of our lives. We rejoiced not only in that deliverance, but in God's love in His Son Jesus Christ, who had delivered us from eternal death by His death on the cross. We wanted to honor God with our lips and in our lives.

Many years later that deliverance on the interstate still stands out in my mind. God is alive. He has power to save. Thank Him for His unfailing mercy!

Prayer Thoughts
Discuss days of trouble when God has delivered you. Thank Him.

Two Kinds of Sinners

Reading: Luke 15:1–10

Text: Luke 15:1–2—"Now the tax collectors and 'sinners' were all gathering around to hear him. But the Pharisees and the teachers of the law muttered, 'This man welcomes sinners and eats with them.' "

What kind of a sinner are you? In Luke 15 two kinds of sinners are mentioned. We could call them "insider" and "outsider" sinners.

Do you feel like an outsider sinner? Perhaps you have lived a life-style in the past which you regret. Even now you may not be fitting in with other church members. As an outsider sinner you either have no desire for repentance and say, "I'm outside and I plan to stay that way. I'm a sinner and I can't change now. Stay away from me, Shepherd. I don't want to be rescued." Or God brings you to Jesus repentant as you say, "I'm lost as an outsider. I'm lonely. I'm sinful. I need help. I want a complete change of heart. Thank You, Shepherd."

The text also describes insider sinners, "the Pharisees and the teachers of the law." They consider themselves righteous because they are lifelong sons of Abraham and obey the Law. Do you consider yourself an insider sinner? You may be a lifelong believer with a well-known family name in the church. You may be active in church leadership. But you may also be puffed up with pride or be lacking in love. As an insider sinner you either have no desire for repentance and say, "I'm OK—a sinner yes, but not too bad a sinner. I don't need help right now." Or God brings you to Jesus repentant as you say, "I have the heritage, but I'm missing something. My pride and lovelessness are as sinful as the open sin of others. I need help from You, Shepherd. In fact, I'm the chief of sinners."

We meet Jesus Christ. He came to die for insider and outsider sinners alike. Shepherd of the lost sheep, Jesus comes to us repentant sinners and fills us with a rejoicing that extends to other sinners everywhere.

Prayer
Father, forgive my sin for Jesus' sake. Amen.

Leading Others to Sin

Reading: Proverbs 1:8–19

Text: Luke 17:1—"Things that cause people to sin are bound to come, but woe to that person through whom they come."

As the word "sex" was once "unmentionable," so has the word "sin" become today. All sorts of milder words flood our language—"mistake," "error," "miscalculation." In Luke 17 Jesus makes no effort to sweep sin under the rug. Exposing three areas of wrongdoing, He deals bluntly with sin.

Jesus first deals bluntly with the sin of leading others to sin. "Things that cause people to sin are bound to come, but woe to that person through whom they come." He adds that it would be better for such a person to have "a millstone tied around his neck" and "to be thrown into the sea" (v. 2).

Leading others to sin. Parents so easily set wrong examples for their children—materialistic life-style, poor church attendance, excessive drinking and smoking, no love between husband and wife. A frightening list when we know our own shortcomings and our influence on our children!

We can also lead others to sin by engaging in gossip. Many times our careless tongue harms the Lord and His church and leads others to doubt their faith. When we engage in false teaching, we lead others to sin. We deny Christ and raise questions about the reliability of God's Word. We may sound skeptical and cynical about God's power today to change lives.

Since many of our sins may lead others to sin, we need to set aside the pervasive sin in our midst. Instead we turn to the great Sin-bearer, Jesus Christ. Sinless in His own life, He went to the cross for us to defeat the power of sin. He offers full forgiveness to us. No millstones for believers in Jesus! "If we confess our sins, he is faithful and just and will forgive us our sins and purify us from all unrighteousness" (1 John 1:9). Instead of leading others to sin, Jesus helps us lead others to Him.

Prayer
Father, keep us from leading others to sin. Amen.

Not Rebuking Sin in Others

Reading: Galatians 2:11–16

Text: Luke 17:3b—"If your brother sins, rebuke him."

Second, Jesus deals bluntly by exposing the sin of not rebuking sin in others. He says plainly, "If your brother sins, rebuke him." We would rather overlook sin in others. If we ignore their sin, perhaps they will ignore our sin. We want them to like us, so we remain silent.

But sin threatens to engulf our world. Abortion on demand results in the murder of millions of the unborn. Pornography corrupts the minds and lives of youth and adults. Homosexuality and other sexual perversions profane God's name and destroy lives. Cheating takes place on a wide scale. Exploitation victimizes people on many levels. People slander others with a constant and uncaring barrage of rumor and innuendo. Church members evidence a coldness of faith and life that deadens the fellowship of God's people and derails His magnificent plan of taking the Gospel to the ends of the world.

Jesus simply says, "If your brother sins, rebuke him." He intends that we rebuke out of love. We hate the sin because we love the sinner. We speak to the offending brother because we recognize our own sin and need for forgiveness. We believe in the power of daily confession and absolution. And we confess the sin of not rebuking sin in others.

Jesus holds the answer for us. He addressed blunt words to the hypocritical Pharisees and drove money-changers out of the temple. But He also asked the Father to forgive His enemies and died for the sins of the whole world. He forgives our sins of not rebuking others. He also lives in us and through us so that we have the courage to rebuke sin in a loving manner. We "carry each other's burdens, and in this way . . . fulfill the law of Christ" (Gal. 6:2).

Prayer

Delay not, delay not! Why longer abuse
The love and compassion of Jesus, your God?
A fountain is opened; how can you refuse
To wash and be cleansed in his pardoning blood?

Failing to Forgive

Reading: Matthew 18:21–35

Text: Luke 17:3c–4—"If he repents, forgive him. If he sins against you seven times in a day, and seven times comes back to you and says, 'I repent,' forgive him."

We have been dealing bluntly with sin by confessing our sins of leading others to sin and not rebuking sin in others. Jesus adds a third area for our consideration, the sin of failing to forgive. He simply says, "If [your brother] repents, forgive him." He expands the instructions to forgive. "If he sins against you seven times in a day . . . forgive him." We like to set standards and impose limits for forgiveness. Our patience wears thin when someone repeatedly sins against us.

The husband leaves a ring around the tub for the hundredth time. The wife squeezes the toothpaste tube in the middle again. Little Billy lets the dog escape through an open door for the third time this week. Forgiveness? They say they are sorry. But we wonder: Why do they keep repeating their thoughtless conduct? Forgiveness comes hard.

Bluntly Jesus exposes our sin. He knows our tendency to keep score on others. He knows we often continue to hold grudges even after we have spoken a word of forgiveness. We confess our sin of failing to forgive.

Clearly Jesus also forgives. He lived in an unfair world, which wronged Him. He opposed sin, but constantly offered forgiveness to others—to the palsied sinner, the adulterous woman, His enemies at Calvary. And He died on the cross to pay for the world's sins. He forgave His disciples and gave them the power to forgive sins for His sake. He forgives our failure to forgive, and empowers us to go the extra mile. Dealing bluntly with sin leads to clear forgiveness from the Savior.

Prayer

Today your gate is open, And all who enter in
Shall find a Father's welcome And pardon for their sin.
The past shall be forgotten, A present joy be giv'n,
A future grace be promised, A glorious crown in heav'n.

Waiting for the Morning

Reading: Lamentations 3:18–26

Text: Lamentations 3:22b–23a—"His compassions never fail. They are new every morning."

When the well-known preacher Peter Marshall had his second heart attack, he said softly to his wife Catherine as he was being carried out of the house on a stretcher, "See you in the morning, darling." That dark night ended in the morning of eternal life, for Peter Marshall died at the hospital. His wife treasured those words in the days of grief which followed.

Jeremiah writes about the Lord's compassions being new every morning. Precious words of comfort in the middle of the gloomiest book in the Bible—Lamentations. Jeremiah in his effort to proclaim God's Word of judgment upon Judah faces continual ridicule and persecution. He is imprisoned, later beaten and thrown in a well. He agonizes, doubts himself, and turns bitter. The root of his bitterness is self-pity. A dark night of the soul.

We often walk in darkness. Externally, we experience illness, family problems, problems on the job. The more we try to be faithful, the more the problems mount. We feel rejected and persecuted. No one seems to understand. At root we are engaging in self-pity. A dark night of the soul.

Jesus Christ understands our dark night of the soul, for He experienced it in Gethsemane and at Calvary, where He cried out, "My God, my God, why have you forsaken me?" (Matt. 27:46). He waited on the Father and won the victory over the powers of darkness. On Easter morning He rose triumphantly from the grave. With Jeremiah we who have experienced God's love can say the words of our text and add, as did Jeremiah, "It is good to wait quietly for the salvation of the Lord" (v. 26). Whether awaiting a new day of God's mercy or the eternal morning of heaven, we can say with Peter Marshall, "See you in the morning, darling."

Prayer
Lord, help us wait for Your morning mercy. Amen.

Repentance and Joy

Reading: Mark 1:1–8

Text: Mark 1:4—"And so John came, baptizing in the desert region and preaching a baptism of repentance for the forgiveness of sins."

Judea, first century. Excitement in the air. A new stirring of life and hope. A rugged wilderness man appearing to proclaim that Jesus the Messiah has come.

We, in the middle of a difficult world—perhaps bleak weather, heavy burdens, discouraging rat race, family problems—pause to remember "the beginning of the gospel about Jesus Christ, the Son of God" (v. 1). We look ahead to Christmas in its true meaning: Jesus has come as the Babe in Bethlehem, the Man from Galilee, and the Lamb of Calvary. He has come for us.

But John's message starts with repentance. A gourmet meal doesn't appeal to full stomachs. Wonder drugs mean little to a healthy person. Great crowds came to hear John as the excitement grew. A stern preacher, he exposed their sins, broke through their facade of self-righteousness and religiosity. Confessing their sins, they repented and humbled themselves in a Jordan River baptism. Forgiven, they awaited the appearance of "the Lamb of God, who takes away the sin of the world" (John 1:29).

Christmas often provides a superficial joy of the tinsel, glitter, and wrapping paper variety. We sometimes come to Christ wearing masks, desiring sin and heaven, too. What secrets lurk in the shadows of our hearts—hidden adultery, a serious drinking problem, cheating on the job, bitterness and hatred toward another. John's message pierces the facade, sweeps away the superficial, and penetrates to our hearts. Confessing, we humbly turn to the cross of Jesus for forgiveness and live daily in the humbling but joy-giving waters of our baptism. True excitement in the air, new life and hope, from the forerunner's message of repentance. Jesus has come—for us!

Prayer

Lord, repentant we seek Your Advent forgiveness and joy. Amen.

Bearing Witness to the Light

Reading: John 1:6–8, 19–28

Text: John 1:7a—"He came as a witness to testify concerning that light."

The lights of Christmas—Advent candles, decorated street lamps, thousands of outdoor Christmas lights in dazzling colors, Christmas tree light strands, Bethlehem stars everywhere. Temporary joy and comfort in the darkness of our world. But do the lights of Christmas sometimes detract from the one Light shining forever to defeat the dreadful darkness of sin?

John came as a man sent from God into a dark world. He came bearing witness to that one Light, Jesus Christ. Many looked to John as the Light. They wanted to label him as the Messiah, or at least as Elijah or the Prophet. John could have accepted the praise and pointed to himself as the shining Light. But he consistently refused to identify himself as more than a "voice . . . calling in the desert" (v. 23). As John's gospel says, "He himself was not the light; he came only as a witness to the light" (v. 8). And how well he served to point to Jesus as the Light of the world!

In the midst of Christmas lights and so many "stars" who draw attention to themselves as famous, important people, we are sorely tempted to seek recognition. We often secretly think that our light does shine rather brightly. But John's example serves to convict us of pride.

On our own, by nature, we live in darkness. We have no light. God's Son has shined brightly through His birth, life, death, and resurrection. He continues to bring light through His Word and sacraments. By God's grace He has shined in our hearts with His light. We now recognize that whatever light we have is only reflected from Him. So we can joyfully bear witness to Jesus Christ, the Light of the world, at Christmas and all year long.

Prayer

The people that in darkness sat
A glorious light have seen;
The light has shined on them who long
In shades of death have been.

Christmas Shallow or Christmas Deep?

Reading: Luke 1:39–56

Text: Luke 2:19—"But Mary treasured up all these things and pondered them in her heart."

Everywhere, at this time of year, we notice that Christmas is near. The decorations, the bells, the carols—all give evidence that the Christmas celebration is already in full swing. But are we celebrating Christmas shallow or Christmas deep?

Too often Americans observe a shallow Christmas complete with tinsel, glitter, holly and ivy, gift buying in crowded department stores, Christmas carols, and, oh yes, silver bells. But these externals, fine in themselves, frequently leave little time for a deep reflection on the true meaning of Christmas.

There by the manger in the still of the night we find Mary looking in wonder at the newborn Christ child and the visiting shepherds from the fields of Bethlehem. Luke writes, "But Mary treasured up all these things and pondered them in her heart." Mary is celebrating a deep Christmas. Already reflecting for nine months on the visit of the angel and the growing new life within her, she now continues to focus on the meaning of this birth for the world. She knows the Savior is born from her womb.

Mary stands as a model for our celebration of *Christmas deep.* We enjoy the sights and sounds of the season along with family and friends. But we take time to kneel at the manger and worship the Christ child who is to die on the cross for our sins. By the Spirit's power, as we worship together during Advent, we treasure up all these things and ponder them in our hearts. Not *Christmas shallow,* but *Christmas deep.*

Prayer
A great and mighty wonder,
A full and holy cure:
The virgin bears the infant
With virgin honor pure!

Eyes Right!

Reading: Psalm 119:33–40

Text: Psalm 119:37—"Turn my eyes away from worthless things; preserve my life according to your word."

Military drills sometimes include the command, "Eyes right!" As one unit, the troops turn their eyes and salute. Only the greatest discipline can control our wandering eyes. We enter a large metropolitan area at night and find ourselves captivated by neon lights, lighted billboards, and colorful marquees. We window-shop in crowded malls and can't take our eyes off the fashionable clothing, elegant furniture, and expensive jewelry. When celebrities come to town, we strain for a glimpse and an autograph.

The psalmist writes, "Turn my eyes away from worthless things; preserve my life according to your word." The world's glitter distracts our eyes from God and His saving Word. When gazing at Jesus, the One who died for us, we can see the things of the world in the proper light, as part of God's gracious creation. But when our eyes wander from Jesus to the glamour of worldly possessions, we lose perspective, and our heart follows our eyes to a new love.

Only God through His renewing Word can turn our *eyes right.* He fixes our eyes on Jesus, on whom our faith depends from beginning to end. We rejoice to see our salvation drawing nigh. We humbly praise and thank Him for life and salvation. We see Him now by faith and will someday see Him face to face eternally.

Prayer

Help us, dear Lord Jesus, to turn our eyes away from the tinsel of the world and keep them fixed on You. Amen.

Announcing the New Reign of God

Reading: Matthew 3:1–12

Text: Matthew 3:1–2—"In those days John the Baptist came, preaching . . . 'Repent, for the kingdom of heaven is near.' "

When the President plans a visit to your community, the word spreads quickly. People gather. You strain to see the approaching helicopter or motorcade. An advance speaker begins. Finally, the President steps to the platform to speak.

Similar excitement gripped Israel as the advance man, John the Baptist, emerged from the desert announcing, "Repent, for the kingdom of heaven is near." With the appearance and authority of an Old Testament prophet, John clearly communicated that the new reign of God was beginning. Israel, dissatisfied with national and personal conditions, longed for this news and turned out in droves. Waiting in the wings was the King, Jesus of Nazareth.

As we begin a new church year, the announcement of a new reign of God stirs us up as well. With long-standing problems in the world, in our nation, and in our personal lives, we long to hear of the King who brings peace and salvation. Unfortunately, like Israel, we often look for material prosperity and earthly peace in the new reign of God—belonging to a nice church with nice people, where nice Christmas services calm our spirits.

But John preaches a strong message of repentance. God wants to rule our hearts and lives. The new reign of God creates obedient servants who are willing to suffer for the King. We are called, not as spectators but as participants in announcing God's reign to the world.

Joyfully, the new reign of God changes hearts. The King, Jesus, arrives on the scene as Suffering Servant and moves from swaddling clothes in a manger, through an upper room foot-washing, to a rough-hewn cross for us and our salvation. Forgiven, we rejoice to participate in the new reign of God.

Prayer

On Jordan's bank the Baptist's cry
Announces that the Lord is nigh;
Awake and hearken, for he brings
Glad tidings of the King of kings!

349

Shall We Look for Another?

Reading: Matthew 11:2–11

Text: Matthew 11:3—"Are you the one who was to come, or should we expect someone else?"

The same John the Baptist, mighty preacher of repentance and announcer of the new reign of God, now lies in prison in danger of execution. He hears word of Jesus' ministry—teaching and healing. Plagued with doubts, he sends messengers to Jesus asking the question of our text.

He expected another kind of Christ, one who would bring judgment upon King Herod, the Pharisees, and all the evildoers in society. John, in effect, wants to control Christ in the direction of judgment. He wonders if his ministry has been in vain. How easily we also expect another kind of Christ. We, too, might prefer more judgment on others—drug dealers, prosperous unbelievers, the irresponsible, Christmas shoplifters. We also might expect a sugary, sentimental Christ, a superficial Christmas celebration with a cute little baby. That kind of Christ wouldn't affect our lives or ask for commitment or devotion. When faced with the real Christ, we ask with John, "Are you the one who was to come, or should we expect someone else?"

God helps us to accept Christ as He is. Jesus replied to John that the Good News was being preached and the blind, deaf, and lame healed—a sure sign that the Messiah had come. Judgment comes to the individual when Christ is rejected, but God wants the world to be saved. This good news of salvation must have reassured John.

The same good news of a crucified and risen Christ comes also to us to heal our hurts and fears. The Messiah has come for us. Forgiven for our judgmental attitudes and our anemic view of a meek and mild Christ, we look to the real Christ and receive power to live bravely for Him.

Prayer

Thus, if we have known him, Not ashamed to own him,
Nor have spurned him coldly But will trust him boldly,
He will then receive us, Heal us, and forgive us.

Accepting Jesus' Birth Announcement

Reading: Luke 1:26–38

Text: Luke 1:38—" 'I am the Lord's servant,' Mary answered, 'May it be to me as you have said.' "

What a momentous occasion when a young wife tells her husband, "I think I'm expecting a child." The doctor confirms the pregnancy. Friends hear the good news. The months pass. The child grows within—morning sickness, weight gain, movement inside, discomfort, preparation for the arrival. Then the words in the night, "I think it's time to go to the hospital." The rush to the labor room. Waiting—breathtaking, exciting, frightening, joyful waiting. Then the words, "It's a boy!" or "It's a girl!"

Mary got the word from an angelic messenger: "You will be with child and give birth to a son" (v. 31a). Overwhelming news. An unmarried virgin giving birth to a child. Mother of the Messiah. Staggering, incomprehensible, frightening, mysterious news. Yet Mary obeys: "I am the Lord's servant." And Mary trusts: "May it be to me as you have said."

We hear the news. Jesus Christ is born in us today. In Baptism we receive the new birth. But what implications! He calls us to service and obedience. We get no credit for this new birth, nor do we control what being a follower of Christ will mean for our life. Staggering, frightening, mysterious news! Will we trust like Mary—"May it be to me as you have said"? Will we obey like Mary—"I am the Lord's servant"? Are we able to accept Jesus' birth announcement in our lives?

Mary had help. "Fear not," she was told. Words like "Holy Spirit," "power of the Most High," and "Son of God" penetrated to her heart with Gospel comfort. God helps us, too, with His Gospel. We can radiate the joy of Mary as we again this Christmas announce the birth of Jesus Christ.

Prayer

O holy Child of Bethlehem, Descend to us, we pray;
Cast out our sin, And enter in, Be born in us today.
We hear the Christmas angels, The great glad tidings tell;
Oh, come to us, Abide with us, Our Lord Immanuel!

White Christmas?

Reading: Galatians 4:4–7

Text: Isaiah 1:18b—"Though your sins are like scarlet, they shall be as white as snow."

Americans dream of a white Christmas. The Irving Berlin song and movie with Bing Crosby set the stage for an annual preoccupation with snow for Christmas. Children wait expectantly. Adults watch endless weather reports on television. Choruses of glee greet the snowflakes.

Certainly snow doesn't make Christmas. When the Son of God was born in Bethlehem, no snow fell in the Middle Eastern climate. The miracle lay in the Word becoming flesh at God's right time to bring salvation to a sinful world. A white Christmas, while beautiful and part of God's creation, belongs with many-colored Christmas tree lights, tinsel, and department store displays as traditions of Christmas which may actually detract from the Savior's birth.

Or perhaps our white Christmases treasured from childhood could remind us of Isaiah's words, "Though your sins are like scarlet, they shall be as white as snow." Exposing the blatant sins of Jerusalem, Isaiah also brings the hope and comfort of God for repentant sinners. He reminds them that God forgives the worst of sins and makes them as white and clean as snow through the promised Messiah who will go to a cross to pay for those sins.

Nothing wrong with a white Christmas, particularly when the snow reminds us of the cleansing power of Jesus' death and resurrection for our sins. Nothing wrong either with a Christmas more barren and brown than white, because the Babe of Bethlehem turned Calvary sufferer still cleanses us from our sins. "Though your sins are like scarlet, they shall be as white as snow."

Prayer

Dear Lord, thank You for making this Christmas white with or without snow through Your forgiveness won on Calvary. Amen.

Green Christmas?

Reading: Matthew 6:19–34

Text: 2 Corinthians 8:9—"For you know the grace of our Lord Jesus Christ, that though he was rich, yet for your sakes he became poor, so that you through his poverty might become rich."

As a takeoff on America's preoccupation with a white Christmas, satirist Stan Freburg produced a jarring recording a few years ago, exposing the commercialization of Christmas. He entitled the record "Green Christmas." A group of advertisers gather to find new angles and pitches for tying their products to Christmas for the coming holidays. Bob Cratchet, owner of a small spice company in East Orange, N. J., objects to their tactics and simply wants to send a card with the Wise Men bearing gifts to the Savior. Drowned by a chorus of protests, he is offered a medley of Christmas tunes which "Deck the Halls with Advertising," ending with the sound of a cash register ringing three times and coins spilling out on the countertop.

Is your Christmas green? How easily we fall prey to centering our Christmas celebration on gift buying and receiving! How often squabbles develop about the checkbook balance, credit card usage, and easy payment plans! Television and newspaper advertising and the glittering appeal of attractive displays in shopping malls often seduce us into a Christmas celebration far removed from the Bethlehem manger.

St. Paul in our text points us to the true meaning of Christmas. The eternal Son of God, wealthy beyond imagination, came to earth as a humble baby, in poverty. He grew up to walk the dusty roads of Palestine with nowhere to lay His head, and ended up with all clothing stripped away on a shameful cross. But through His death He offers us forgiveness and the endless treasures of heaven. We don't need a green Christmas. We worship the Babe of Bethlehem, our Savior, and give Him our costliest treasures.

Prayer

We are rich, for he was poor; Is not this a wonder?
Therefore praise God evermore Here on earth and yonder.

Anger on Trial

Reading: Ephesians 4:26–32

Text: Matthew 5:22—"But I tell you that anyone who is angry with his brother will be subject to judgment."

Many spectacular murder trials have filled the television screens and the pages of the local newspapers. We gasp at the brutal, premeditated slaughter of innocent people. But Jesus in His Sermon on the Mount, while upholding the commandment against murder, probes deeper into the emotions and places *anger on trial:* "Anyone who is angry with his brother will be subject to judgment."

Suddenly we move from the spectator gallery to the trial bench. How often have we felt anger welling up inside us! Often we explode and lash out verbally or even physically at the person closest to us. Sometimes we maintain outward control but burn inside and find ways to get even with the other person. Other times we internalize the anger and find ourselves gripped with depression or experiencing peptic ulcers and migraine headaches. But anger affects all of us and too often leads to direct sin against the brother or sister. Who can forget Cain, angry with his brother and ignoring God's warning about sin crouching at his door, murdering his brother Abel in the field?

Recognizing anger as a valid emotion, we nevertheless confess our mishandling of it, leading to sin against brother and sister. We turn to Jesus. Angry at the sin of the Pharisees and money changers in the temple, He nevertheless loves every sinner. He stood trial for our anger and for the world's hatred and murder. He was convicted of our sin and paid the full price on the cross.

Forgiven and free, we rely on His power to manage our anger. We recognize our anger, don't let the sun go down on it (Eph. 4:26), confess our sin to God and the offended person, and receive His daily forgiveness. God can help us control our anger in constructive ways.

Prayer

Dear Father, forgive us for uncontrolled anger, which harms others and ourselves. Help us to deal with it on the basis of Your Son's death and resurrection. Amen.

The Angel's Message to Joseph

Reading: Matthew 1:18–25

Text: Matthew 1:20a—"After he [Joseph] had considered this, an angel of the Lord appeared to him in a dream . . . ."

Joseph needed convincing. Mary, his betrothed, pregnant. Shocking news. God acts unexpectedly in history—the miraculous birth of the Messiah to a virgin, a poor, humble Galilean girl. Joseph assumed the worst, that Mary had been unfaithful to him. Joseph also engaged in narrow thinking: He could not see the uniqueness of this birth nor its cosmic significance. Yes, Joseph needed help.

And so do we. God still acts in history to carry out His plan for the world in the midst of nuclear armaments, terrorist attacks, economic woes. We tend to think the worst. Obviously the boss or the world leaders or the pastor or the husband or wife should be blamed! We also engage in narrow thinking: Immediate concerns of Christmas preparations, gifts, and eating the next meal dominate our thoughts, and we fret. We cannot see God's great plan for the world through Jesus Christ with its Great Commission challenge. Yes, we need help too.

God helps Joseph through an angel appearing in a dream: "Joseph . . . do not be afraid to take Mary home as your wife, because what is conceived in her is from the Holy Spirit. She will give birth to a son, and you are to give him the name Jesus, because he will save his people from their sins" (vv. 20b–21). Joseph, believing the message, obeys and gladly plays his role in God's saving plan by taking Mary as his wife.

God helps us through His powerful Word. As we worship together in these Christmas days and immerse ourselves in study of the Bible, God points us to His Son, Jesus, who has saved His people from their sins. Believing God's saving message of the crucified and risen Christ, we take our place in His worldwide plan and live for Him in the midst of a wicked world.

Prayer

Dear Father, open our doubting hearts to Your clarifying message of Jesus the Savior, so that we may participate in Your plan for the world. Amen.

Advent Preparation: Quiet or Haughty?

Reading: Luke 1:26–38

Text: Psalm 131:1a, 2a—"My heart is not proud, O Lord, my eyes are not haughty . . . . But I have stilled and quieted my soul."

Christmas looms ahead—a great festival occasion, the celebration of Christ's birthday—but it often poses a dilemma for the Christian. On the one hand, we need to get ready for the family celebration, which means crowded stores, heavy traffic, gift-buying, and decorating the home. The Christmas rush. On the other hand, we desire to prepare our hearts for meaningful Christmas worship. Advent quiet. How does one reconcile Advent quiet with the Christmas rush?

The psalm contrasts quiet not with rushed but with haughty. Perhaps Advent quiet and the Christmas rush present false alternatives. The question: Are we haughty in both rush and quietness? Haughty when rushing: "I can do it on my own. I must be busy so that my family will have a nice Christmas. Everything depends on me!" Haughty when quiet: "I am a very religious person. I will go to all the special services during Advent and Christmas. We will have daily devotions during Advent and religious ornaments on our tree. I will find quiet time with God if it kills me!"

If we can be haughty during Advent either while rushing or seeking quiet, then what does Advent quiet mean? Psalm 131 suggests a quiet dependence on the Lord for everything. Admitting our pride and confessing it, we look outside of ourselves for a solution to the Christmas dilemma. God sent His Son for us, to be fed at His mother's breast. He lived for us and died for us so our sins could be forgiven.

Whether we head for the shopping mall or attend a midweek Advent service, we need to depend on Him. He can then bring His Advent quiet into our rushing and our quiet times. Begone, haughtiness! Enter, quiet dependence on the Babe of Bethlehem!

Prayer

As your coming was in peace, Quiet, full of gentleness,
Let the same mind dwell in me Which is yours eternally.

Advent Preparation: Strength in Quietness

Reading: Isaiah 37

Text: Isaiah 30:15—"In repentance and rest is your salvation, in quietness and trust is your strength."

Every year American Christians wrestle with Advent preparation because of the Christmas rush. Meanwhile, the problems of the world continue, along with daily personal and family struggles. Where can we find strength to cope?

Judah faced similar problems in our text. The northern kingdom had been destroyed, and Judah was subjugated to the Assyrians. Judah faced some tempting opportunities to make alliances with Egypt and Babylon. If an alliance could be formed with one of these other countries, perhaps she could throw off the Assyrian yoke. Isaiah warns against such folly.

How often do we seek strength in alliances, hopes for world peace, military armaments, or new economic proposals! Just around the corner, we think, lies a solution to our problems if we use clever tactics. We even turn to the magic of the Christmas season and hope that our frantic activity will somehow eliminate our continuing problems. Such folly to rely on our own strength!

Isaiah points to the only solution: strength in quietness. Isaiah told Hezekiah that Assyria would be destroyed by God, and alliances should be shunned. True to Isaiah's word, when Sennacherib's army threatened Jerusalem, the angel of the Lord destroyed the army. Trusting quietly in God, Hezekiah saw a marvelous victory.

Repentant, we quietly kneel at the manger and trust God. He used Caesar Augustus' decree to bring about the Savior's birth in Bethlehem, foiled Herod's plot against the infants, and arranged for Jesus to be crucified under Pontius Pilate. Jesus Christ has won the victory over sin and death. He rules the world. In this Advent season the key to world and personal problems lies in the same words of Isaiah, "In quietness and trust is your strength."

Prayer

Dear Advent Lord, come to our hearts with Your strength as we wait in quietness. Amen.

The Art of Rejoicing

Reading: Philippians 1:12–20

Text: Philippians 4:4—"Rejoice in the Lord always. I will say it again: Rejoice!"

"Rejoice . . . always." Really? How? Why? Rejoice sometimes. That's plausible—on the wedding day, at the birth of a child, because of the new job or the promotion or the large salary increase, during the thrilling festival worship service, when a loved one comes to believe in Christ. But rejoice always? Impossible—when the car accident occurs, when the tornado rips a path through the neighborhood, when divorce shatters a whole family, when the factory closes its doors, when a teenager runs away from home. Surely Paul doesn't mean what he says!

But somehow Paul's words stand. The whole Letter to the Philippians overflows with rejoicing. Paul writes from prison. He may soon lose his life. He knows that he lives in an evil generation. He realizes that Euodia and Syntyche are feuding in the Philippian church. Yet he writes, "Rejoice . . . always." How? What secret art of rejoicing does Paul possess?

He explains, "Rejoice *in the Lord* always." He treasures the surpassing greatness of knowing Christ Jesus as his Lord. He knows Christ's servant death and the power of His resurrection. He rejoices that Christ lives in the Philippian Christians as they reach out to him and others. He awaits the return of the Savior, who has already given him citizenship in heaven. He receives strength from Christ to do everything. Paul practices the art of rejoicing in the Lord always.

We, too, can rejoice in the Lord always—in His cross and resurrection power, His presence in the love of the Christian fellowship, His daily strength, His promised return. Deeply rooted in the Gospel, dependent upon Christ's power in every situation, we learn the art of rejoicing in the Lord always.

Prayer
Rejoice, my heart, be glad and sing,
A cheerful trust maintain;
For God, the source of ev'rything,
Your portion shall remain.

Waiting for the Lord

Reading: Luke 2:25–35

Text: Psalm 27:14—"Wait for the Lord; be strong and take heart and wait for the Lord."

Waiting does not qualify as an American virtue. Impatient motorists change lanes precipitously in order to gain a car-length advantage. Food-laden grocery carts race for a favored place in the checkout line. Crowded airports feature well-dressed travelers clawing for a final seat on a departing plane. Waiting patiently seems to imply weakness and lack of assertiveness. We live impatiently. College graduates want a top-paying job immediately without starting at the bottom. Newlyweds want a fashionable home with all the modern conveniences. When obstacles arise to our plans, we want them removed at once and at any cost.

The psalmist seems to be learning a lesson in patience. He finds himself surrounded by evil men. His enemies attack. False witnesses accuse. Perhaps his own parents forsake him. Certainly these circumstances could describe young David on the run from an angry, jealous Saul, constantly in physical danger, unsure of enemies and friends, fearful for his life. But David also makes a beautiful confession of faith in a God who will keep him safe, permit him to worship in the house of the Lord, and enable him to see the Lord's goodness.

God pierces our impatience with enemies, roadblocks, uncertainties, and failures. He brings us to our knees, helpless and hopeless. Then through David He asks us to wait for Him. But He also bestows what He asks. In the fullness of time after centuries of waiting, God sent His Son to be born of a virgin. Jesus waited for the right time to begin His public ministry. He willingly endured the cross, drinking the cup of suffering. Risen from the dead, Jesus asked the disciples to wait for power from on high. Our fast-paced society only serves as a foil to build patience in our lives.

Prayer
Enter now my waiting heart,
Glorious King and Lord most holy.

Not Worthy to Untie His Sandals

Reading: John 1:19–28

Text: John 1:27—"He is the one who comes after me, the thongs of whose sandals I am not worthy to untie."

"Who are you?" asked the messengers from Jerusalem. John the Baptizer, the target of their question. A rising religious leader, someone to take seriously, cut in the mold of the great Old Testament prophets. How will he answer? He gets a choice of Christ, Elijah, or one of the prophets. Important company.

"Who are you?" ask today's messengers. Apparently our Christian life is showing. We seem to be effective, successful, caring people. An opportunity for witnessing. How will we answer?

Our answer: "A good church member, regular in attendance. Even serve on a board." Pride. Self-righteousness.

John's answer: "I am the voice of one calling in the desert . . . I am not worthy to untie [His sandals]." Pointing to Jesus Christ as everything, John points to himself as nothing. Only slaves did the work of carrying shoes after a man or taking them off his feet. And a Hebrew slave was not even obliged to perform such a menial task. John the Baptizer, therefore, places himself even lower than a slave. Why? He knows himself as a sinner. He knows the Messiah as true God and the Savior of the world. No pride in John's answer. Only humble dependence on Jesus Christ.

The question again: "Who are you?" Humbled by our pride in the presence of the Christ who took on the form of a servant and became obedient even to death on a cross (Phil. 2:7–8), we answer with John, "I am not worthy to untie [His sandals]." We rejoice that the Lamb makes us worthy by His death to stand before God and to receive His body and blood in Holy Communion, a foretaste of the feast to come. This royal gift empowers us to live as humble servants, pointing to the Christ at Christmastime and throughout the year.

Prayer
Lord, I humbly bow at Your feet. Amen.

Mary's Visit

Reading: Luke 1:39–45

Text: Luke 1:39a–56—"At that time Mary . . . entered Zechariah's home and greeted Elizabeth."

Mary accepted the angel's word that she would give birth to the Messiah, impossible as it seemed. But now as the period of waiting for Jesus' birth stretched on, God used a visit to Elizabeth as a faith strengthener.

Mary's faith was, first, confirmed by a friend. She needed someone else with whom to share. Suspect in Nazareth for being pregnant out of wedlock, she greatly needed her three-month stay with Elizabeth, who welcomed and affirmed her. We also need our faith confirmed by Christian friends. When faced with problems, we find strength and comfort from Christian friends who listen and understand.

Mary's faith was, second, confirmed by a sign. The baby leaped in Elizabeth's womb. Although a normal occurrence, Elizabeth saw the timing as a definite indication that Mary was to be the mother of the Messiah. While our faith is not based on signs, God often uses events in our lives to confirm His loving care and plan. Again Christian friends help each other.

Mary's faith was, third, confirmed by the Word of God. Elizabeth told her by the Spirit's power that she was blessed among women and would give birth to the Savior. Mary was greatly strengthened, and she rejoiced, praising God with the Magnificat.

We also need to have our faith confirmed by the Word of God—spoken by a friend, preached in a sermon, sung in a hymn, taught in a Bible class. That Word points us to the Christ Child who came to save us from our sins. That Word assures us of God's promises for us in the midst of life's problems and challenges.

Mary's visit to Elizabeth strengthened her faith in God's promises. We also are strengthened through the Word of God working in our Christian friends and the events of our lives.

Prayer

Lord Jesus, visit our home with Your love through friends, events, and especially Your saving Word. Amen.

Come to the Manger!

Reading: Luke 2:8–20

Text: Luke 2:11—"Today in the town of David a Savior has been born to you; he is Christ the Lord."

Picture yourself on the Judean hillside with the shepherds and hear the compelling message of the angel. Incredible glory. Incredible message of good news. Far beyond the daily routine of the shepherds. Far beyond their understanding.

What if the shepherds had decided to stay with their flocks? They could have absorbed all of the glory and been dazzled— brilliant light, angel message, angel choirs. A great story to tell their grandchildren! Then a fading memory. Without a visit to the manger that glorious hillside experience would have been empty.

What if we decide to stay in the Christmas glow? The magic of Christmas. Visions of sugar plums. Anticipated gifts. Warm family times. Glorious Christmas Eve services, almost like angel choirs with carols and candlelight. A great story! Then a fading memory. Without a visit to the manger that glorious Christmas experience would be empty.

But the shepherds did not stay. They said to one another, "Let's go to Bethlehem and see this thing that has happened, which the Lord has told us about" (v. 15). They came with haste and found the babe. Worshiping the Christ, their lives were changed. They "spread the word" about what they had seen and "returned, glorifying and praising God" (vv. 17, 20). No fading memory, the manger visit continued to motivate them.

The Spirit works in our Christmas celebration so that we want to go and see what the Lord has done. We come again to the manger on bended knee and see the Christ Child. Our lives are changed. Through His birth, death, and resurrection Jesus has won salvation for us. Sins forgiven, we rise to spread the Good News and to glorify and praise God. No fading memory, the manger visit continues to motivate us for witness, service, and praise. Changed lives change the world, for we have *come to the manger!*

Prayer
Lord, bring us to Your manger again. Amen.

No Room for Them in the Inn

Reading: Matthew 8:18–20

Text: Luke 2:7—"She wrapped him in cloths and placed him in a manger, because there was no room for them in the inn."

Crowded department stores. Last-minute shoppers. Pushing to find a place in line for a final purchase. We know the feeling of waiting in line and being passed by someone bolder and pushier.

The holy couple comes to Bethlehem. Mary needs a place to rest and deliver her baby. But Luke simply tells us that "there was no room for them in the inn." Conditions were crowded in Bethlehem and accommodations inadequate. No room in the inn for a pregnant woman, for the mother of the Messiah, the eternal Son of God.

The humble, lowly birth of the Savior symbolizes His ministry. Mary and Joseph soon had to flee Bethlehem for Egypt. Herod had no room for Him in Israel. When Jesus began His public ministry, He was not welcome in His hometown of Nazareth. In our Bible reading Jesus says that "the Son of Man has no place to lay his head." He would even be crucified outside the city walls of Jerusalem and be buried in a borrowed tomb.

Is there room for Jesus in our hearts and homes? Sometimes our crowded celebration of Christmas, with gifts, baking, and decorating, leaves no room for the Savior who makes Christmas possible. We may find ourselves giving Jesus room in the corner but not at the center of our lives.

Yet God has room for all in His heart and home. He desires all people to be saved. The angel brings good news for all, including common shepherds and foreign Wise Men. Jesus died even for the innkeeper, Herod, and the Roman soldiers. The Word made flesh dwells among us (John 1:14). He who died and rose is truly present in Holy Communion. He welcomes us as His forgiven children. There is room for Him in our hearts and homes, because He has room for us always.

Prayer

Enter now my waiting heart,
Glorious King and Lord most holy.

A Shepherd's Tale:
Hearing the Good News

Reading: Luke 2:8–14

Text: Luke 2:8—"And there were shepherds living out in the fields nearby, keeping watch over their flocks at night."

Amidst the overpowering sights and sounds of Christmas, is the Good News of the Savior's birth penetrating to your heart this year? For the next three devotions, remove yourself from the blur of modern Christmas preparations, return to the fields near Bethlehem, and listen to the tale of a shepherd:

"I am a shepherd from the hills of Bethlehem. I have come to tell you about the birth of the Christ Child. Behold, I have seen, and I believe. One evening we were resting by our campfire as we watched the sheep nibble the closely cropped grass of the hillside. Suddenly a great light appeared, and as we cringed in the shadows a radiant figure clothed in white stood before us and said, 'Do not be afraid. I bring you good news of great joy that will be for all the people. Today in the town of David a Savior has been born to you; he is Christ the Lord.' And suddenly thousands of other figures clad in white appeared before our eyes and began to sing a beautiful song. The words they sang were unforgettable: 'Glory to God in the highest, and on earth peace to men . . .' They were trying to prepare us for a visit to the Baby who was born in Bethlehem."

What an impact on the shepherd! How unexpected the angelic visit and the joyful news of Christ born in the city of David! Does not the shepherd's tale move us to joy and expectation in these days before Christmas? Does not the quiet of the hillside after the angels' visit give pause for a simple focus on the Babe in the manger, our Savior from sin? The shepherd's tale continues tomorrow.

Prayer
Angels we have heard on high,
Sweetly singing o'er the plains,
And the mountains in reply,
Echoing their joyous strains.
Gloria in excelsis Deo.

A Shepherd's Tale: Hurrying to the Manger

Reading: Luke 2:15–16

Text: Luke 2:15b—"The shepherds said to one another, 'Let's go to Bethlehem and see this thing that has happened, which the Lord has told us about.' "

The tale of the shepherd continues: "That was the most glorious thing I have ever seen. When the angels left the skies, darkness filled the air again. Almost immediately we all said, 'Let's go to Bethlehem and see this thing that has happened.' We went as fast as we could and found Mary and Joseph and the Baby just as the angel said we would. I don't think any of us thought much about what would happen to the sheep. We just wanted to hurry to Bethlehem. Preparation? We didn't have time to prepare. God spoke to us, and we wanted to move as fast as we could.

"When we reached Bethlehem, none of us knew what to do or say. We entered quietly and saw the man and the woman and the manger cradling the little Babe. I fumbled for words. I shuffled my feet. Finally, I knelt awkwardly at the manger and gave thanks in my heart for the wonderful Child, the Savior."

How would you describe the unfolding story of your Christmas celebration this year? Dazzled by the angelic glory or overexposed to Christmas glitter? Deeply moved by the Messianic message or exhausted by hectic preparations? Hurrying expectantly to the manger or continually sidetracked by baking and shopping and decorating and partying?

Hear the shepherd's tale. God has come to our world in Christ. The infant Savior went to the cross to pay for our sins. He lives and will return again. We enter His presence again this Christmas, and His love forgives us, quiets us, and fills us with joy and thanksgiving.

Prayer

Come to Bethlehem and see
Him whose birth the angels sing;
Come, adore on bended knee
Christ the Lord, the newborn king.
Gloria in excelsis Deo.

A Shepherd's Tale: Sharing the Savior's Birth

Reading: Luke 2:17–20

Text: Luke 2:17—"When they had seen him, they spread the word concerning what had been told them about this child."

The tale of the shepherd concludes: "I arose and pressed the hands of Mary and Joseph in my own. I felt like a helpless child in the presence of this Child who I knew was the true Son of God. But still I felt perfectly secure and happy in His presence. I left the stable a different person. My friends and I scarcely spoke a word to each other for quite a while. But we shared the same thoughts. We realized that we had seen a great sight and that we had experienced true joy. We looked at each other with bright eyes. Then, all of a sudden, we all began to talk at the same time. Gradually our words began to fit together into one story, a story of peace, of joy, of love, of the birth of the Son of God.

"We told this story to everyone whom we met along the way— the local carpenter, the short, barrel-chested man who sold fresh fish, the shabby, one-eyed beggar half asleep on a doorstep, the rich noble with the gold ring and the long robes. Why don't you rejoice with me, my friend, and help me spread the Good News?"

What an agenda for our Christmas celebration! We hear again the angel tidings. We journey with the shepherds to the manger. Transformed by the Christ, we arise to share the Good News with our family and friends, our neighbors, our co-workers. Like the shepherds, we speak only because God has spoken to us in Christ and through His Word empowers us to share with others. And the telling further strengthens us to share more of the Good News.

Thank you, shepherd, for your tale of Christmas tidings. We will help you spread the message.

Prayer

Shepherds, why this jubilee?
Why your joyous strains prolong?
What the gladsome tidings be
Which inspire your heavenly song?
Gloria in excelsis Deo.

The Slavery of Christmas

Reading: Galatians 4:3–7

Text: Galatians 4:4–5a—"But when the time had fully come, God sent his Son, born of a woman, born under law, to redeem those under law."

Could Christmas for us at times be a form of slavery? We set up standards to evaluate the success of our celebration—managing to buy just the right gifts for our children, preparing just the right dinner, attending all the church services.

Galatians describes a type of slavery that is close to the heart of the problem. Paul preached the freeing Gospel to the Galatians. Later false teachers came, insisting on again observing Jewish rites. "It's fine to believe in Christ," they said, "but you must also be circumcised as the Law says and obey Sabbath regulations. Then you will be saved."

In the white heat of anger Paul writes against such ideas. He knows that the Galatians are in danger of exchanging their new Gospel freedom for the old slavery of the Law. They were losing Christ.

As Christians we easily become slaves to the Law. Despite the Christmas Gospel we, like the Galatian Christians, tend to put ourselves back under the Law. But, as our text reminds us, the whole purpose of Christmas is to free us from slavery to the Law. Christ became a slave to make us sons and daughters of the King. He was born under the Law, lived in the world as an outcast, and died as a common criminal. This slavery of Christ was the price God paid in order to make us His free children.

God's Spirit can free us from Christmas slavery by reminding us again through the Christmas story that we are free children of God through Christ.

Prayer
From the bondage that oppressed us,
From sin's fetters that possessed us,
From the grief that sore distressed us,
We, the captives, now are free.

A Sign: Cloths and a Manger

Reading: Luke 2:33–40

Text: Luke 2:12—"This will be a sign to you: You will find a baby wrapped in cloths and lying in a manger."

Signs of Christmas all around. Santa Claus and Rudolph, silver bells, candlelight, carols, and roasting chestnuts. But the only sign that counts was given to the shepherds in the Judean hills—cloths and a manger.

The shepherds, you see, lived in a rough world with daily hard work and a struggle for survival. Very little tinsel and glitter in their lives! Yet God came to them with His realistic sign, "You will find a baby wrapped in cloths and lying in a manger." Swaddling cloths—a square of cloth with a long bandagelike strip coming diagonally off from one corner. The Child was first wrapped in the square and then the long strip was wound round and round about Him. Manger—smelly feed trough for animals. What a sign! The Messiah was born in a down-to-earth place of humble origin, very much in the real world. The wood of the manger prefigured the wood of the cross on which Jesus was to die for real sins. Strengthened by their visit to the manger, the shepherds returned to their real world to live for Jesus.

We also live in a rough, wicked world filled with major problems, drudgery, hard work, and sins. To us also comes God's enduring sign—swaddling cloths and a manger. The manger lies in the shadow of the cross. God's Son joined Himself to our flesh, lived and died in our real world, and triumphed over death and sin. Like the shepherds, we kneel at the manger, receive strength from the Lord, and return to our real world to serve Him and those in need.

Prayer

To you in David's town this day
Is born of David's line
A Savior who is Christ the Lord;
And this shall be the sign:
The heav'nly Babe you there shall find
To human view displayed,
All meanly wrapped in swaddling clothes
And in a manger laid.

Why a Partridge in a Pear Tree?

Reading: Psalm 145:1–9

Text: Luke 2:19—"But Mary treasured up all these things and pondered them in her heart."

"Four mocking birds, three French hens, two turtle doves, and a partridge in a pear tree." The 12 days of Christmas. Who observes them anymore? Christmas, December 25, ends the celebration. Everyone returns to work and begins thinking about the New Year's Eve party. Decorations are taken down. The live tree, already brittle after three weeks in the house, is consigned to the garbage heap. Gifts are put away in drawers and closets.

This somewhat somber dismantling may be delayed for two or three days, or perhaps (for some faithful souls) from December 25 until January 6, when we celebrate Epiphany and the journey of the Magi to Bethlehem. The 12 days of Christmas provide us opportunity to continue celebrating the Savior's birth. Still fresh in our minds are the visit to the manger, the message of the angels to the shepherds, the joy of Mary and Joseph. After weeks of Advent preparation with repentance and hopeful anticipation, the church bursts forth in a sustained chorus of praise, just getting started on Christmas Day.

Whether or not we formally celebrate Christmas for 12 days, or how long the Christmas tree remains decorated, does not really matter. But the idea of celebrating Christmas continually, pondering the birth, has considerable merit. One thing is certain: The joy of Christmas continues; the angel songs continue to ring out in our world. Jesus is right beside us on the job, on the highway, in our home. He offers forgiveness, strength, and joy.

Yes, we can sustain the joy of Christmas, even without leaping lords, waiting ladies, golden rings, and a partridge in a pear tree.

Prayer

Dear Lord, help me to continue celebrating Your saving presence. Amen.

The Ironies of Christmas

Reading: Matthew 2:1–18

Text: Matthew 2:3—"When King Herod heard this he was disturbed, and all Jerusalem with him."

A baby born—Jesus the Savior of the world! Angel messages, running shepherds, adoring Wise Men, and a jealous, furious, vindictive King Herod. There are many ironies about Christmas.

One year on Christmas Eve, sometime after midnight, vandals stole a wooden plaque and wreath from the front door of a large Midwestern church. The beautiful plaque, a memorial gift from the daughter of the former pastor, pictured the three Wise Men bearing gifts to the Savior. Ironic.

But are there not also ironies in your own home during the Christmas season? Children squabble beneath the Christmas tree about who gets to use the new Christmas toys. Tempers flare about cleaning up the mountain of discarded wrapping paper. These little Christmas irritations are ironies because they don't seem to fit a season of peace and goodwill.

These examples serve as minor reflections of worldwide evil. Nothing really changes much over the holidays. Nations that hated our country still hate it. Politicians still undercut one another. Crime continues. In the face of these ironies, should we decide to abandon the celebration of Christmas next year?

No, indeed. The presence of evil explains why God chose to send His Son in the first place. Only the birth, death, and resurrection of Jesus Christ could bring forgiveness into a fractured and broken world. And the message of Christmas takes on deeper meaning against the background of a stolen church plaque, squabbles over Christmas toys, and global bitterness and hatred. This year once again we perceive a real need for God's Son. And God continues to love us in Christ.

Prayer
Oh, the joy beyond expressing
When by faith we grasp this blessing
And to you we come confessing
Your great love has set us free.

Simeon's Christmas

Reading: Luke 2:25–35

Text: Luke 2:25—"Now there was a man in Jerusalem called Simeon, who was righteous and devout."

How well did your Christmas celebration go this year? St. Luke helps us evaluate by describing to us Simeon's Christmas—his preparation, his perception of the Christ Child, and his praise.

Simeon was prepared for the Messiah's birth. He was righteous, righteous in God's eyes by faith. He was devout, that is, conscientious about his worship. "He was waiting for the consolation of Israel," even though many years had passed since God's original promise.

Our preparation, as we know only too well, usually leaves much to be desired. May God help us learn from Simeon!

Simeon's perception of the Christ Child was shaped by his patient waiting. The Spirit revealed that he would not die before seeing the Lord's Christ. Led into the temple when Mary and Joseph arrived, Simeon took Jesus in his arms, recognizing Him as the Messiah. Later Simeon described Jesus to the parents as "a light for . . . the Gentiles" (v. 32) and "a sign that will be spoken against" (v. 34). He perceived Jesus both as the Savior of the world and as the Messiah who would have to suffer and die.

How clear is our perception of the Christ Child? So often we don't see the Christ Child as the Savior of the world, but perceive Him as a sentimental child, not as the One who was crucified for our sins.

Simeon's praise filled the temple. Based on God's faithfulness to His promise of the Messiah, Simeon overflowed with witness to Him.

How was our praise for the Christ Child this Christmas? Despite our poor preparation and narrow perceptions, God remains faithful to us. Christ's forgiveness, won on the cross, helps us to praise Him fervently.

Prayer

Dear Father, help us learn much from Simeon. Amen.

Purified for Love

Reading: 1 Peter 1:13–25

Text: 1 Peter 1:22—"Now that you have purified yourselves by obeying the truth so that you have sincere love for your brothers, love one another deeply, from the heart."

Another year draws to a close. Time for reflection on the old year and anticipation of the new year. Think of the above verse with the theme *Purified for love.*

The verse gives the standard: "Love one another deeply, from the heart." Love is described as "sincere" and as "deep." Has your love held steady or fluctuated erratically during the past year? Think of your relationships at home, on the job, in church, in your social contacts. I fear that my "love thermometer" registers lovelessness, inconstancy, selfishness.

Enter God's purifying process for the new year. We are purified by the blood of Christ (vv. 18–19). He came as the Father's love incarnate. He consistently loved friends and enemies alike, even to His death on a cross for us. His "love thermometer" registers warmth, sincerity, and depth at all times. He purifies us in our Baptism. That process continues in our lives as new creatures. His Word cleanses us. The Holy Meal cleanses us. He then purifies us in our obedience to the truth through trials and suffering (1 Peter 1:3–7). In short, God, who forgives our lovelessness of the past year, promises to purify us for love in the new year as we look to His loving Son.

Prayer

Love divine, all love excelling,
Joy of heav'n, to earth come down!
Fix in us thy humble dwelling,
All thy faithful mercies crown.
Jesus, thou art all compassion,
Pure, unbounded love thou art;
Visit us with thy salvation,
Enter ev'ry trembling heart.